PENGUIN BOOKS

SACRED GAMES

'[Gerald Jacobs's] achievement is a considerable one. After a painstaking five years of research, he has managed to bring to life not only the facts, but the atmosphere of the events described ... *Sacred Games* is one of a handful of books of stature on the Holocaust produced by British writers' – Zev Ben-Shlomo in the *Jewish Chronicle*

'A remarkable book' – Chaim Bermant in the *Daily Telegraph*

'Should rightly become obligatory reading ... as graphic as Spielberg's *Schindler's List*, reminding us that the written word can be more vivid than images on screen. It is also as objective as any scholarly work on Hitler's Final Solution' – Louis Heren in the *Hampstead & Highgate Express*

'Constantly gripping and frequently horrifying' – Tibor Fischer in *The Times*

'Fascinating ... disturbing ... makes the enormity of the Holocaust experience a personal journey which helps the reader absorb the magnitude of the Final Solution' – Julia Pascal in the *Scotsman*

'A modern equivalent of the Book of Job' – David Pryce-Jones in *The Times Literary Supplement*

Sacred Games

GERALD JACOBS

PENGUIN BOOKS

PENGUIN BOOKS

Published by the Penguin Group
Penguin Books Ltd, 27 Wrights Lane, London w8 5tz, England
Penguin Books USA Inc., 375 Hudson Street, New York, New York 10014, USA
Penguin Books Australia Ltd, Ringwood, Victoria, Australia
Penguin Books Canada Ltd, 10 Alcorn Avenue, Toronto, Ontario, Canada m4v 3b2
Penguin Books (NZ) Ltd, 182–190 Wairau Road, Auckland 10, New Zealand

Penguin Books Ltd, Registered Offices: Harmondsworth, Middlesex, England

First published 1995
1 3 5 7 9 10 8 6 4 2

Set in 12/15 pt Bembo Monophoto
Printed in England by Clays Ltd, St Ives plc

To Hannah, Ben, Rebecca, Joseph and Amy

'Who will wipe this blood off us? What water is there for us to clean ourselves? What festivals of atonement, what sacred games shall we have to invent?'

from *The Madman* by Friedrich Nietzsche
(translated by Walter Kaufmann)

Acknowledgements

In my capacity as literary editor of the *Jewish Chronicle*, I have frequently been approached by Holocaust survivors with stories to tell. Some are painful, some poignant. Each is a unique slice of the most bitter experience of life in the twentieth century. And each deserves to be known; to be part of a record of horrific events which is at once a memorial to those who perished and a lesson to subsequent generations.

Unfortunately, whether through fallible memory, inadequate powers of communication, resistance in the publishing world, or for other reasons, many of these stories fail to emerge from what T. S. Eliot – no hero, incidentally, to these victims of anti-Jewish scorn and hatred – called 'the small circle of pain within the skull'.

It is humbling and frustrating when one is unable to offer any constructive assistance to such people. It was therefore enormously appealing when Nicholas (Miklós) Hammer came to me with his personal story, which he later substantiated with vivid, detailed recollection. Not only had he endured particularly dramatic experiences, but he was also able to convey them through a powerful intelligence and personality.

Over a period of four years, I spent one or two evenings a week in his company, recording his life as a young man. Ready access to the *Jewish Chronicle* library enabled me to augment my researches, but so comprehensive was the original source material from Nicholas that comparatively little extra investigation was necessary.

During the entire period of the book's preparation, I enjoyed the magnificent hospitality of Sonja and Nicholas Hammer. I was also Nicholas's guest on a trip to Poland for the purpose of visiting the Birkenau and Auschwitz sites. For this and much more, I should like to record my thanks.

I am also very grateful for the encouragement I have received from Xandra Hardie; for the many suggestions of Laura Phillips, who acted as a 'sounding board' for the early sections of the book; and to my indefatigable typist, Dolores Karney.

Sacred Games

I

The knock at the door was soft, almost tentative. Inside the room, the young girl was quick, alert; the man and woman silent and suspicious. The evening's fragile repose was broken.

The girl opened the door before her mother and father had moved. They looked across the room at the man who stood there. Another intruder. Not like the others. Gentle. From a different world. But still an intruder.

The apartment, on the ground floor at 19 Wesselényi Street, had seen better days. Music had echoed from its walls. There had been laughter.

All the apartments had been alive with the intimacies and hostilities of husbands and wives, parents and children, brothers and sisters. And rich with the fragrances of the kitchen. Braised goose liver with onions. Sausages with green peppers and paprika. Boiled beef with sauerkraut. The sweetness of home-prepared cherry or apricot preserve. Almond cake and tea with sugar and lemon.

But all that had faded away in the 1930s. This was 1945. The fare was more frugal now. All the former tenants had disappeared. Wesselényi Street, in the old Jewish quarter, was part of the official Budapest ghetto designated by the Nazis. But though the Nazis had gone, few of the Jews who remained had breath enough to sigh in relief. Their sighs for the most part came from the deeper recesses of the soul.

The man was in his twenties, tall and gaunt with sparse hair and a grey complexion. He wore spectacles and a well-tailored, though rather

shabby, woollen suit, which looked far too warm for the weather. He
held a cap in one hand. His manner was stiff, but polite.

'Rabbi Hammer?' he inquired.

'Yes, I am Rabbi Hammer. What is your business with me?'

David Hammer stood up and walked across to the doorway, where
his daughter remained by his side, rooted with curiosity at the sight of
this strange, formal young fellow, calling at such an unusual hour.

The present occupants of the apartment, Rabbi David Hammer,
his wife Rosa and their fifteen-year-old daughter Alice, were
used to a little more space.

From 1932 until another knock on another door in October
1944 they had lived two or three miles away in a larger flat at
34 Murányi Street, near the city park. Rabbi Hammer had been
entrusted with the spiritual needs of the local community. His
income was modest but he and his family had lived comfortably
enough. They even had a maid – Julia, a shy young gypsy girl.
And, for most of that time, the two other children, Miklós and
Ibolya, had been with them.

Frequently, in the old days at Murányi Street, a bed would be
made up in the hall for some visiting, out-of-town relative, such
as Dani Friedman from Tiszabüd. Dani was David's favourite
cousin, a large man with a red face and plump hands, a self-
taught thinker, passionately well-read in foreign literature.

By trade a food merchant, Dani Friedman always brought
bags of fruit which he would distribute piece by piece with much
ceremony to individual members of the family. Within minutes
of his arrival, he would plunge into a game of chess with Miklós
or 'Ibi', all the time keeping their little sister Alice amused and
shouting his news to David or Rosa in the next room.

A married man with two children of his own, Dani would
come to Budapest three or four times a year, staying for a week
or more. He came mainly for business, but now and again
simply for pleasure. And the principal part of his pleasure
would be his discussions into the night with his rabbinic cousin,
debating some fine point of folklore or Talmud.

One night, the whole household was kept awake until four in the morning by an argument over the proposal to establish a new Jewish homeland in Palestine.

'But we Jews are a *nation*.' Dani summoned up all the powers of emphasis at his command, beads of sweat bubbling across his forehead.

'We Jews are a people,' rejoined David. 'The Lord's people. In so far as we are a nation, we are a holy nation, with holy work to do. We are to be a light unto the earthly nations, not gather ourselves to become one of them, to aspire no higher than the squalid foothills of politics. The gathering-in will take place when the Messiah comes. You are the great reader of profane books around here. Doesn't one of your poets say something about serving God by waiting?'

'Ha! I don't believe it! You are talking of Milton. An *English* poet. How have you come by such "profane" trifles? Imagine, David Hammer using an English poet to support his arguments. And what he wrote was, "They also serve who only *stand* and wait." An argument for idleness, perhaps. Do you need to remain passive to be holy? Don't we have to *strike* this light unto the other nations? Or if we simply lie back, does it shine out of our Jewish eyes?'

Warming to his theme, he addressed himself beyond David, through an open door: 'Imagine, Rosa! Your revered and scholarly husband tries to win this debate by seeking the help of a heathen English poet.'

'Is that any worse than *your* heathen,' the rabbi, forefinger stabbing the air, ignored this call to his wife, 'that ignorant Hungarian, Herzl?'

'Ignorant? Herzl? A cultured, educated man. He had no time for backward-looking superstitions, that's all. A man of vision. A true Jew. An *active* Jew. And no less of a Jew for knowing no Hebrew. Where it matters, in the heart and the mind, he was completely Jewish. And as for Milton, he was a Christian!'

'He must have had a Jewish soul.'

'I'll tell you what he was. I'll tell you why he wrote that line. He was *blind*.'

On these occasions David Hammer was motivated by a benign tolerance, a sociability otherwise rare in him. His religious knowledge was far greater than his cousin's and he inclined more to solitude. His fondest pleasure was to sit alone, his black *kipa* perched on his bushy hair, in the tiny, book-crammed room which overlooked the courtyard and served as his study, reading his beloved Rambam or Nachmanides, the *Tractates of the Talmud*, or tales of ancient Hebrew travellers.

Fully bearded, with resolute, dark brown eyes, he was physically imposing, taller by several inches than the rest of his family, and solidly built. But his chief power lay in his intellect.

He had excelled at his studies at the *yeshivah* at Bratislava, where he was awarded a number of prizes before emerging with his rabbinic diploma in 1916. Two years later, he married Rosa Rothman, the delicate, small-boned daughter of a store-keeper made penniless by the Great War.

The young couple moved to Budapest from the east Hungarian countryside. David ministered to a small congregation and oversaw the *kashrut* of its meat. Though his standards were strict for a generally lax community, he was respected for his learning. His knowledge of Talmud won him the esteem of his congregants. His lack of worldliness, however, laid him open to the financially unscrupulous among them.

'My name is Imre Löwy, sir,' the stranger continued. 'I have something important to talk to you about. But I have to speak to you alone.' And he asked David to go with him into the street. Now, for the first time, Rosa stood up, and examined Löwy cautiously. 'Wouldn't you like to come in and have a glass of tea?' she asked him with elaborate courtesy.

'No, thank you very much,' replied Löwy. 'I must speak to your husband on a very important matter.'

Childbearing had had a weakening effect upon Rosa Hammer's

slight frame. Doctors expressed concern at the condition of her heart. She became diabetic.

Rosa doted upon her first-born, Miklós, and reassuringly wrapped maternal arms around him whenever her husband reproached him for straying beyond the traditional path.

The rabbi's own relationship with his son was more complex. Miklós loved music and sport. He listened to the radio and read newspapers and non-religious story books. All these things troubled the rabbi. 'How can you live a proper Jewish life among all this nonsense?' he would ask. Or he would say, 'It's all *distraction*,' spitting out the word with contempt.

At the age of eleven, Miklós went to the Jewish high school. Here, in the mornings, the pupils studied Hebrew, the Bible and Talmud. In the afternoons they learned Hungarian language and literature, Latin, mathematics and other secular subjects. It was an intensely academic establishment, run by high-minded, old-fashioned schoolmasters.

Miklós, having inherited something of his father's outstanding mental abilities, was one of the brightest of an exceptionally glittering collection of students. At the end of his first year, he was awarded a leather-covered copy of the *Torah*, the holy law, for being placed first in Talmudic studies in a class of thirty-four boys. He knew 100 pages by heart.

Rosa shared her son's pride and delight in this prize. When her husband came home that evening she was unable to restrain her excitement. She pushed Miklós forward with his news and his leather-bound booty.

The rabbi examined the book, slowly nodding as he did so, and then turned to his son with a distant, almost hostile expression. 'So, you are becoming a scholar,' he said. 'Let us see tomorrow, after Sabbath supper, just how much you have learned.' And on the following Sabbath eve, Rabbi Hammer questioned his son in a manner so exacting that it would have had his cousin Dani Friedman loudly and laughingly protesting. Miklós did not laugh, though he did protest at his father's dismissal of him with a wave of his hand as 'an ignoramus'.

'What do you want of me, Papa?' he piped in a high voice through his tears. 'That I should be like the Vilna Gaon?' – referring to the celebrated sage reputed to have committed the entire Talmud to memory by the time he was eighteen.

'No harm would come to you if you were.' David Hammer was a man who hid emotional weakness behind a severe exterior. In fact, he leaned upon Miklós to an extent he could not admit even to himself. With a frail, sickly wife and two daughters to care for, Rabbi Hammer looked to the only other male in the family as a source of the strength he needed to shoulder his worldly responsibilities. He was determined that no childish frivolity would encroach upon the serious business of his son's life.

Miklós would sometimes resent this and, as with the incident of the school prize, begin to cry. But he would never break. For most of his childhood he strove to win his father's approval.

Despite the rabbi's strictness, the atmosphere in the flat on Murányi Street was generally cheerful. Rosa and the girls shared the habit of humming to themselves whenever absorbed in some occupation – Rosa at her embroidery, making rugs or sewing curtains; Alice doing her homework; Ibi sitting on the floor, her back against a chair, with a novel or book of short stories propped up on her knees.

Miklós relaxed completely only when his father was away at the synagogue or on communal business. Or in the regular Sunday afternoon games of football in the park at the end of Murányi Street, where he had his only contact with non-Jewish boys of his own age.

Ibi teased Julia, the maid, about her boyfriends. Julia would blush while Ibi laughed playfully. Rosa scolded Ibolya for her behaviour which, she said, was unbecoming in a Jewish young lady. Ibi took this in good part and loved her mother all the more for her concern, even though Alice – 'cheeky', mischievous Alice, who conspired with Miklós to put strange objects in Ibolya's bed or to hide her books – was always let off lightly.

In August 1945, however, in the closer confines of the ghetto flat, Alice at fifteen betrayed few traces of the carefree girl she had been throughout that previous decade at 34 Murányi Street. She and her mother were still capable of a sort of serenity, of absorption in domestic tasks, but it was no longer wholehearted. In this it resembled the animated chatter on the streets outside, which now carried an edge altogether absent in the brighter, pre-war days.

David, Rosa and Alice were eager to return to Murányi Street, but they knew it would take months for Budapest to reorganize itself. And, in a city of fragmented families, the Hammers, too, were looking for their lost pieces.

Every day, new lists were posted outside the office of the Jewish board of deputies at 12 Sip Street. Every day, David went to check them. For just one morning he had been part of the ripple of celebration which daily broke through the ranks of anxiety. On a list of survivors soon to return from Bergen-Belsen he saw the name, 'Hammer, Ibolya', and raced home to tell his waiting women.

Each subsequent morning he scrutinized the lists for the name of his son, Miklós, whom he had not seen since the previous year when the twenty-four-year-old had boarded a train to rejoin his colleagues in the *Arbeitsdienst*, the Hungarian army's Jewish labour brigade.

The reward for those who survived the rigours of service in the *Arbeitsdienst* had been deportation to the East. And now, more than two months after the end of the war, Rabbi David Hammer needed to look deep into his faith to find a way to deal with the absence of his son.

A mass of anxious thoughts tangled themselves in David Hammer's brain, but his general sense of fear was allayed by Löwy's meek appearance. Turning to his wife, he told her not to worry. Then he asked Alice to bring him his hat, jacket and shoes, and beckoned Löwy to wait inside the room while he put them on.

A few minutes later the two men turned the corner of Wesselényi into Kazinczy Street and Löwy broke the silence. 'Sir, I am a survivor of the Nazi camps,' he explained. 'I was with your son Miklós in Buchenwald.' And, seeing the rabbi's eyes widen, 'I realize you probably have had no news of him. I didn't want to say this in front of your wife. I am afraid I have come to tell you that the Germans shot him. He is dead.'

Some time in the mid 1930s, to his family's great surprise, David Hammer took up painting as a hobby. Although he steered clear of portraits – tantamount to idolatry in the eyes of many orthodox Jews – he occasionally peopled his raw, naïve landscapes with recognizable glimpses of humanity.

He quickly developed a distinctive style, characterized by bold, heavy brush-strokes and muted colours. Certain aspects of his pictures were severely geometric but, having established a context with such forms, he would from time to time release his imagination into more vivid colours and a profusion of shapes, whether in flowers, trees, or even, sometimes, in the suggestion of a crowd of faces clustered in a corner or hovering at a window.

His subjects were chosen from the surrounding neighbourhood or from memory. Although he shunned the human face and body, he would often depict a place indelibly associated with some particular person or persons. Like the little house next to the synagogue, where his parents used to live. Or the stretch of river bank along which he and Rosa had walked shortly after being introduced. Or Murányi Street, by the park entrance, where Hedi the madwoman used to stand in her black cape and hood.

Normally modest about his ability, the rabbi was always eager to show his latest effort to Dani Friedman. He would smile indulgently when Dani would use the occasion to launch into some weighty topic like 'the noble traditions of European painting', or 'the failure of nerve of the Jewish artist'.

Apart from these perorations of Dani's, David's paintings were never talked about. He hoarded them in his study or in a hall cupboard and they were seldom seen by anyone outside the family circle.

He was unable to paint in the ghetto apartment. There were no materials available. But he had taken one of his pictures to Wesselényi Street. A dark, sombre street scene, it was his favourite painting, the one of which he was most proud.

Rosa thought it cheerless: the colours were mainly greys and muddy browns, with splashes of black. But David considered it his most creative work. It gave him a sense of achievement. He felt the picture had some serious, if mysterious, purpose in it. He wished he could have shown it to Dani Friedman.

Rabbi Hammer's head pounded. For some reason he found himself thinking about his dark painting of the street. Noticing, too, that the buildings around him suddenly seemed to have lost their fixed solidity, to be themselves part of a painting. The sky darkened. His arms and legs were shaking. His throat felt as if it was in the grip of some inhuman monster.

But to Löwy, whose grey face wore an expression of patient respect, Rabbi Hammer preserved a calm and dignified manner as he expressed his quiet appreciation to this grim messenger. Löwy shook his hand and gave him a piece of paper on which was written his name and address. 'Please get in touch with me at any time if there is any way I can help,' he said. And he turned and walked away, leaving the rabbi wondering what to say to his ailing wife and fifteen-year-old daughter.

He walked the short distance home like a drunkard trying to look sober, measuring each step too carefully. His mind was a volcano. His heart, which had warmed at the news of Ibi's survival, froze at this revelation of Miklós's fate. At first, in a cloud of darkness, he wanted to die. But a combination of guilt and responsibility towards his wife and daughters quickly fought off such submissive thoughts.

A mental camera shutter threw up scenes from Miklós's infancy and schooldays: standing on Rosa's lap, looking out of a train window; bringing home his first school report; David's own regretted anger at some transgression. Miklós's matriculation. The moment of his first departure for the Arbeitsdienst.

How was David Hammer to convey this shockingly reported ending to Rosa, whose adoration of her son was the central force of her life;

9

which perhaps even kept her heart from failing? Or to Alice, Miklós's devoted former playmate?

By the time he had arrived back at number 19, he had resolved to keep the news from them. As he stepped through the door he tried not to meet their eyes. Alice's anxiety was the keener and she came towards him and laid her hand on his arm. Still he couldn't look at her, and spoke over her head.

'Such a mystery the man makes.' They both tried to pretend there was no catch in his voice. He placed his arms around Alice's shoulders, for him a rare display of affection. Now he was meeting Rosa's stare. Her expression was confused, puzzled, angry even at this unwarranted disturbance of domestic calm.

In contrast, Alice's face showed a dread expectancy. Perhaps she was convinced by her father's shrugging off of their mysterious visitor, perhaps she wasn't.

Rosa, busy with questions, seemed contented with her husband's curt replies. It was a business matter, he had said, something to do with the communal accounts; Löwy was an official from the revenue office.

And when David said he was tired, that it was getting late, and perhaps they should all go to bed, Rosa agreed readily.

But David Hammer was unable to rest. Throughout the night he looked several times at the sleeping figure of his wife in her bed adjacent to his. Remembered clearly her pride and pleasure, twenty-five years earlier, at the birth of their son. More than once he almost woke her, without knowing quite what he would say, whether or not he would tell her what Löwy had revealed. But he resisted and turned his head back to his own pillow, inwardly — and for the first time in his life, almost disbelievingly — calling on his maker for strength and guidance.

He rose shortly after dawn and, with Rosa and Alice still sleeping, dressed and left the apartment. He made his way to the address Imre Löwy had written on the piece of paper. Despite the hour, Löwy was already up, wearing the previous day's same pale shirt and woollen trousers, when David Hammer knocked at his first-floor apartment door.

'Forgive me for disturbing you so early in the morning,' said the rabbi.

'Not at all, my dear sir. Please come in.'

'No, thank you, I won't. I just, if I may, want to ask you one question.'

The two men presented a solemn tableau in the clear, August morning light shining through a window on to the landing outside Löwy's flat, the elder stooped and fatigued, the younger taut and grave.

There was barely any expression in Rabbi Hammer's eyes as he asked Löwy: 'Tell me, did you actually see my son die?'

'No, I wasn't actually present. It was a separate group of prisoners. But they all died. Without exception. I saw them taken away. None returned.'

The rabbi persisted: 'But you never saw Mik . . . my son's body? Please be frank and don't try to spare my feelings.'

'No, I never saw him dead with my own eyes but . . .'

David Hammer interrupted him: 'Then I still have hope. We are in God's hands.'

2

By the time Miklós Hammer was about fifteen or sixteen years old, a philosophical divide had already begun to open up between himself and his father.

Rabbi David Hammer's conception of Judaism was not only intellectually rigorous but also generous and humane. Notwithstanding the depth and volume of his scholarship, he defined Jewishness simply, by behaviour, not rule; attitude, not appearance.

'A Jew,' he once told his son, 'is somebody who, at least once in his life, utters the *Shema*, the declaration of belief in the one true God, with complete sincerity.'

In practice, however, he regarded Jewishness as a pure state, always open to contamination from external sources. Though firm in his own belief, he sought to shore up his family's observance by denying validity to secular ideas. He refused access to any influence in his home which failed to conform to the highest Jewish religious standards.

Neighbours; schoolfriends of the children; Jews prominent in politics or the arts; even the occasional member of the congregation – any of them could be condemned with a wave of the hand as 'not from a religious family'.

Miklós, stretching his wings and beginning to realize how important his own bedrock of confidence was to his father's emotional security, found the rabbinical outlook too constricting, the way too narrow. The boy wanted to match Spinoza with those who rejected him, to balance Maimonides with Marx, the music of the Psalms with the glories of the great Germanic composers.

Meanwhile, he continued to make his mark at the Jewish high school. He excelled in science and in languages. In addition to the basic Hungarian and Hebrew, he acquired a good knowledge of Latin, German, Italian and – at home with the help of a dictionary, a grammar book and the regular broadcasts of the BBC – English.

So far as his father was concerned, the time spent on this last subject took Miklós away from the only meaningful course of home study: Judaism. They began to quarrel and the boy increasingly took to shutting himself in his room.

Although the rabbi no longer held such authoritarian sway over his assertive son, the father's word was still law in the Hammer household. Rather than cross his father, Miklós began to pursue his growing list of frowned-upon interests in secret. He spent many hours in the public library and read Spinoza, Kant, Tolstoy, Otto Weininger and Havelock Ellis. With his mother's complicity – and small change – he attended concerts. From high up in the 'gods' at the Vigadó concert hall he saw Hubermann, Kodály, Bartók, and the young Menuhin.

Though aware of the sensual pleasures to be derived from a Mozart concerto, a Beethoven sonata, a Shakespeare sonnet, or indeed the promise afforded by Havelock Ellis of unlocking the enticing mysteries of sex, Miklós tended to devour his interests in the intellectually serious manner imparted to him by his father. This had been communicated both directly, as a deliberate part of his upbringing, and, more subtly, through the fact that Miklós, from a very early stage of his life, was party to his father's intimate thoughts.

For years, Rosa's elder brother Leo subjected David Hammer to a great many financial and other pressures. Money was borrowed and not paid back. Leo's schemes often failed but when they did occasionally flourish the time was never right to pay David.

'It has to grow,' Leo would explain. 'You are an investor – in the family business – not a moneylender. You have no head for figures, David. That's why you find it hard to manage for cash.

That's why you are a rabbi. Your intellectual gifts, I envy. Honestly. Ordinary wealth you'll never have, but *spiritually* you are overflowing. In this respect my sister is a lucky woman.

'If only I had time to come to you about religious matters. And if only you had time to come to me about business matters. Between us we could make Rosa a happy woman. Please God, her health should improve.'

Leo Rothman was adept at blurring the distinction between legal and familial obligation, heaping guilt and anxiety upon his unfortunate brother-in-law.

One Saturday afternoon, unable to speak freely to Rosa about her brother's impositions, the rabbi took his young son for a walk in the park. And, while other children ran wildly along the paths and played on the grass around him, Miklós held his father's hand and listened to his father's voice release a tide of troubled feelings.

With nobody else to turn to, David spoke to his young son as if he were an adult. He felt better for doing so. Perturbed Saturday afternoon walks became almost routine events until, at sixteen, Miklós was being called upon to advise his father in the management of his personal and professional affairs.

His adolescence was anything but lighthearted. Until he was almost twenty, girls belonged to the romantic past of William Shakespeare or the equally distant future promised by Havelock Ellis. Close female company was confined to that of his mother and two sisters.

Despite Miklós's rejection of his father's narrowness, his own social life was circumscribed by his orthodox Jewish background. There were certain of his companions whose homes he could not visit since, although they were Jewish, they ate non-kosher food. Similarly, there were friends whom it would have been unthinkable to invite to the Murányi Street apartment; boys who would never wear a *kipa* at the dinner table, or whose less religious upbringing or bearing would be subjected to Rabbi Hammer's too-apparent disapproval.

But this did not prevent Miklós enjoying a large circle of

friends. Quite apart from the fact that his school was entirely Jewish, he lived in a city with a Jewish population of almost a quarter of a million, a cosmopolitan city with an international reputation for art, drama, good food and entertainment. Its citizens called it 'Paris on the Danube'. Jews – certainly in the capital – tended to assimilate into the mainstream. In commerce and banking, the press and the theatre, Jews helped significantly to shape the image in which Budapest chose to see itself.

This still left room for thousands of self-contained religious families, on the margin but generally at ease with their status and sense of well-being within the Hungarian nation.

The cold winds blowing in from Germany following the advent of Adolf Hitler failed at first to unsettle this structure. In spite of the fact that the father of Zionism, Theodor Herzl, was a Hungarian, and an assimilated one at that, his philosophy did little to dislodge the Hungarian Jewish feeling of security, of belonging.

Zionism's biggest impact within the Hungary of the 1930s was upon the younger generation of Jews. And although Miklós Hammer and his friends came together from a shared religious background, what excited them most as a group was Zionism. Young Zionist societies – Betar, Dror, Klal Zion, Hashomer Hatzair – sprang up across Budapest. Meetings were addressed by guest speakers from Poland and Germany.

From the age of fourteen, when he first went along with his friends Gavriel Stein and Victor Sternberg to a gathering of young Klal Zion supporters in a large room above the local post office, Miklós attended meetings avidly. The dream of a Jewish homeland gave his youthfulness its element of romantic longing.

His Zionism and that of his friends was in part a reaction against the conservatism of their parents. The older religious Jews largely remained entrenched in their niche within Hungarian society and regarded Zionism as godless and Zionists as wild political upstarts.

Even as the repressive anti-Jewish laws were passed in tandem with Hitler's approach, the orthodox Jews preferred to put their fate into the hands of God rather than in the keeping of immature idealists. To certain of the relentlessly traditional Chasidic sects, the very idea of establishing a Jewish state before the coming of the Messiah was a heresy.

Miklós, whose religious life was outwardly observant but inwardly inactive, felt no such inhibition. He and his father had many arguments over the merits of Zionism and the Zionists, arguments in which Miklós was frequently confounded by his father's strong, forbidding faith.

Miklós's attendances at Klal Zion and other meetings became part of his secret life, along with the concerts and the visits to the library and the theatre.

In the religious sphere, too, he often acted in secret defiance of his father. He read the Cabbala, the collection of mystical Jewish theological writings, forcefully condemned by David Hammer for its superstition and its unseemly tampering with the tenets of Judaism as he saw them – simple, and uncluttered.

Miklós was also attracted to services at the majestic Dohány Street synagogue, with its regular gatherings of 4,000 congregants and its rich, swelling organ music accompanying a choir of mixed male and female voices, anathema to souls like David Hammer.

Another negative spur for the Zionism of Miklós, Gavriel, and some of the others, was their perception of anti-Semitism in the society around them. Sometimes, during a game of football in the park, one or two of the Gentile boys would shout and complain about 'the bloody Jews'. Vicky Sternberg and others could laugh it off, but for Gavriel and Miklós it would provide more fuel for their burning ambition to settle in the new promised land. As would every disdainful glance from ordinary Hungarians in the street that Miklós might fancy to be directed at his parents' mannerisms or style of dress.

But these were mere drops. The deluge was to come.

Miklós Horthy, the Hungarian regent, dismissed the liberal aristocrat Count Károlyi as prime minister in 1932, and set up a series of quasi-Fascist governments, firstly under Gyula Gömbös and later, Kálmán Darányi, who introduced – and severely enforced – a range of anti-Jewish legislation.

Miklós's first taste of official discrimination came after his matriculation. He wanted to study medicine and become a doctor. His school career left him well qualified to do so but he fell foul of the *numerus clausus* law. This imposed a quota system whereby universities and other institutions could allow only five per cent of their intake to be Jews.

Prior to the introduction of this legislation it had been common for there to be 200 Jewish students among Budapest University's annual admission of 500. Following *numerus clausus*, those Jewish parents able to afford it sent their children to universities abroad: to Brno in Czechoslovakia, to Bologna, Vienna or Paris. Otherwise, the quota was quickly filled by those whose fathers carried some influence with the academic administrators or – in the case of the medical school – were themselves doctors.

Provision was made for a few others to become 'affiliated' students: on payment of a negligible fee, a handful of Jewish young men and women were allowed to attend lectures. Affiliated students were not, however, entitled to take part in practical work, or to enter examinations.

Among the hundreds of young Hungarians afforded a privileged opportunity to attend university by the enforced absence of Jews, a sizeable number turned against the very group they had displaced and from whom their good fortune thereby derived. Fascist clubs were established by the students. There were marches and military gatherings. Anti-Semitic slogans were daubed and chanted across the university campus.

One of the non-Jewish boys with whom Miklós played football in the park was Sándor Gabos, an uncomplicated, brawny youth always happy to throw himself headlong at the ball, a bludgeon in football and in life. He was the same age as Miklós and lived in the same building on Murányi Street, where the corridors would often resound with his uninhibited singing and shouts of greeting. Miklós's father sometimes exchanged a few words on the landing or in the street with Sándor's father, who was a pharmacist. But neither man ever entered the other's home.

Sándor Gabos became a beneficiary of the quota system. Without it he would have been well out of the running for a university place, but in 1938 he found the doors of Budapest University medical school open to him. And this in turn helped Miklós.

Since Sándor's father had connections at the medical school, he was able to ensure the acceptance of his son's Jewish friend as an affiliated student. And Sándor, being a boisterous, gregarious individual, gave Miklós an entry into the main currents of student life. Sándor lent him his library ticket and took him to the cafeteria. In return, Miklós helped Sándor with his essays and examinations.

One morning the two of them were drinking coffee together in the cafeteria. A third student was sitting with them, complaining about the teaching style of his physiology tutor. After a while, this other student, a nervous, self-absorbed young man who seemed to turn everything – even the drinking of coffee – into a struggle, downed his cup and left.

Sándor leaned across to Miklós and placed a hand upon his arm. 'Miklós,' he said in an urgent tone. 'You must keep away from the university tomorrow.'

'Why?'

'Some of the boys will be looking for trouble.'

'Trouble? What do you mean? This has nothing to do with me. I intend simply to come to the anatomy lecture in the morning and go straight home afterwards.'

'*Miklós.*'

'Tell me what you mean, *trouble*?'

'It's just that a group decided to organize themselves. A sort of gang. And you know, go around *looking*.'

'For Jews?'

'I don't know what will happen but I think it's better if you stay at home.'

Miklós's expression of thanks was compounded of irony and frustration. And it was interrupted by five or six other students, friends of Sándor's, swaggering up to the table.

'Well, who's this then?'

'What are you doing with him, Sándor? Don't you know that he's *Jewish*?'

'Of the *Mosaic* persuasion.'

'A member of the tribe.'

'A yid.'

'I wouldn't start feeling too clever, my friend. You Jews have got it coming to you.'

Here, Sándor broke in with a shrug and an eloquent, open-palmed gesture: 'Hey, Miklós is my friend. Leave him. He's a good fellow.'

'Your *friend*? Your *Jew*, don't you mean?'

The incident dissolved in laughter, a smiling Sándor with his arm around an anxious Miklós, thereafter referred to in certain circles as 'Sándor Gabos's Jew'.

The next day, the few knots of Jewish students in and around the vicinity of the university buildings were cornered, taunted and, in three or four cases, beaten with sticks and planks of wood. An affiliate medical student had his arm broken. Miklós, however, had decided to forgo the anatomy lecture.

In the summer of 1938, along with Gavriel Stein and several other friends, Miklós made an application to the University of Jerusalem. Forms were available at the Jewish Agency offices in central Budapest and the young Zionist groups distributed them freely at their meetings. Miklós virtually sprinted home with his to obtain the necessary signature of consent from his father. This was delivered in an abstracted manner, the rabbi purporting to treat the matter as of slight consequence, muttering in an offhand way: 'What's all this? Jerusalem? University? What do you want me to sign? Such notions.'

Every week at the Klal Zion meetings two or three delighted young people would race in shouting, clapping, and waving aloft letters of acceptance forwarded to them by the Jewish Agency. On the day Gavriel Stein received his, he and Miklós drank brandy in a bar until they were sick.

Gradually it seemed as though all of Miklós's young Zionist acquaintances had heard from Jerusalem, and all of them with an offer of a place. One exception was Vicky Sternberg. His father, more alert than most to the coming danger, had arranged for him to leave Hungary to live with relatives in England.

But Miklós heard nothing. Eventually he went along to the Jewish Agency and asked the secretary, Miklós Krausz, why he seemed not to have been accepted by Jerusalem.

Krausz was surprised: 'What are you talking about? Your acceptance came through three, four weeks ago.'

'What!'

'You mean you didn't know?' Krausz went on. 'Your father came here to withdraw his consent.'

At home, a disconsolate Miklós confronted his father in his study, pleading for an explanation. Angry that David had not mentioned his intervention, Miklós was more forthright than he might normally have been.

'Why did you stop me going to Palestine? Why did you withdraw your consent? All of my friends are going. This was the chance of a lifetime for me. What do you care? Just because you disagree with me. You can't decide my whole life for me. What happens to me should be my decision, my responsibility. With you, religion has to dictate everything. Life's not like that any more!'

Out of breath, seeing the sadness in his father's eyes, he knew he was spent.

'Life will *always* be "like that", Miklós. Judaism is all about life, everything you do, your work, your home, your family, your friends. But this is not the point, my son.' Rabbi Hammer sighed and rubbed his eyes wearily. He asked his son to sit next to him at his desk before continuing.

'I am most concerned for your mother's health. You know how special you are to her. I'm not sure that she could have taken the news of your leaving without suffering, physically and mentally. She has been very weak lately. She tries to hide it but I can see. Frankly, I'm worried. And if – the Blessed One forbid – something were to happen to her while you were all those miles away, if she should be taken seriously ill, it would be unbearable for all of us, including you. And then there are your sisters. Still young girls. You are the only man in the family to help me. We must weather the storm together.'

In February 1939, soon after the day of the anti-Jewish attacks at the university, Miklós made a second attempt to get to Palestine. Another Jewish affiliated student, David Goldberg, had secured himself a passage aboard one of the *Aliya Bet* immigrant ships at that time sailing around the Danube and the Black Sea. He offered to try and find a place for Miklós. One afternoon, the two of them went to the Jewish Agency offices to meet an *Aliya Bet* representative who wrote down the bare details of Miklós's name, age, address and the fact that he had been offered a place at the University of Jerusalem.

This time Miklós kept his plans to himself. He was given five days' notice of the ship's departure and secretly put by a set of clothes and other basic essentials in the corner of his wardrobe.

The *Aliya Bet* ships were the subject of much whispered rumour among the local Jews. Garment workers, professors, housewives, students and shopkeepers became filled with romantic, escapist longings which they magnified against the increasingly dark reality of everyday life. It was in this spirit that Ibi's friend Hannah Goldberg shared her excitement about her brother David going on the same ship as Ibi's brother Miklós.

Within minutes of Ibi's arrival home that day, Rosa was almost hysterical. She pleaded with her husband and she begged her son not to leave them. Ibi and Alice were both drawn in, crying and hugging each other.

'You see, Miklós.' David Hammer held up an open hand towards his wife and daughters. 'You are needed here.'

3

In the autumn of 1940, as Miklós Hammer began his third year as an affiliated medical student, his father found him a job at the Jewish Hospital in Budapest. This was a huge institution, packed with medical men of the first rank not allowed to practise elsewhere. It was administratively overstaffed too, with many otherwise unemployable Jews working in shifts in its kitchens, laundries and offices. David Hammer was responsible for overseeing the food, ensuring it was kosher, and, with a group of other rabbis, offering spiritual comfort to the patients, not all of whom were Jewish.

David recommended his son for a clerical post in the department responsible for ordering food supplies. It was an attractive proposition. Not only could Miklós carry on attending lectures at the university but he was also allowed to watch the occasional operation at the hospital. There was free food, agreeable company and even a little pay.

Miklós had grown into an engaging young man. Physically, he inherited equally from both parents. Dark-haired and dark-eyed like his father, he had about him a softness and delicacy that was his mother's. Like his father he was solidly built, though not as tall. He inherited his father's intent, concentrated frown. But this would frequently dissolve in an open, friendly smile that was a replica of his mother's.

The hospital gave him his first real taste of freedom. He was employed in a shift with four other men, Jews from a range of backgrounds wider than he was used to. There was very little work to do and they spent a lot of time just sitting and gossiping.

Each day brought news of the Nazis' progress. Families gathered around their radio sets, seeking comfort in the broadcasts from Moscow and London. Rabbi Hammer came ultimately to bless his son's 'profane' study of English, since it enabled him to translate Churchill's speeches. But in the Jewish Hospital, life was full of purpose. It was a separate world, with its own routines, too active and localized to suffer interference from outside events.

Miklós's four colleagues were all older than he was. The eldest, Molnár, a man in his early fifties, had been a lawyer but was no longer able to carry on his profession in the repressive atmosphere of Budapest. The others were all cheerful working men, pleased with the sanctuary and slender means of living which the hospital gave them.

Miklós was by far the most outgoing and vocal of the group, readily asserting himself to make up for the age difference. Their discussions usually polarized, with Miklós's optimism set against Molnár's sometimes sour view of events. The other three always tried to encourage the younger man's youthful exuberance.

Molnár was especially despondent about what he termed 'Hitler's hold over Stalin'. This was a phrase he repeated constantly, giving rise to many hours of political analysis in the food supplies section of the Jewish Hospital.

Miklós argued forcefully for the inevitability of evil's collapse. Molnár, on the other hand, was heavy with foreboding, even after the Nazi–Soviet alliance was in ruins and Hitler had invaded Russia.

But not all the talk was of the war's progress. With their duties promptly and easily disposed of, the men found various ways to amuse themselves. Miklós was teased for his youth, Molnár for his lawyer's correctness. Hospital politics were debated as fervently – with the added relish of gossip – as those larger issues on which their survival hinged. Women were a constant topic; women in general and women at the hospital.

'What do you think of that new nurse along the corridor?' one man would ask.

'With the big breasts and the hair?' another would reply. 'Nah, she's fat.'

'Fat? What're you talking about? She's womanly, voluptuous, a *real* woman. Fat, he says!'

'Like a barrel.'

'I'd like to get my hands on her, I tell you.'

'Ach, you're such an animal. You've got no culture.'

'And you? You'd like to read poetry to her, I suppose?'

'I've told you, she's too fat. The tall redhead in the men's ward is my idea of a woman.'

'That beanpole?'

The department became a kind of social club. Administrative staff, porters, nurses and even doctors would join in the arguments and jokes.

Miklós enjoyed meeting the young female nurses. He learned to flirt with them, but anything more made him nervous. It required the initiative of Nurse Theresa Levy to suggest a concert trip together. There rapidly followed a second and a third, as well as walks by the Danube, visits to the theatre, a café or bar. There was even a memorable birthday party at the home of one of the other nurses.

At first the friendship between Miklós and Theresa provoked ribald comments on the part of his companions. But once it was established and he became less gauche, Theresa was welcomed as just another member of the crew, the food supplies section's inner debating circle.

The emotion that Miklós experienced most when he was with Theresa was a feeling of liberation, a step further away from the confines of the nest; part of the same novel sensation he enjoyed in his daily chatter with Molnár and the others. He was slightly in awe of her. Though she was a year younger, she was more sophisticated and had been out with other men.

He was struck most of all by how neat and smooth she was. Her soft, brown hair was cut very precisely, always with a mathematically straight fringe. Her clothes were always clean and smart, never overtly fashionable. Her olive-coloured skin was soft and clear; her mouth perfectly, invitingly rounded.

A pattern emerged from the outset. Each new phase of the relationship was entered into at her instigation, gradually allowing Miklós to take over by paying for drinks or commenting knowledgeably about a painting or piece of sculpture in an art gallery. Then she would take his hand and he would blush. But once it felt right to place his hand in hers he would proudly swing arms with her along the street. She first kissed his cheek, stroked his hair, embraced him.

After a few months, in the heady atmosphere of her friend's birthday party in October, Theresa boldly revealed that she had a cousin planning to go out of town on business for a day or two. She had a key. Why didn't they take advantage of the cousin's absence and spend an afternoon there? This question was delivered with a coy but unmistakably erotic flicker of the eyes; a moist curl of her tongue around those perfect, round lips.

Shy, not to say terrified, Miklós fumbled for an answer and later, an excuse. But the next day he was saved anyway. Papers arrived at his home summoning him to appear in two days, on 11 October 1941, at 7.30 a.m., at the central distribution centre of the Hungarian Jewish Labour Battalion in Buda.

He was entering the *Arbeitsdienst* a virgin, though his spirit already bore more than a few marks of maturity.

It was an odd gathering that collected that morning at the 'distribution centre', a former elementary school. Row upon row of bewildered and apprehensive young men assembled in the old playground. Religious Jews and non-religious Jews. Others who did not regard themselves as Jewish, even some practising Catholics who'd had no idea of their Jewish antecedents.

Almost every conceivable physical type was there. Athletic fellows built like oxen mingled with thin, pallid *yeshivah bochers*. Bearded and clean-shaven, bare-headed and with hats; many wore a lost look, fearful at this new turn in their lives.

Some appeared to relish the outdoor masculinity of the occasion, the issuing of uniforms, the lining up in ranks, the discipline and collective impression of power. As they were slowly called and placed in alphabetical order, little clusters formed among those waiting. They made jokes and exaggerated their laughter. They stamped their feet and beat their arms against their coats to fend off the early morning cold.

Miklós reflected upon the preceding few days, the abruptness of his departure from the hospital; the short, impersonal list of 'essential items' – shaving brush, razor, toothbrush, mug, spoon, knife and fork – that had accompanied his call-up notice; the hesitant encouragement from his father; the fussy attentions of his mother, masking her concern. He wondered what Gavriel Stein was doing, having long since departed for Jerusalem. And Vicky Sternberg in London.

He looked around for familiar faces. There were a number of his classmates from the Jewish high school. As they were put into alphabetical groups he saw his cousin Siggy, who'd been training at the *yeshivah* to become a rabbi. They greeted each other warmly.

'Hey, Miki. What do you know of this set-up, this *Arbeitsdienst*? All us Jewish boy soldiers.'

'I presume, since it's a labour battalion, we'll be slaving away somewhere for the army. Shovels instead of rifles, that sort of thing.'

'Ploughshares instead of swords!'

'That's right. It suits me.'

'Me, too. I have no desire to fight for an unjust cause.'

Neither was daunted by the prospect of hard, physical work. Labour could be viewed as something noble, even when performed at the behest of tyrants.

Their uniforms – of a coarse, khaki material – were issued to them by a fat, middle-aged and toothless soldier with a country accent. He laughed continually, like a baying animal, at the sorry band of recruits passing before him as he handed them their tunics from the heaps randomly piled into 'small' and 'large'.

26

By about 11 a.m. the sorting and other preliminaries were concluded and the new members of the *Arbeitsdienst*, the Jewish labour brigade, were herded into the school buildings. The Budapest battalion consisted of four companies of between 200 and 250 men. Each company had a commanding officer, a Gentile seconded from the regular Hungarian army, and a dozen or so non-Jewish, non-commissioned officers.

The NCOs seemed to be everywhere. They yelled incessantly at the new recruits, shoving them into loose formations, and passing on orders handed down to them about loyalty, routine and discipline. The commanding officers, in contrast, were rarely to be seen.

Miklós's company was placed in what had been the school gymnasium. They were given blankets and pillows and allocated sleeping spaces on the floor. For the next three weeks they were drilled by the NCOs, spending a great deal of their time exercising and marching around the playground.

Miklós was amused by the sight of such skinny, bookish specimens as his cousin Siggy being forced to push their ungainly limbs into some semblance of co-ordination. After a week, however, Siggy was taken ill and transferred to the hospital

On Sundays they were allowed home for the day. Miklós surprised himself by feeling quite proud to be wearing his uniform as he sat among his family.

The recruits were also allowed to bring back food to augment the bare rations at the centre and Rosa sent her son away each Sunday evening with an inevitably bulging bag.

Rabbi Hammer was concerned about the religious welfare of the battalion. Miklós couldn't bring himself to tell his father of the almost total lack of observance. The strangeness of their circumstances had led most of the recruits to suspend normality. A few could be seen early in the mornings binding *tefilin* to their arms and foreheads. Some even blessed their bread and prayed together on Friday evenings, but these activities were peripheral.

In the course of twenty nights, Miklós read six books, wrote several letters to his family and played innumerable games of chess. He also wrote to Theresa, thanking her for their time together and stating that he was sure she realized 'nothing more would come of it'. She never replied.

On the last Sunday, he went to visit Siggy at the hospital and tried to find Theresa. But she wasn't there.

At the end of the third week, Miklós's company was called together in the gymnasium by a heavily built, pock-marked NCO. This was Gergely, a gypsy, who had already made his mark as the bully of the outfit. He told them they were to leave the next day for 'a destination to be determined by the army'.

The following morning they were marched to the station, where they boarded a train of cattle trucks lined with straw and blankets. After a couple of hours the train pulled out. There were sixty men to a truck. They made regular stops to refresh, relieve and wash themselves. The atmosphere was like that of a children's holiday outing. There was a lot of loud, excited talk and even singing.

It was something approaching a toughened and eager unit of men that arrived forty-eight hours later at Szeretfalva, in central Transylvania.

Three of the four companies were to be stationed in Szeretfalva village. The fourth, to which Miklós belonged, was billeted in the nearby hamlet of Mezökövesd. Their task was to build a section of railway and thereby help improve communications between eastern Europe and the Reich.

Although the locals spoke only Romanian, they clearly comprehended the situation. They appreciated who were the overlords and they sided with the obviously subordinate Jews.

Some of the local inhabitants were ejected from their homes by officers seeking the best accommodation, and had themselves to move in with neighbours. They were people of the land, mostly shepherds and a few modest farmers, none of whose dwellings was in any way grand. So, although the officers commandeered the largest houses, even these were little more than cottages, plainly furnished, with no real luxuries.

Miklós and six companions were placed with a farmer, Károly, a man of thirty or so with a wife and three young children. A brawny, good-hearted soul, Károly welcomed his uninvited guests with genuine hospitality, even though he and his family were forced to sleep in an outhouse while the seven conscripts occupied two bare and simple rooms inside.

Between the outhouse and the men's quarters stood the kitchen, in constant use by all. Miklós and his colleagues slept on bales of straw, covered with sacks. They all warmed to Károly's unaffected cheerfulness. He knew two words in Hungarian: 'Very nice.'

Although the sleeping quarters were cramped, they all had the freedom of the large kitchen and were generally more comfortable than their fellow battalion members scattered around in their various billets. Károly's farmyard, too, was of a fair size and the men were able to stretch their legs among the pigs and goats.

One man in the billet, Stefan Bergel, who at thirty was a kind of father figure to the young conscripts, was able to speak Romanian. Not only did this give them the inestimable advantage of an interpreter, but it speeded up their acquisition of such basics of the local dialect as the words for 'bread', 'drink', 'women', and 'bastard NCOs'.

Two other members of the billet, Nándor Wieder and Paul Justus, had been at school with Miklós. The three of them, together with Stefan, formed a team capable of quite adventurous forays into the social life of Mezőkövesd.

Paul was the schemer, exactly as he had been in their schooldays. Nándor Wieder's father was a successful manufacturer of razor blades, whose wealth enabled him to preside with expansive contentment over a conspicuously religious family life. His son's antics in Mezőkövesd would have shocked him.

Several evenings a week, many of the villagers went to one or other of two rudimentary inns on the road between Mezőkövesd and Szeretfalva. Here they drank cheap beer and vodka, but mostly steaming glasses of coffee. These were evenings of good-humoured high spirits, where the visiting battalion conscripts would learn a few peasant songs and pick up local scraps of gossip and superstition.

While the officers tended to keep to themselves, ordering refreshments to be brought in to them, the NCOs formed a self-regarding circle at the larger of the two inns.

The Jewish recruits primarily amused themselves after their day's labours in such quiet pursuits as cards, chess and reading, enjoying the nocturnal freedom to visit each others' billets. But some of them, including the quartet of Nándor, Miklós, Stefan and Paul, often preferred the company and conviviality of the inn, usually avoiding the one favoured by the NCOs.

They became especially friendly with a large, extended family from Szeretfalva village. This included a young couple, a farmer and his wife, of strikingly contrasting temperaments. While the farmer was a dour individual, most of whose contributions to conversation took the form of quaint agricultural aphorisms (often involving the appearance of the angel of death at harvest rituals or family celebrations), his wife was as playful as a child. She initially would hide behind a veneer of shyness, but that would evaporate as her husband grew more withdrawn.

They appeared to operate in a kind of inverse partnership. As he inevitably became sleepy and taciturn over the course of an evening, so she flowered, singing lustily and laughing coquettishly at the city Jews' attempts at rural Romanian dialect. Her laughter came in short, staccato bursts which she would break off with a sudden smile in which the humour lingered enticingly around her eyes and mouth.

'I was telling my dear wife,' the farmer announced one evening, 'the coming of you foreign people, you Hebrew tribes, is a sign. I seen it in the stars also, last harvest.'

At this, several of his cousins and neighbours nodded like an assembly of lawyers.

'I was telling my dear Maria. "Mark my words," I told her. There will be disturbances around here.'

'You did, you did!' The said Maria laughed gaily before being hushed by her elders and her spouse.

'Oh, 'tis a serious matter,' the latter resumed. 'A sheep in Szeretfalva village gave birth to a two-headed lamb last spring.' He allowed this part of his narrative to sink in while he took a sip of beer and lit his pipe. A gulp, a blow on the match, a baleful cast of the eyes and, 'One head was white, the other . . . black.'

This had its effect. Shocked gasps from the women (except his wife Maria, who was trying like a schoolgirl to suppress a giggle), low moans and shaking of heads from the local men. The young Jews at the table made encouraging noises and feigned astonishment.

His point made, this agricultural raconteur sat back and smoked his pipe, satisfied to let others take up the theme he'd given them and to withdraw into the mysterious corners of his imagination.

A few nights later, Nándor invited this farmer and his Maria, and the range of aunts and cousins that went with them, back to the billet. Károly knew the Szeretfalva family by sight and offered them mugs of tea.

The three Jewish conscripts who hadn't been at the inn moved into the smaller of the two 'spare' rooms to continue their game of cards. Paul drifted off to join them and the husband from the inn decided to depart the company too, leaving them with a valedictory aphorism about the moon, darkness and the devil. The safe return of his wife was entrusted to a pair of cousins.

In her husband's absence, Maria's laughter was more spontaneous, less controlled. She sang along with Nándor's roguish versions of Romanian songs and let him teach her some scurrilous Hungarian rhymes. At the end of each little burst of singing, she slapped Nándor's hand playfully and pushed her head against his chest as she laughed.

The following night, all six of Nándor's colleagues moved into the next room after he managed to bring back the laughing Maria on her own.

4

Miklós and Nándor had the good fortune to be appointed to the 'hospital' – a room at the railway station about twenty feet by twenty feet square. Miklós, on account of his training at the university and the Jewish Hospital, was made medical superintendent and Nándor was his orderly.

Having been promised such posts before leaving Budapest, they'd had the foresight before departure to stock up on aspirins, bandages and other basic medical supplies at the Jewish Hospital. Without these, treatment at the Mezőkövesd 'hospital' would have been still more of a haphazard, amateur affair than it undoubtedly was.

There was a set routine. The conscripts rose at around six and reported for work in the station yard at seven. They were given hot coffee and then the workforce marched away under the direction of the NCOs. Anybody who wished to report sick had to convince that day's hospital duty NCO. Few would risk feigning symptoms to these men, several of whom overcame their boredom with casual sadism. Those who were able to show they were ill then came to Miklós for treatment.

Tending the sick and writing reports for the company medical officer normally took until noon, sometimes longer, and then Nándor and Miklós would spend the afternoon cleaning the room from floor to ceiling.

The medical officer, a vaguely affable former professor of medicine at a provincial university, visited regularly. He was a round-faced man of a florid, broken-veined complexion hinting at a deep fondness for alcohol. But, despite this, and a generally unkempt personal appearance – his thick moustache was unruly and stained, his tie and uniform invariably undone – he insisted upon Miklós's 'hospital' being immaculate.

One way and another, Miklós was kept busy and the fact that, like the barber, the cook and the battalion secretary, he was exempt from the hard labour which was the *Arbeitsdienst*'s *raison d'être* in no way diminished his popularity with the men. As the resident 'medic' he was frequently consulted after hours by conscripts suffering from a range of ailments, physical and psychological, real and imagined.

Some of the local peasants even came to him for medical help. One night, at about three in the morning, he and his room-mates were awoken by an urgent knocking at the window of Károly's house. Károly himself went to investigate and brought in a young farm worker who was running his hands through his hair in a state of agitation.

Károly explained that the man's wife was in labour. Miklós got dressed, followed the man to a rough hut on the edge of a farm half a mile away, and helped bring a baby girl into the world. The grateful young peasant rewarded him with twelve newly laid eggs.

Even the NCOs reacted favourably to the resident medical man. Two of them, the pock-marked gypsy Gergely and his friend Márai, had especially good cause to be well disposed towards Miklós. Among the supplies he and Nándor had obtained from the Jewish Hospital was a case of sulphur. It was used for the first time when Gergely and Márai presented infections after two or three visits to a pair of village girls who quickly became known throughout the battalion as the 'sisters of mercy'.

Gergely introduced what became the standard form of punishment for conscripts who failed to report on time in the mornings, or who were unable to convince the hospital NCO that their sickness was genuine.

This involved stringing up the victim by his hands to a high post or tree, leaving his feet skimming the ground. The poor wretch would inevitably pass out and then Miklós or Nándor would be called upon to throw water over him and cut him down.

Out on the site, where the men were digging the railway, anyone caught not working was beaten with a rifle butt. A few suffered severe injury in this fashion and one, a small, delicate youth whose father had shared rabbinical duties with Miklós's father at the Jewish Hospital in Budapest, never recovered.

At least once a week, Miklós wrote to his parents. Before leaving Budapest he and his father had devised a code so that he could be kept informed about what was happening in the city and in the war at large without arousing the authorities' suspicions. The two of them had correctly anticipated that the *Arbeitsdienst* conscripts would have no access to radio or newspapers, and that their correspondence would be subject to censorship.

Rabbi Hammer had an old friend called Wiesner, a distinguished religious scholar who became Chief Rabbi of Munich. Another friend of the family was a businessman called Freilich, who had gone to live in London before the war. In their letters, Miklós would regularly inquire, and his father report on, how Wiesner and Freilich were doing.

In reality, David Hammer had long lost touch with both men and was using their names to indicate the respective fortunes of Germany and Great Britain in the conduct of the war, with similar cover for the Russians and the Americans.

At New Year, Miklós was allowed a week's leave to visit his family. About one in ten of the conscripts was granted this occasional privilege and would be urged by his comrades to deliver and gather news and collect small trinkets, photographs or items of food.

After a tiring train journey with many halts, at which Miklós had to show his train pass and identification papers to a series of identically brutish militiamen, he arrived in Budapest on a crisp and frosty Monday morning.

The city seemed to have changed. People walked faster along the streets, bent into their coats. They greeted each other curtly, if at all, and rarely smiled. Loudspeakers had appeared on street corners.

The concert halls and theatres remained open, however, and Miklós went to see a performance of the Tchaikovsky Violin Concerto by a young Polish virtuoso, and of a play by Hungary's premier playwright, Ferenc Molnár.

No longer did he bother to hide the purpose of these excursions from his father, though he did keep secret a visit to the old headquarters of the Jewish Agency. Here the only person he could find to speak to was a deaf and elderly caretaker who could tell him little about the extent, if any, of Zionist activity in the Hungarian capital.

At home, Rosa remarked upon how 'toughened up' her son seemed. He was a good deal leaner, and more upright. To his sisters and his father it was apparent for the first time that this young man in his army-issue greatcoat and tunic had left boyhood far behind. Ibolya, in particular, was quieter and more restrained towards him, less physically demonstrative.

Rabbi Hammer wouldn't talk about the war in front of the family. Instead, he got Miklós to accompany him on several walks, where he expressed a God-trusting, but grave, fatalism.

'Our worries increase all the time,' he told Miklós once they were clear of the apartment building on the first day. 'Shortages. Restrictions. Your mother isn't getting any stronger and I'm not getting any younger. The synagogue is now a haven for a handful of dreary old men. Four or five of them – old Stern, Izidor the hatmaker and a couple of others – seem to spend their whole time there. But somehow the more they pray, the more it seems to me their devotions are automatic. It's as if the most important thing, the spirit, has died inside them.'

He shrugged. 'Ah, Miki, I don't know. We are at least still alive, all of us, still ticking away, blessed be the Holy Name. We have much to be thankful for. I'm still painting; your mother still enjoys her sewing. News of the many battles is not good just now but evil men have always been in the world.

'We are now learning the lessons our ancestors learned. We

35

can appreciate their experience more deeply, be at one with them in the remarkable wholeness of Jewish history. Understand that God is good and profit by the closeness of wrongdoers. Learn to stand apart from such people and realize all the more strongly that our ways are righteous ways. These times will pass, Miklós, with their cruel men, these Nazis.'

Miklós kept a stiff silence throughout this speech. He knew that his father wanted no answer. And although they walked side by side neither looked at the other's face. Miklós replied only to direct questions, those his father asked him about life in the *Arbeitsdienst*, who his colleagues were, what kind of families they came from.

Miklós told him about Nándor, about raucous evenings at the inn, about the card games. The rabbi hardly seemed to listen.

On subsequent walks, Miklós asked about family matters.

'How is Uncle Leo?'

'We don't much hear from him these days. He has worries of his own, I suppose.'

'What about money?'

'Money . . . everybody has problems with money.'

On the day before his return to Transylvania, Miklós went to the synagogue with his father. It gave him a chance to bring into focus the thoughts and impressions which were crowded and confused in his mind. His mother's poor health. Ibolya's new and more respectful attitude towards him. The concert where the music appeared to transport the soloist, orchestra and audience away from reality for a short, wonderful period. As he'd joined in the thunderous applause at the conclusion of the Tchaikovsky he had experienced a totally new and intense emotional release.

He half listened to his father's sermon, which was confined to biblical matters, scrupulously avoiding any reference to the way the world stood in January 1942.

Leaning heavily on the reading desk, David looked up at the synagogue's dark, wooden ceiling rather than down at the faces below him. He quoted Moses's warning to Pharaoh.

> *Send now and gather your cattle and all that you have in*
> *the field; for upon every man and beast which shall be*
> *found in the field, and shall not be brought home, the hail*
> *shall come down upon them, and they shall die.*

Rabbi Hammer drew no parallels from the ancient book of
Exodus, no message for his congregants to consider.

> *He that feared the word of the Lord among the servants of*
> *Pharaoh made his servants and his cattle flee into the*
> *houses. And he that regarded not the word of the Lord left*
> *his servants and his cattle in the field.*

To Miklós Hammer the parallels came easily. He thought,
for the hundredth time, about Gavriel Stein and others of his
friends in Palestine, and about Vicky Sternberg in England.
He recalled his mother begging him not to leave on the *Aliya
Bet*.

He found himself missing Theresa Levy and then longing for
the company of his companions at Károly's cottage in Mezökovesd. He left with a vague feeling of disquiet.

In June 1942, Miklós's entire battalion was uprooted from
Transylvania and transferred back to Budapest. Those, like
Miklós, who had families in the city were allowed to sleep at
home, while a makeshift few were housed once more in the old
school gymnasium. Uniforms were surrendered in favour of
yellow armbands, and even these were abandoned in the evenings when the conscripts were left to themselves.

They were much more scattered than they had been in
Mezökovesd. Miklós was at first appointed medical officer at
the Military Geographical Institute on the outskirts of town,
moving in August to the more central military academy, where
Nándor had already been given a more privileged clerical
position. The great majority of the other recruits were dispatched to various labouring and menial operations.

At the end of their working day, these young men attempted

to shake off the austerity of the city. Miklós became a regular again at the Vigadó concert hall, met up with groups of friends in cafés and bars, and even went dancing. For the first time, he was enjoying a full social life.

Most of the weekends were spent with his family. His father presided over a full table once more for Sabbath meals (though there was less food now) and the two men even sang Sabbath songs together. On Sunday mornings they went as a family to stroll in the park, where they listened to a brass band playing Hungarian and German folk tunes.

Budapest lay in a heavy, expectant calm. The thick, humid July afternoons felt ominous. There were relatively few adult men on the streets and, of those that were, most were in uniform. Many Hungarian troops had been posted to Russia. The lid was finally closing down on 'Paris on the Danube'.

Rabbi David Hammer was no longer able to conceal his unease from his family. While he continued to make statements of steadfast spiritual optimism, the table talk was weighed down with foreboding.

'Surely this war is no business of the Jews.' Rosa made this point regularly. 'Why should it affect us? With whom are we picking a quarrel?'

'We are fated to observe the world's woes.' Her husband tried to reassure her, adding, 'And eventually . . . to triumph.'

Ibolya pitched in: 'How can you talk of the Jews triumphing in the middle of all this fighting, when they are spread all over the place without weapons, their noses either stuck in books or in barrels of herring?'

'Ours will be a *spiritual* triumph. The Lord will remember his people, Israel, because they remember their Lord.'

'But they will *all* turn on us,' rejoined Ibi. 'Germany, Russia, *Hungary*. Because we are such an easy target. Because they all hate us.'

'How do you get such silly ideas in your head?' scolded Rosa. '*Hungary!* Germany, yes, maybe. Poland. There's no love for Jews there. My cousin Rivka tells me in her letters. Such people they have to live amongst. But surely not Russia, in the end. That's all history. And Hungary is your *home*.'

Miklós was standing away from the table when this exchange took place, his back to the room. He was gazing out of the window at two young Jewish men whom he recognized from the *Arbeitsdienst*. They were locked in some heated argument. He couldn't hear what they were saying but their gestures described their mood eloquently.

They were standing by the park railings directly across from the Hammers' flat. If either man had looked up he would have caught Miklós's gaze, but each was too intent upon the dispute. After a minute or two they were interrupted by a third man, a frail, elderly Jew who crossed the street in order to intervene. He seemed to plead earnestly with one of the younger men in particular. Suddenly, this latter reached into his shirt pocket and pulled out his *Arbeitsdienst* yellow armband. He crumpled it into a ball, threw it into the face of the old man and ran off.

Miklós felt himself shudder. Before he could react further the other young man looked up and caught sight of him, causing him to step back abruptly into the room.

Most conversation was bolstered by rumour, in which fear and hope mixed more or less equally. Throughout August 1942, one particular rumour began to obsess the *Arbeitsdienst* conscripts. With many regular Hungarian soldiers serving in Russia, word began to spread about the possibility of an imminent posting to Stalingrad.

This amounted, more or less, to a death sentence. Jews in such locations were sent out over suspected minefields, scampering to their deaths like helpless rabbits.

Nándor Wieder soon discovered that this rumour was not without foundation. At the military academy, he befriended a boastful recruiting sergeant named Bakos. A drinker, an amusing companion whose tongue loosened a little more with each glass, Bakos became a useful source of information to Nándor and Miklós when they met him once or twice a week in a quiet bar discreetly positioned off Margit Körut Street, a block or two from the academy.

One morning at the beginning of September, Nándor met Miklós in a corridor at the academy. In the brief moment they were alone Nándor told him, 'It's official. Bakos has seen the orders. The battalion is leaving on October the 19th for Stalingrad.' And, as they became engulfed in the gathering tide of workers and military personnel – 'Meet me tonight in the park.'

The next few hours were perhaps the darkest Miklós had known. As he went about his duties – he was again a medical officer – he mentally wrestled with despair as he sought practical remedies for this new situation. He eventually resolved to urge Nándor to leave Budapest with him, go to his cousins at Tiszabüd, hide for a while and either return or seek work on a farm.

But when the two met that evening, sheltering from a shower in the park bandstand where the Hammers listened to brass band melodies on Sundays, his friend offered a more immediately practical means of escape.

'The list of names will be issued in two weeks,' he told Miklós. 'It will not necessarily contain every name in the battalion.' And, it seemed, Bakos could be their deliverer.

'I need to give him money,' explained Nándor. 'For five only. You, me and three others. A thousand *pengö* each. Can you arrange it?'

Miklós ran home as the rain abated. The fresh moisture on his face made him feel almost exultant. Wet and panting, he went to his father's study. He sat in an armchair and caught his breath without speaking. The rabbi looked up from his book, pushed his spectacles up over his eyebrows and, still holding his book open, turned to his son.

'Yes, Miki, what is it?'

'Father, you are reading the holy scriptures.'

'Yes . . .'

'I need, myself, to play God.'

'Whatever do you mean, son?'

'The battalion is to be posted to Stalingrad and certain death.'

David Hammer started, closed the book and came forward to stand over his son.

'A thousand *pengö* can keep me off the list of recruits.'

It was a minute or two before his father spoke.

'How . . . how can we raise the money?'

'We must.'

'We will. In the morning I'll ask your mother to speak to Uncle Leo.'

'Dad, *nobody* must know. It is absolutely vital. We can only save five.'

David fixed his eyes upon his son's, turned away, picked up the book he had discarded and blessed the name of God through the open window.

The next evening, after work, Miklós made three visits. He called at the homes of Ede Kaller, Imre Goldberg and Siggy Zweig. Kaller was a good friend from his schooldays. Goldberg and Zweig were newer but equally trustworthy comrades in the *Arbeitsdienst*. Each came from a sound, respectable family, capable of discretion, and of gathering 1,000 *pengö* without too much fuss or difficulty.

In each home, Miklós was able to speak directly to father, mother and son as they sipped coffee around a table. And, on each occasion, the parents' reaction was more shocked than the son's. Ede Kaller's mother was visibly appalled at Miklós's blunt words. Imre Goldberg's elderly father stood up without saying a word and turned his face to the ceiling as his chest heaved and tears flowed down his face.

No questions of morality came into these conversations. Miklós concentrated on the two urgent topics – money and secrecy. Bakos had given Nándor a fortnight to find the money. Miklós gave his own and the three other families ten days.

To spare David Hammer added mental turmoil, Rosa prevailed upon him to let her brother Leo know exactly what the money was needed for. In deciding to do this she had to balance the risk of Leo's indiscretion against the manipulative hold he would have exercised over David as the price for his ignorance. In the event he was flattered, and even moved, to accept the role of his nephew's saviour.

On the evening of 14 September, Miklós handed 4,000 *pengö* to Nándor in the park bandstand. There followed, for the five families, fourteen anxious days of silence. Leo attended the two Sabbath evening meals of that period which, since neither Ibolya nor Alice knew of the ransom, served only to increase the tension.

On 28 September, letters were sent to the homes of more than 500 young Jewish men in and around Budapest, ordering them to report the following week to the distribution centre. Simultaneously, full lists were posted at the centre as well as at the military academy and various Jewish community buildings.

Most of the Szeretfalva conscripts were included, but not all. Among the names missing were Imre Goldberg, Miklós Hammer, Ede Kaller, Nándor Wieder and Siggy Zweig. For the first time, Miklós revealed to his family the names of his four companions.

On the morning of 19 October 1942, hundreds of Jewish labour battalion members duly left Budapest for Stalingrad. None returned.

5

The battalion members left off the Stalingrad list were absorbed
into another unit. Miklós was kept on at the military academy
but in a more menial role. Both he and Nándor found
themselves cleaning dormitories and sweeping courtyards.
Then, in January 1943, they were once more posted to
Transylvania.

This time they were further from home, at Bereck on the
Romanian border, 400 miles from Budapest. The whole area
was frozen, several degrees below zero, and the men were
housed in huge concrete bunkers, formerly warehouses for the
Romanian army.

There were six of these bunkers, each containing a company
of around 200 men. Beds, consisting of straw and sacking, were
arranged around huge central stoves. Narrow window slats ran
around the top of the high walls. Water taps and latrines were
situated in the yards outside.

The food ration consisted largely of an anonymous gruel-
like mixture, supplemented by potatoes, bread and coffee.
With the thermometer constantly registering lower than minus
twenty, it was ruled too cold to work, so the men remained
cramped together, day and night, in blank, collective apathy.

Miklós was attached to the medical section again, though this
time he assisted two qualified doctors and had nothing to do
save hand out stomach pills of indeterminate origin. Nándor
Wieder was in a different bunker, but Ede Kaller was billeted
next to Miklós and the two of them kept up each other's spirits
with shared memories of home and their plans for the future.
At least, they reasoned, they were still in Hungary. Budapest

43

still seemed accessible. Surely there was a chance of the odd week's leave to see their families?

When the thaw came, the six companies were dispersed through the surrounding countryside. Miklós and his colleagues were taken from their bunker and put up in a small village. He and Ede, along with a dozen others, slept in a barn. The two doctors were posted elsewhere, so Miklós once more became the medical man. Ede and the rest dug anti-tank ditches.

The company had the good fortune to be presided over by a genial and educated captain, a sensitive man in his mid-forties who made no secret of his contempt for the Nazis. Although the labour was hard and the NCOs the usual coarse bullies, the fact that this sympathetic officer was in charge, coupled perhaps with the long winter lay-off, made the men more resilient.

One day Miklós was sent to the nearby town of Cluj to collect supplies from the hospital there. In the morning he was summoned to the captain's quarters in a beautiful old house at the heart of the village.

'Hammer, good morning. You have your travel documents in order, I assume? And the requisition papers for the hospital?'

'Yes, sir. I have them with me.'

'While you are in Cluj I'd like you to deliver these letters for me. They are for members of my family. Please be sure to do this correctly.' Then, as Miklós turned to leave with all his letters and papers, 'Hammer, tell me something. Do you think we will win the war?'

'It depends who "we" are, sir.'

'This is what I find myself wondering these days. All right, you can go ... I believe you are interested in music and literature?'

'Yes, sir, I am.'

'You may spend the whole day in Cluj. Report back to me upon your return this evening. We might even have a little chat about our favourite writers and composers.'

Miklós passed an agreeable day in Cluj. He had enough money to visit a café, where he sat for a couple of hours drinking tea and watching the locals pass by. Otherwise, having completed his errands, he strolled the streets with a long-forgotten feeling of freedom.

Upon his return that evening he reported to the captain as directed. However, it wasn't music or books they discussed but the manner in which Miklós had been transferred to Bereck rather than Stalingrad. It appeared that Bakos, the recruiting sergeant, had got drunk back in Budapest and begun to spend money loudly and prodigiously. He'd boasted of how he'd 'milked the Jews for gallons of cash' and was now to face a court-martial which Miklós and Nándor had been ordered to attend as witnesses.

'I think you should seek advice from a military lawyer,' the captain suggested. 'You will catch a train on July the 2nd and remain in Budapest for the duration of the court-martial – a few days. The court will not take a kindly view of your conduct but remember, on this occasion at any rate, you are a witness, not the accused. Good luck.'

In the event, the hearing was a perfunctory affair and the case was postponed for some months. Miklós had no access to a lawyer, military or otherwise, but hardly needed one. He was merely asked to state his name, number and the locations of his postings with the *Arbeitsdienst*.

So far as he and Nándor were concerned, it was simply good to be back in Budapest. They were exuberant. They called on two girls they'd met during their last stay in the city and spent each evening glorying in their civilian clothes and the uplifting sights and sounds their home town still had to offer them.

A week later they were back in the small village in Transylvania.

Once or twice that summer the friendly captain happened to pass Miklós in the village street. 'Ah, Hammer,' he would say. 'We must sit down and talk about literature. Perhaps listen to music.'

Autumn came. The days passed into winter in an unruffled

routine. Then, on 4 January 1944, the company was transferred to Volóc in the Carpathian mountains. With his medical duties having dwindled, Miklós spent half his time with the other men digging anti-tank ditches designed to impede the now relentless progress of the Russians from the north.

Still under the command of the friendly captain, the discipline in this north-eastern outpost was relaxed. There was a substantial Jewish community in Volóc and the conscripts were allowed to visit local families on Friday nights and enjoy Sabbath-eve hospitality.

On one occasion, Miklós, Nándor and Ede were allowed time off to go to a Saturday morning service at the synagogue. As he listened to the wizened old rabbi conducting the prayers in a feeble voice, Miklós wondered if his father appeared to others as this old man did to him now. Perhaps his father's congregants regarded their minister with the same detached superiority. And perhaps his father's energies were wasted, his learning of no more account than the insincere gabblings of shallow old men like Izidor the hatmaker.

Sitting with his two friends in the picturesque old Volóc synagogue, he recalled the last time in Budapest when he'd heard his father preach: the unmade connection between the war and the Book of Exodus. He felt conscious of himself as a spectator, before whom one curtain had been raised and another lowered.

At the end of January, he was called in by the captain to receive another summons back to Budapest to participate in the postponed prosecution of the recruiting sergeant. Nándor was also required, as was Ede. Presumably Imre Goldberg and Siggy Zweig, too, were being summoned from somewhere.

Upon arrival in Budapest, however, Miklós, Nándor and Ede were met by military policemen and marched away separately. Miklós was placed under guard in barracks in Buda. He was kept there for several weeks, confined to quarters, breathing fresh air only twice a day on half-hour drill marches around the compound. His parents were allowed to send him food parcels and he could write to them.

On 19 March, the Germans overran Budapest. Miklós's regime was immediately relaxed by his preoccupied captors and he was allowed outside the building almost at will. There were a few political prisoners around, with whom he had the odd, desultory conversation, but mainly it was a solitary existence.

German soldiers were everywhere. Bakos's court-martial seemed to have been forgotten. Miklós, too, felt forgotten. Occasionally he thought of his comrades in Volóc. One day he learned they had all been taken to the Russian front.

One of the guards, a paunchy, easy-going, middle-aged fellow, told him. 'You're a lucky man. Nobody survived.'

'Not even the captain?'

'Not a man. I told you.'

'We never did have our literary discussion.'

'What's that?'

'Oh, nothing. Just a memory.' He recalled the captain's concern for the safe delivery of his letters in Cluj and then remembered with pleasure his own day out, drinking tea at the little café.

The war was moving towards a climax. New developments daily altered its complexion. One day that spring, Miklós, still under guard in Buda, looked up to see the sky darken with a phalanx of American bombers. Their intended target was a munitions factory a mile and a half away.

As the barrage began, a stone ricocheted and struck Miklós between the eyes. In the unreal no-man's-land of the barrack compound, a small, sharp piece of reality had hit him. It left a tiny physical scar but a large mental impression. He even laughed. 'They're on the run,' he said to himself. 'They're on the run!' And laughed again.

On the morning of 10 May, the paunchy guard handed Miklós an envelope. 'These are your orders, my little Jewish soldier.' He smiled, almost affectionately, at Miklós. 'You're getting out of here. Back out to do some honest work in the East somewhere. But first you are being granted eight days' leave. The Hungarian army is good to you, young man. You'll be able to see your family today.'

'But what about the court-martial?'

'I know nothing of that.'

As he made his way home, Miklós felt himself to be in a different city from the one in which he'd grown up. He heard German spoken on the streets almost as much as Hungarian, and spoken loudly and confidently. There were very few young Hungarians to be seen and the older men and women, the ordinary working people, seemed to have about them an unnatural dullness and severity. It was apparent in their clothes, their gestures, and in the scraps of conversation he heard in queues outside the shops and along the pavements.

At the corner of his street two women passed each other and exchanged brief nods before hurrying on. Normally such women would have stopped for half an hour or more at that same corner, complaining about the price of meat, the pains in their limbs or the behaviour of the neighbours.

And, at the courtyard entrance to his own apartment block, a German soldier leaned against the wall, listlessly eating an apple and spitting out pips as if in contempt for the building's occupants.

When Miklós eventually entered his own home, the atmosphere was funereal. They had been ordered to surrender their radio set to the authorities. No more gathering round to listen to the BBC.

His father's cheeks had lost their smooth roundness; his skin was sallow, his eyes tired and watery. His mother appeared shrunken and bent; her face pinched around the mouth. Both his sisters were sullen and withdrawn.

He opened the hall cupboard to hang up his jacket. His father's paintings were piled up at the bottom, gathering dust. Above them hung the family's clothes. Each of their outer garments, including some dresses, had a crude yellow star sewn on to it. It was like a wardrobe of costumes for amateur theatricals.

48

In a little under two months, the German clerk in charge of all this reorganization, Adolf Eichmann, had delineated and isolated the Jews of Budapest with the utmost efficiency. Miklós learned of two uncles and a cousin who had been evacuated from the city 'for the purposes of the war effort'. But where? 'To the East'. There was no official information. The cryptic rumours always distilled into 'the East'. All needs and explanations were located in two words and one direction: 'the East'.

Rosa was in a particularly troubled state. No longer was she refusing to believe that the war would encroach upon their lives – she had seen with her own eyes. No longer did she upbraid Ibi for suggesting they were threatened on their very doorstep. No longer did she find refuge in passivity or patriotism.

David Hammer continued to try to rally his family and his dwindling congregation. But it was all done with a heart full of foreboding. He could make no public reference in the synagogue to the direction the war was taking, but at home he tried to reassure his wife and daughters that the nightmare would soon be over. The liberators were on their way. The Russians. The Americans. Above all, he told them, the Lord would provide for his people.

But the sounds and smells of war had never been this close. Germans were barking orders in the street. The air was charged with bombs and bullets. The contagion of inhumanity, the acrid odours of fear, had spread into the remotest corners of Budapest. And for those who were not, like Miklós, conscripted to the military effort, the only way out was to be prised out.

Miklós's parents had at one time discussed the possibility of temporarily joining his father's sister or his mother's aunt in the country. Instead, they had found themselves sending parcels of bread, jam and a few vegetables to these provincial relatives to help them cope with food shortages.

They were caught, all these Jews. The teachers and the doctors, the tailors and the lawyers, the bankers, writers and musicians. Caught like butterflies in the net of the boring little lepidopterist, Eichmann.

Alice asked her father why people spoke so much about 'the East'. The phrase had become an incantation, which hung in the air, unadorned, almost revered.

'Ah, rumours,' he would say, as dismissively as he could manage. 'These gossipings are just rumours. They are calling some people up to the army, to help them in their war. Like Miklós, here. And they are fighting these days mostly in the East. And losing. May our cousins be working for a losing cause!

'All this fighting, this uncertainty, is bound to make people worried. And when people are worried they spread rumours. They know nothing. But soon it will be over. We will all lead proper lives again. Without these indignities heaped upon us.'

At these last words, he waved derisively towards their clothes hanging in the closet, daubed with their yellow patches of felt. And when he spoke in this way Rosa could not look directly at him, or at her youngest child going on with her questions.

Though she said nothing, Rosa inwardly agonized. She had an instinct about 'the East', and mourned her missing cousins in dreadful, unspoken anticipation. While her husband found words to reason himself out of a corner, while her child gave voice to her confusion, she screamed in silence.

Miklós intervened to try to rescue his parents from despair. He, after all, was already part of the effort out East. He told them of the companionship in the *Arbeitsdienst*, the optimism, the easy life they led.

He didn't tell them about the annihilation of this life of ease, of the passing of the friendly, cultured captain and all his comrades from Volóc. Nor did he refer to Stalingrad.

He discovered that Ede Kaller was also on leave, and the two of them spent three or four evenings together. They enjoyed each other's company and joked a lot. Miklós was glad to get away from the gloom at home. But there were no celebrations this time, no concerts and no girls.

Their leave came to an end in mid-May. Ede and Miklós arranged to meet at the station. Miklós left the apartment at eight in the morning. He hugged his mother and kissed her lightly on the forehead. He smiled affectionately at Alice and squeezed her cheek. His father and Ibolya went with him to the station, a short walk and bus ride away.

The sun lit up the day. It was bright, hot, and the barest of breezes ruffled the leaves and gently lifted the corners of posters that had been slapped on to almost every wall. The city itself seemed to be thrown into stark relief, its cold, hard greyness in angular contrast to the flowing warmth of the day.

Miklós was disturbed by a sensation of change. The mood and identity of his native city seemed to have been altered irrevocably. The German occupation simply sealed an already established process of transformation. Only the Danube remained its eternal self.

His departure somehow bore the marks of a ceremony, an auspicious passage. This feeling was reinforced by his father kissing him farewell at the station gates. While Ibolya walked on a few steps towards the platform, David stopped, clearly unable or unwilling to go any further.

Miklós turned to face him and, as he did so, the stiff, physically undemonstrative rabbi pulled his son to him and kissed his face in a surge of love and helplessness. He remained rooted to the spot as Miklós and Ibolya walked towards the train.

After a few seconds Miklós turned and saw his father still standing there, arms hanging by his sides, apparently unable to wave goodbye. He wore an old, much-repaired jacket, on which the sun seemed to be reflected in the yellow splash of felt at his lapel.

Miklós turned away for the last time and marched alongside his sister, her expression steady and serious. By now they could see Ede, his thin, white face showing signs of too little sleep. He waved eagerly. Miklós greeted him in return.

'I must go back to Daddy,' said Ibolya. 'I won't wait for the train to leave. God bless.'

She leaned forward and embraced her brother. He returned

her kiss and, like her, avoided saying goodbye. Both had tears in their eyes. They could find no more words. Ibolya smiled faintly and ran back to join her father.

Although the train was crowded, Ede and Miklós managed to find seats. They were both more inclined to fall back on their own thoughts than to carry on a conversation, and they spoke few words over the course of the journey.

Ede quite quickly drifted into sleep. Miklós tried to read a newspaper but found it hard to concentrate.

A couple of the other passengers in their compartment, a hollow-cheeked youth and a fat, matronly old Romanian woman, carried baskets of food, which they ate avidly and, in the boy's case, noisily.

Their other travelling companions were a pair of Hungarian merchants, plainly bored by a life spent travelling. A group of German soldiers, two or three compartments away, launched into song every so often. Somewhere in the corridor a child cried and a woman giggled intermittently.

Progress was slow; there were many halts. Officials and military personnel boarded and descended from the train at almost every town. At a couple of stops the passengers were encouraged to leave the train for coffee or exercise. Miklós and Ede declined and on one occasion found themselves alone in the compartment for an hour or so.

Food vendors prospered, proffering their wares through the train windows at each station. Eventually, as they drew nearer to the Romanian border, the engine settled into a regular rhythm. Day gave way to night and the sounds of the train became more nocturnal as people shuffled and dozed in their seats or squatted against baggage in the corridors.

Miklós removed his coat and kicked off his shoes as he stared at the window, which offered a shadowy view of the country-side and a much clearer reflection of the six occupants of the compartment.

Ede was asleep. The hollow-cheeked boy appeared to be staring at Miklós, or perhaps he too was trying to look through the window. The old Romanian woman and the merchants had long since left the train. Their places had been taken by three taciturn young men in Hungarian army uniform, who had previously been standing in the corridor. Even in the imprecise reflection of the window, Miklós could detect the nervous tightness on each of their faces.

Suddenly the train screeched to a halt. Passengers were jolted awake. There was a murmur of startled agitation. Lights flashed; a dog barked outside. They were at a station: Nagyvárad.

A pair of Hungarian paramilitary gendarmes boarded the train and slowly threaded their way along it checking the passengers' papers. Eventually one of them came into the compartment and carefully scrutinized the papers of the three soldiers and the youth.

As he examined Ede's papers, the officer, a stocky, low-browed individual with tiny eyes narrowed behind wire-rimmed spectacles, stared hard at him and breathed out sharply through his nostrils.

Ede held up his hand to take back his papers but the man held on to them and turned to Miklós. He checked Miklós's documents much more rapidly and abruptly ordered Miklós and Ede from the train.

Both men shook themselves from their sleepy postures and protested. 'We are military personnel,' cried Miklós in an outraged tone. But the man ignored their protests and their questions. Keeping a firm hand on their papers, he simply beckoned to them to collect their bags and follow him.

6

Although it was well past midnight, the station platform was thronged with a ragbag of people and possessions, including several conscripts who, like Miklós and Ede, had been on their way to join the labour battalion.

Miklós and Ede were escorted by the bespectacled gendarme into the waiting-room. Here, they found themselves among a dispirited crowd, packed along the benches and spilling on to the floor. Many had clearly been there for hours.

Miklós recognized at once that all of these people were Jewish, even though only a handful wore the yellow star. The gendarme immediately left them without returning their papers.

'Why have they stopped us from rejoining our battalion?' said Ede. 'What is the point of it?'

'We have been taken prisoner because we are Jews,' said Miklós.

Confused and demoralized, his palms became damp and his stomach tightened. He could see that Ede, too, was frightened, even though he tried to joke about their abrupt removal from the train – which had since continued on its way without them.

They remained in the waiting-room for about two hours. It was dreadfully quiet, possibly because of the time of night. A few people were snoring and most of those left awake spoke in whispers. Miklós looked around the room at the assembled women, children, middle-aged and old people – several of them invalids – and muttered to Ede, 'I can't see many of this lot being of use in the *Arbeitsdienst*.'

Ede shook his head and laughed. 'Maybe they are going to

give you a proper hospital this time, and these are your first patients.'

Eventually, an armed Hungarian militiaman appeared at the entrance to the waiting-room. Those who were sitting or lying down were ordered to their feet and the entire complement of bewildered Jews was herded out in pairs, Ede and Miklós forming one link in a long, straggling chain, slowly moving away from the station towards the town.

Those who had been waiting outside on the platform formed a larger, advance contingent. There was a gap of about 100 yards between the two groups, each of which was escorted by five or six militiamen.

After a mile or so, they arrived at a large synagogue, in grounds protected by iron railings. They were made to go through the gates and assemble in the courtyard. Several more militiamen were running around, pushing the new arrivals into clusters, like so many bundles of dirty clothes.

The darkness was broken by a yellowish glow from a first-floor window above the synagogue entrance. A single light-bulb was burning in what appeared to be an office.

'You! Over here!' Sharp voices pierced the night air.

'Line up. You are under orders now.'

'Come on, you lazy scum. Stop snivelling.'

'Quickly!'

Nobody seemed to be in charge. The militiamen shouted, swore and laughed. They seemed disorganized, unruly, quite unlike professionally drilled soldiers.

After a few minutes, Miklós recognized the gendarme from the train, the man with the wire spectacles. He was carrying a pile of documents. Perhaps, thought Miklós, his and Ede's were among them. The gendarme went into the building and emerged a quarter of an hour later, empty-handed, accompanied by another man.

This latter was bare-headed and wore a white shirt with plain civilian trousers and shoes. He had no jacket and his shirt and tie were undone. He walked with a deliberate slouch. One of his hands occasionally tugged a cigarette from the corner of his mouth; the other was thrust deeply in his pocket. He spoke native Hungarian.

He asserted his authority over the man in spectacles and the rest of the uniformed guards by ostentatious movements of the head. A pencil-thin moustache coated his upper lip, which he drew up in contempt and revulsion at the weary humanity before him.

The Jews mostly stood in silence but here and there a child whined, at which this swaggering, shirt-sleeved commander would yell, in the general direction of the sound, for that child to be kept quiet.

He sucked on his cigarette one last time and, in the same movement with which he tossed it aside, waved his hand for the uniformed guards to take away their captives.

They were marched off to a yard at the rear of the synagogue. From here they were sent in batches into the building and upstairs to the room where they had seen the light on. It contained an ancient filing cabinet, a wooden table and two chairs, at which sat a young German officer and a white-haired Hungarian gendarme.

On one wall was a roughly drawn street plan of Nagyvárad. On the back of the door was pinned a Hebrew calendar, an incongruous reminder of the building's original purpose.

The German officer, with the older Hungarian's sycophantic assistance, was allocating accommodation to the new Jewish arrivals. Miklós and Ede were sent to an apartment a street or two away, where they were joined by several other men from different companies of the *Arbeitsdienst*.

It was in a three-storey building which had been recently vacated by local families. The occupants were packed into spaces designed for a quarter of their number.

Straw beds were arranged around the floor. There were some tables, a couple of chairs and the odd cupboard and shelf, but for the most part the place had been stripped bare.

Miklós dropped gratefully on to his bed and rested for several uninterrupted hours, though both he and Ede were too hungry to sleep properly. They spoke fitfully to the other men in their apartment. All told the same story of being plucked without warning from the train. All were tired, hungry and mystified.

One man, a religious Jew, put his head in his hands and wept. Nobody reacted. It was just part of the overall adjustment to new circumstances.

'What's happening in this place? What do you think they are going to do with us?'

'How should I know? I am as baffled as you. I was on my way to the labour battalion and . . .' The grey-faced man, with several days' more growth of beard than the rest of them, shrugged with eloquent resignation.

'But what do they want with us here? Just lying around.' The youth with the nervous tic pressed on in his anxiety.

'Lying around is better than digging trenches and being spat at by ignorant pigs of guards.' The older man looked ready to meet any new turn of events with deep and worldly cynicism. He lay on his straw bed, his hands behind his head as he leaned against the wall, one leg drawn up at the knee, the other stretched out.

The younger man sat alongside him on the floor, his bony shoulders hunched forward, his head cocked for any morsel of reassuring information.

The two of them occupied positions close to Ede and Miklós. Miklós felt sorry for the boy but was at the same time fascinated by the tic in his face and relieved to see some of his own fear reflected and redoubled in the eyes of another.

'What do you make of that bastard in the white shirt?' The boy's grizzled companion brought Miklós into their conversation. 'What an arrogant swine! A Hungarian, too. I'd like to have stubbed his cigarette out on his arse. Who does he think he is? Ach, some jumped-up peasant.'

'I have only seen one German,' said Miklós. 'The one who directed us to this apartment.'

'Yes, but there seem to be a lot of civilians running things.' Ede joined in. 'Do you think they can all be Hungarians?'

'Hungarians, Germans. Do you think it matters?' Their cynical neighbour screwed up his face. 'They're all ready to kick the Jews in the balls.'

This again provoked the twitching boy. 'Why should they want to harm the Jews? We're not their enemies.' His voice was high, his speech rapid.

'Oh, but we are,' said the older man emphatically. 'And this is not a question of petty border disputes. We've never signed any treaties with them. We are their enemies simply because we exist under their noses. It doesn't matter where you were born, you will always be the unwelcome stranger putting his feet under *their* tables, eating *their* bread, making them smell *your* shit under *their* roofs.

'Oh yes, my young friend, we are their enemies. To them – maybe to ourselves – we are a nation. And a nation which lives within the boundaries of another nation is all too easily seen to be a parasite. And a parasite, my boy, is the worst kind of enemy. You don't merely want to defeat him, make him surrender. Him you have to destroy, because he knows you from the inside. All your secrets and your fears. All your stinking sores and scabs and rotten little dirty tricks.

'And we are always the parasites. Forget that we've lived in our homes for centuries. Longer than them, often. Forget that we play our part in the culture of the country, its economy, its pride, its honour. Forget our children's stake in its future. Parasites! Ach, destroy them.' One arm dropped from the wall, swatting the air.

'But I *am* a Hungarian,' the boy protested, his tic and his voice insistent. 'Hungarian is my native language. How can you be an enemy of war in your own native land?'

The older man shrugged again, with both hands back behind his head. 'You are a Jew, you poor fool. The Hungarians allow you to be there under sufferance. The war has given their Fascist bullies the excuse they were waiting for. And whatever is happening to us in this God-forsaken place, it's better than remaining in Budapest.'

'But my father was a high-ranking police officer in Budapest.'

'Oh? And does he now wear the yellow star upon his shoulder?'

'No. He died a few years ago.'

'Yes, well, I'm sure when the proper authorities find out whose son you are you will be given privileged treatment.' The older man's sarcasm was not quite enough to dispel the boy's confusion. His family had, after all, been model Hungarian citizens. What was he doing being rounded up with these others like a common criminal?

Miklós spoke again, directing his question at the unshaven face still cushioned against the wall: 'Don't you think the people running this place – your friend in the white shirt for instance – are the same types as the Fascist gangs in Budapest?'

'Probably.' His head at last came forward from the wall. 'But there seems to be some official sort of arrangement out here. Not that I'm in any way impressed with these militiamen. Still, aren't we all useful members of the *Arbeitsdienst*?' He held out his left arm grandly, to indicate the dozen odd souls in the room.

'But what about all those women and children and old people with us out in the courtyard?' cried Ede suddenly.

The debate was now taking the edge off the grizzled campaigner's languor. He sat up on his mattress and turned a pair of surprisingly bright green eyes on Ede, his face up close to within an inch or two. 'You must learn to look out for yourself, my friend. As you say: what about those women and kids? What indeed? Who gives a shit? There's nothing we can do, so just forget them. They've been put in some other building.

'Admit that you only mentioned them because you were worried about your own skin. This is a time and place for basic honesty, friend. As long as you can keep yourself going, the rest is shit.'

And then more gently and more generally, easing away from Ede, 'And anyway, they gave us all plenty of dinner, didn't they?' His laughter was too much for the nervous young man, who – his tic throbbing madly – returned to his own bed across the room, looking as though he could vomit at any moment.

They had been left alone for most of the twenty-four hours they had been there. Just once, they had been summoned to the main administrative building. For lunch. This had been substantial enough, a potato stew with even a suspicion of meat in it. And there had been coffee with bread in the morning and soup with bread in the evening.

The only orders they had received were for them to remain in the apartment at all times unless called out by a guard or official. So far, lunch had been the only occasion for this. Otherwise, guards had appeared with the coffee, the soup and, once, silently to check the men were all still there.

Miklós's cynical neighbour was Weisz, a tailor. Miklós pictured him back in his workshop in Budapest, entertaining his customers with a bitter view of the world as he measured their arms and chests, swathing them in checks and stripes and sharing crude jokes over the steaming trouser-press.

Here in Nagyvárad it was Weisz who held that dejected roomful of men together, even though some of them despised him for it. Miklós admired him, learned from him as he stitched together that patchwork of souls as expertly as he ever could have wielded his tailor's needle. After two days, their ranks were swelled by an assortment of civilians. Older men, including a couple of rabbis, who'd been nowhere near any labour battalion. This influx seemed to depress Weisz. He treated the rabbis especially with undisguised contempt.

As Weisz withdrew into himself, Miklós began to realize how much he had begun to depend on the older man, to need his sharp focus, his way of stripping them all of illusion yet reminding them of the hard, consoling fact of their existence as individuals.

But now things were changing. Along with the increase in

numbers came a freedom to wander the streets of this artificially defined township at the edge of Nagyvárad, this Hungarian ghetto of Jews who'd always been content to consider themselves Hungarians, albeit, some of them, 'of the Mosaic persuasion'.

Weisz was one of the first to take advantage of the new liberty – 'to get away from these rabbinical beards, running with their unctuous spittle'. During daylight they hardly saw him. And in the evenings their discussion was no more than a brief preliminary to sleep.

Miklós and Ede stuck together determinedly, constantly analysing their situation, reducing it to essentials, not appreciating how much Weisz had influenced them in little more than a day of talking and arguing.

'Whatever Weisz says, Budapest is better than this.' Miklós was bent on escape.

'We are in prison here,' he continued. 'Disposable like all the old men and the women. No longer of use to them. But if the war drags on they will need us young ones. We must keep ourselves together. Keep ourselves tough. Eventually get back to Budapest. There they will need our strength one day, Ede.'

Ede trained himself to control his desperate longing to be away from there, to be home, to be safe and unthreatened in the bedroom of his parents' house; a longing which drowned his sleep at night and rose in his gorge by day, a scream rising against the sides of his throat.

'We must explore the ghetto,' he would say a hundred times a day. 'Find a hiding place. Bide our time. Await our opportunity.'

Each day they made plans. They tried to remain calm amid the turmoil. Resourcefulness, patience – these were the watchwords with which to hold back the tide that seemed to be sweeping towards them.

The ghetto seethed with its overcrowding, its mass anxiety, its lack of structure or any organization beyond the initial allocation of beds in the bare apartments.

Children ran wild in the streets, their parents no longer

bothering to keep them in check, knowing at least that they could not run away. Men, and even women, fought each other in public, egged on by their companions, sometimes over the possession of a book, a packet of cigarettes or an article of clothing; sometimes over nothing. Food supplies began to run low; stew became soup and no longer tasted of meat.

Suitcases had been confiscated on arrival, though families were allowed one bag of possessions. Each person had one basic set of clothes and, with little sanitation, the increasingly rank odours led these enforced neighbours to care little for their personal hygiene or appearance.

The perimeter of the ghetto was formed by the high back walls of apartment buildings in the main town, linked to makeshift wire and wooden fences, often stretched across roads turning them into abrupt culs-de-sac. It was possible to see through these fences at certain points but uniformed guards patrolled them, preventing the Jews getting too close a look at the local populace.

On the outer side, however, children and old men would sometimes stand by the fence and peer through at the crowds of Jews wandering the streets, the children shouting and pointing, the old men staring blankly through rheumy eyes. The guards usually shooed them away, waving a rifle butt at them, but now and then one of them would laugh along with the children.

Inside the ghetto, there was no shop, no post office, no official building of any kind except the administrative block adjoining the synagogue; only apartments crammed full with Jews from all parts of Hungary.

On the fourth day, one of mocking sunshine, Miklós and Ede were walking along a street when a commotion broke out in one of the buildings. Two old women stood in the doorway, one wailing and beating her breast in biblical fashion, the other yelling as if to outdo her, 'They are lucky, they are lucky! If only God would show such mercy to us!'

The two women were sisters. Two of their brothers had died

in the ghetto apartment in quick succession, the second within the past few minutes. The two men given the job of collecting bodies in the ghetto were already upstairs about their business with the corpse.

These two, the half-simple son of a kosher butcher and a scrawny youth, pallid and bent at eighteen from too much study, had been authorized personally by the man in the casual white shirt – a colonel, it was now rumoured, in the Hungarian secret service.

A few minutes passed and the unlikely undertakers staggered into the street with their load, which they heaved on to their cart. Slowly, sweatingly, they dragged the lifeless bundle to the same lime-covered ditch in which the first brother lay luke-warm. One sister sobbed in the doorway, the other followed the cart, still calling out to whoever would listen: 'They are lucky! They are lucky!'

Later that day, a man from among the second batch of arrivals in Miklós's apartment was taken away by a guard. He didn't return until well into the evening, when the rest of the men were beginning to doze in their beds. He was brought back draped like a yoke around the necks of a uniformed militiaman and one of the mysterious civilians, assumed in the daily gossip to be secret service men working for the 'colonel'.

Their charge was dumped in the centre of the room. He seemed broken. His name was Kertész. A studious bachelor in his early forties, he had occasionally contributed some optimistic note to the evening conversations before falling asleep quite peacefully.

Now he looked far from peaceful. His mouth hung open, a trickle of blood drying at one corner. There were cuts, too, around his eyes, the lids of which were drooped, neither open nor closed.

Weisz, Miklós and a third man, a tall, strong-looking battalion recruit, carried Kertész to his bed. He was limp in their arms, wincing slightly at any pressure upon a cracked rib or an ankle which might well have been broken.

'What happened?' Weisz whispered the question for all of them once he and his two helpers had carefully laid down their battered companion.

There was no reply. Weisz stroked the man's brow, the first sign of compassion he had given, and repeated the question. Kertész slowly shook his head from side to side. Weisz urgently searched his pockets, looked around him and then went over to one of the elderly orthodox Jews.

'You,' he urged one old man, beckoning him with one hand, gnarled fingers held tightly together. He removed the old man's greasy *kipa* from his head and folded it into a sort of handkerchief. He spat on it in front of the old *frummer*, who had no power to stop him. Next he bounded back to Kertész and wiped his face with the stained and moistened ball of cloth, spitting some more to get rid of the blood.

He turned back to the bareheaded owner of the *kipa* and stretched out his arm, dangling at the end of it the ancient skull-cap, black as ink. As the man timidly retrieved it, his head strangely naked until he wiped the *kipa* on his sleeve and replaced it on his crown, the green eyes flashed. 'Thank you,' said Weisz.

It was half an hour before Kertész could fully open his eyes. An hour before he eventually responded to Weisz's patient questioning. All the time, Weisz took great care to make Kertész as comfortable as possible, untying his shoes, stroking his face, propping up his head.

At last, under cover of darkness and the spluttering sounds of old men sleeping, Kertész quietly and slowly told his story to Weisz, Miklós, Ede, Zoltán Klein – the boy with the tic – and about a dozen others forming a semi-circle around the bed like an audience at some intimate revue.

Kertész had been taken, he said, to the headquarters building for 'interrogation'. Puzzled, he had resisted: 'What for? I have done nothing! I am a loyal Hungarian, a labour battalion veteran.' All irrelevant, all ignored. This was, it seemed, an inexorable process.

He was placed on a chair in a dimly lit basement room. Then the 'colonel' had appeared with another civilian. The colonel was in his familiar guise: unbuttoned shirt, neatly trimmed moustache, a sneer through cigarette smoke.

Then it had been: 'Tell me about your money, Kertész? Your jewellery. Where have you hidden it, eh?' A slap from the colonel, a kick from his similarly plain-clothed assistant, the uniformed guard standing by, not quite at attention.

'No money, Kertész? Nothing valuable? A rich man like you?' And the cigarette stubbed out on his navel, a torrent of punches to his chin, a boot in the ankle, a fist in the eye.

And so it continued, Kertész coughing out his denials, protesting he was not a wealthy man, until he recalled for them a small bundle of banknotes he had tucked into a suitcase taken from him the first day.

One last slap, a grin from the colonel, his uneven, discoloured teeth a grotesque contrast with his neat moustache, and then Kertész was carried back by the civilian assistant and the uniformed guard.

Years later, some of these men – there were to be only a handful of them – would remember Kertész's gasped account with more horror than the routine bestiality to which they were later to become accustomed. For those blows to Kertész's face had awoken them all.

A ghetto was something which belonged in the stories told by their grandmothers. They had believed themselves to be under the protection of fellow Hungarians, officials of the State. Suspended for the time being from normal life, it was true, but this was to be expected in wartime.

And so, despite the ominously worsening conditions in Nagyvárad, these Hungarian citizens had refused to believe in the implications of their plight, in the fences across the roads, the slouching colonel and his wayward henchmen.

Until Kertész's return from 'interrogation'.

7

Miklós was greatly affected by Kertész's experience, one that was to be repeated for scores of victims over the ensuing days. He felt like a man who, waking from a grisly nightmare and opening his eyes in expectation of the relief and comfort of familiar surroundings, finds instead that the dream was true. That the walls of his room are those of a condemned cell.

As early as the following afternoon he learned more about the techniques of interrogation.

A number of single women were housed in the ground-floor section of his block. At first this had fuelled the erotic imagination of the men upstairs and the odd liaison was formed. But in the main this small cross-section of womanhood, from a seventeen-year-old student to a sixty-three-year-old kindergarten teacher, quickly became just another set of grim and faded faces.

Miklós struck up an acquaintance with one of these women, Bertha Kaufman, a well-educated pharmacist of about forty. She had a high forehead, large grey eyes, and a soothing manner. Their conversations were brief and pleasant interludes in the general run of ghetto life.

The morning after Kertész, had introduced the fearful concept of interrogation to Miklós and the others, Bertha Kaufman was also taken to the colonel's basement room. Miklós, equating her case with Kertész's, was anxious to find out what had happened.

'I can't understand what this is *for*. These people must know you could not possibly be a spy or anything like that. What were they saying to you? What did they do?'

'Let me just tell you I shall never be able to get over this experience.'

She remained silent for a while, staring straight ahead. She'd had enough of being questioned. But Miklós persisted with the rawness of youth.

'What happened? What were they trying to find out?'

She closed her eyes as she answered. 'Oh, whether I had anything valuable here with me. I told them I hadn't except for the ring I was wearing, which they examined but made no attempt to remove.'

'But why did they not let you go then? What did they do to you? Were they Germans?'

At this, she opened her eyes and shook her head before replying. 'My dear friend, there was not a single German around. They were all Hungarians. Not a word of German spoken, not a sign of a German uniform. They put me on a table. They stripped me, they beat me and eventually they . . .' She bit her lip.

'They what?'

The look she gave him was both weary and compassionate. 'They grabbed my finger with the ring on and said they wanted to know where I had hidden the rest of my jewellery. Then they placed electrical pencils into various parts of my body.'

As the days passed, he sought out new acquaintances in other buildings. But he did not forsake Ede. Whenever they spent a morning or an afternoon apart, the two of them would report back to each other, hoping always to pick up new pieces of information or ideas for escape.

On the day they encountered the two grieving sisters, Miklós had noticed in the crowd milling round the funeral cart a middle-aged man greatly concerned about a large bag his wife and daughter were carrying between them.

At first, Miklós had thought this contained something with which the man could console the mourners, a bottle of medicine perhaps, or even a prayer book, and he offered to help carry the bag. But this made the man even more agitated, until his wife patiently explained that her husband was a diabetic and the bag was filled with medicaments and needles for his injections.

Miklós nodded sympathetically, told her that he was a medical student and that his mother too suffered slightly from diabetes. The woman and her daughter seemed very grateful for this spark of understanding before moving on and leaving him with Ede to witness the bizarre spectacle of the ghetto's first cortège.

The family's name was Grosz. Miklós found out where they were housed and began to visit them. The woman and her daughter − Eva, an eighteen-year-old with long, straight black hair and a pale, sad, beautiful face − were always pleased to see him, though the man was usually irascible, bitterly concerned lest his needles be mislaid. Miklós told them about his family, how he and his sisters used to play tricks on their mother and Julia, the maid.

For the odd, brief half-hour a semblance of domestic normality was regained, the four of them sitting together, sometimes with coffee, around a table in a bleak, bare kitchen. The wife's face muscles, clenched with the task of caring for her sick husband, would relax a little, smiling as Miklós the comedian strove to impress.

This was, they all knew, mainly for Eva's benefit. She acknowledged the attention she was being paid by raising her eyebrows, or coughing gently, her lips too firmly closed to allow any laughter through.

Eva's family was typical of many in Nagyvárad. Torn from a comfortable and cultured existence (Eva's father, Dr István Grosz, was a formerly prosperous accountant, his wife the daughter of a distinguished mathematician), they had no idea how to adapt to the situation in which they found themselves. Or even to accept that it was other than an aberrant interlude in their ordered lives.

Their humiliation increased as they became objects of contempt instead of respect; as they suffered cruelty or witnessed it at close hand. Apart from the torture of 'interrogation' and the street-fighting among the prisoners, the guards raped and assaulted at will. To the colonel and his undisciplined rabble, these captives were less than human.

Courtesy, learning, religious observance, all counted for nothing. This terrible inversion of values reinforced the desperate confusion of men like Eva's father. They were like stunned animals.

The two young burial men became busier and busier. One of the rabbis in Miklós's apartment building managed to commit suicide by hacking at his throat with a belt buckle. Old people simply found the conditions unbearable, and died.

And then the overcrowding ceased. The intake of newcomers slowed to a trickle. Teams of guards began to evacuate sections of the ghetto, apartment by apartment, tossing the old and weak to the burial cart and marching the rest out through the synagogue gates.

One evening, Miklós and Eva found themselves alone together in the kitchen of her apartment. Her parents were sleeping in the next room. In whispers, Eva spoke of her worries, for her parents – especially her father – and for herself. Miklós tried to encourage her, to urge her to find in her youth and her beauty the strength to keep going.

But neither of them were prepared to delude themselves. They had heard about the 'transport'. They had seen the steady procession out of the ghetto. They knew that they would be joining it in due course.

Miklós referred optimistically to the clearly regimented efficiency of the German officers whom they had seen supervising the evacuation. They would be better off with them, he argued; know where they stood instead of being subject to the whim of the ragged bunch of Hungarians in charge of the ghetto.

For most of their conversation her head was bowed, her hands in her lap. Suddenly she raised her eyes to him. 'Miklós,' she said, now placing one hand on the table between them. 'I know at least one thing that is going to happen to me soon. It is happening to all the young girls here, even those from the most religious homes. Some of them even invite it.'

She looked down again and then once more turned her face to his. Her eyes, the way she held her head, the tone of her voice, all indicated a deep fear.

'Miklós, I want you to be the first. I want you to be the man to take me. Not some drunken secret service man. Not one of those SS officers. Not even one of our silly, wild Jewish boys. Please, I am ready. I can't bear the thought of being *defiled*' — she gave the unfamiliar, unexpected word an involuntary emphasis — 'by these people who are destroying everything we love.'

The room grew darker. Neither of them could speak for several minutes. Miklós couldn't even look at Eva. He knew he would have difficulty controlling his voice if he tried to say anything.

He remembered how he had desired her, showing off to her in front of her parents. For this he now felt painfully guilty. She had become for him an object of untouchable, unattainable purity. Even to hold her hand would be an act disloyal to the emotions he was experiencing.

Eventually, he broke the silence, huskily. 'You must not say such things. You must not *think* them.'

He sensed she was crying, though she remained silent and still.

'Eva,' he whispered. 'Eva, you are young and strong. You will get over all this. We both will in time.'

She didn't reply but stood up and went to join her parents in the next room.

One morning that week there was a disturbance at the gates that led into the synagogue courtyard. A crowd gathered, pushing and shoving to try to see what was happening. Miklós managed to peer through a gap in the railings.

A local man, a huge labourer with a loud voice, was pulling along two young girls by their arms.

He was declaiming self-importantly to a couple of uniformed guards who stood idly smoking by the front of the synagogue building. They ignored him at first but then became amused by his brash, naïve manner as he dragged the two girls behind him like a poacher with a pair of rabbits.

'Hoy!' He was shouting at the guards although he had

stopped barely a yard away from them. 'I've brought you a couple of Jewish prostitutes.'

The guards laughed. One slapped the burly labourer on the back.

Miklós turned to look at the girls, two terrified creatures of fifteen or sixteen, feebly trying to free themselves from the man's grasp. Thin and ungainly in plain black dresses and shoes, they seemed a long way from becoming women.

But somehow they had succeeded in running away from the ghetto. If they had given any thought to the sympathies of the local populace, they had clearly misjudged them. Their captor was proud of himself and stood expecting a reward.

The guards took the two girls from him and, raising their rifle butts, struck them with careless violence about the head and arms. The stranger stood by, nodding approvingly. The girls, neither of whom would even have heard the word 'prostitute' before, were taken weeping and screaming into the administrative headquarters.

One of the guards acknowledged this big citizen's deed with a curt nod of thanks. This seemed to satisfy the man, who thereupon held up his fist and shouted, 'There you are!' to nobody in particular, walking backwards a few steps before swinging round to make an untidy and belligerent exit.

As Miklós returned to his block, he found himself walking alongside a Pole he'd heard about from Weisz, a man in his forties who had lived as a Gentile in Warsaw before coming to Hungary. The Hungarian authorities had discovered his Jewish origins and packed him off to Nagyvárad.

'You people have no idea of what is waiting for you,' he snapped sharply in Miklós's direction.

'What do you mean?' asked Miklós. 'Here in this place, or the labour camps?'

'Labour camps?' The Pole gave a hollow laugh. 'Yes, labour camps.'

'Do you know something about the labour camps? That is where the transports will take us, isn't it? Are they hard? What about the women and children?'

'Such camps exist in Poland. Run by the Germans. The women and children go there too. You won't be able to survive it. If I were your age' – here more confidentially to Miklós – 'I would do everything in my power, *everything*, to get out. Escape.'

'It isn't possible to escape from here. You saw what just happened to those two poor girls.'

'Yes. They were such little girls. But at least they tried.'

At this point one or two of the others in the small crowd of people around them began to decry the Pole.

'Ah, he talks nonsense!'

'I know this man. Always the same. Nothing but doom.'

'He hates himself because he is a Jew. He tried to pretend he was one of the *goyim*. He hates *us* because we are Jews.'

The Pole stared hard out of his haggard, anaemic face and repeated: 'You people have no idea of what is waiting.'

Later that day, Miklós was striding around the perimeter of the ghetto with Ede, pointing out where the two girls had been handed over (nobody had heard what had become of them since) and telling him of the strange encounter with the Pole.

'He's right, you know. We should be doing all we can to get out of here.'

'Like the two girls?' Ede was finding it hard to feel sanguine.

'All right, but now at least we know we cannot count on help or shelter from outside. But if we are being treated like animals here, how do you think the Germans will treat us? Ede, this man has seen people being taken to those camps. He has heard about them in Warsaw and on his travels in Poland. It is a dire situation.'

'But if we can work, we can at least escape torture . . . or death.'

'Ede, we have lost our identities here. They have taken away our papers, our possessions, our self-respect. We are just numbers. It's not like Budapest. Your parents, mine, had their radios taken away. We've got *nothing*. And if we go even further away, in these transports, we ourselves will become nothing.

Slaves. They could kill us. Nobody would know. At least in Budapest we mean something. We are *somebody*.'

'Miki, how do you expect to get to Budapest? Stroll down to the station, buy a ticket and board a train?'

'Look, the ghetto is thinning out daily now. As each transport leaves, there is more room to hide.'

'Do you think they won't search the place to see that everybody is gone?'

'They can't search everywhere.'

'And even if they don't find us, what then? What are their plans for Nagyvárad? More Jews to be shipped in? The locals let back into their homes? They'll take very good care of us, I'm sure.'

'Look, Ede, I've served my country in the military. I have obeyed the laws. My family has paid its taxes. I have kept clear of trouble. The whole of Hungary cannot be a prison for me.'

'Then possibly, Miklós, we should carry on obeying the laws. Keeping out of trouble. Go peaceably to those labour camps. After all, we are young and strong.'

'Ede, we are *in* trouble. This ghetto is trouble. Those camps are worse trouble. I felt terrified when I heard that Pole speak. I can't tell you.'

'Miki, what does he know? Really know? He heard rumours. If things were as black as all that, he'd be trying to escape himself instead of telling others to. You and I are used to labour. The *Arbeitsdienst*. Maybe it won't even be as bad.'

'Ah, I don't know. Perhaps you are right. It's possible. I heard that people in some camps even sent postcards home to say they were doing well. Perhaps you are right. I'm not even sure about Budapest at this moment. They don't seem to be doing much about us.'

'How would we get back there, Miklós? No money, no proper clothes. Look at us! And two fellows of our age not in military uniform – we'd hardly go unnoticed. In here at least we are still being fed.'

The two of them had stopped to sit on a low wall. Miklós

continued. 'Bertha told me that her torturers were Hungarian. No Germans were present. Kertész, the others; more or less the same story. How hollow the anti-Zionist arguments of the rabbis sound now! I feel betrayed. My *fellow* Hungarians. Ha! What a sick idea. You've seen those German newspapers – *Der Stürmer, Der Völkischer Beobachter.* I thought it would be different in Hungary. "Horthy is not Hitler," my father used to say. "Horthy is not Hitler." No, but it doesn't stop Hungary flushing us out like rats. Our guards here are not the SS, but that doesn't stop them *interrogating* us like spies – for *pengö*, for trinkets.'

'Did you hear what happened on the first floor yesterday afternoon, while you were out – when the new batch arrived?'

'Still new batches are arriving? I thought the traffic had dried up.'

'Yes, so did I, but this batch came in yesterday. Just six men. One of them looked particularly upset at his predicament. And as he walked through the door, one of the fellows who'd been there since the first arrivals went crazy. He jumped up and shouted, pointing his finger at this new person. "You, you!" he shouts, and laughs like a madman.

'Then he runs off to the next building to get his friends from the same district. They all crowd into the room and scream with laughter at this miserable newcomer. "I can't believe it," yells one of the men, over and over.

'It seems this man was known in their locality as a Jew-hater. And it turns out he's a Jew himself without knowing it! Way back somewhere in his family he clearly hadn't been pure enough. His parents were good, baptized Christians, but probably his *grandparents* . . . the room was in uproar.'

On the evening of 27 May 1944, a guard burst into the apartment room in which Miklós and Ede were sitting, along with Weisz and young Klein – his nervous tic by now a permanent tremor.

'Everybody get up! You are to leave here. Now! One minute. Out. You, come on! All of you!'

'It is our turn for the transports at last,' muttered Weisz. 'Do you think they'll have any tailoring work for me in the Ukraine or Poland or wherever it is we're going?' As usual his sardonic attitude unsettled Klein, whose facial muscles seemed completely out of control.

'Perhaps I'll inject bodies and you'll sew jackets with the same needle,' Miklós said to Weisz, and the two of them laughed.

The guard was in a hurry and prevented some of the men from collecting their meagre belongings heaped against the walls. Among the debris of scarves, socks and well-thumbed books scattered across the floor, the departing occupants picked their way through abandoned religious objects – dusty packs of phylacteries, stained fringed vests and shawls, grubby *kipot*.

This was to be the last round-up in Nagyvárad. As enforced departure followed on enforced arrival, the population had dwindled dramatically. Now, Miklós and his room-mates joined a procession of several hundred people filing towards the synagogue courtyard.

One man walking with him was moaning aloud, calling out two women's names. 'Leah, darling! My darling Leah! Rachel! Oh, my little Rachel!' Presumably his wife and daughter, or possibly a sweetheart and a little sister. Miklós thought of his own sisters, and of his mother, pleased they were in Budapest and far from Nagyvárad.

He felt thankful he had no sweetheart, wife or children. And he felt ready for the transport, for a new regime of labour, though he realized he would be unlikely to enjoy the privileged position of medical superintendent this time. Nothing, however, could have prepared him for his last few hours in Nagyvárad.

The line slowed almost to a halt as Miklós and his companions reached the edge of the courtyard. From here they could see that this large last group of ghetto prisoners was being shepherded into the synagogue itself, shuffling through the entrance in twos and threes under the disdainful eyes of the Hungarian guards.

The synagogue was a square, two-storey brick building. At the front, the first floor above the entrance was taken up by administrative offices. Even now, Miklós could see through an open window into the room where he had been taken on arrival to be allocated to his temporary ghetto address, the same single, bare light bulb burning.

The rear part of the upper storey was mostly given over to a gallery, which opened out on three sides to afford a view into the well of the synagogue downstairs. This gallery was where the Jewish women of Nagyvárad had formerly worshipped, peering from serried rows of benches at their menfolk below, the men swathed in prayer shawls rough as blankets, swaying, chanting, closer to the apparently masculine heart of the ancient Hebrew mystery.

On this May evening, the gallery was filled to overflowing, men and women indiscriminately bundled along the gangways and the benches. Some of them yelled greetings to friends below, who shouted and gestured back.

Miklós and Ede were herded into the main area downstairs. The heat from the mass of bodies was already oppressive. A murmur of voices was rising with panic and excitement. A few men at the front of the stalls were praying, an act of sublime incongruity. More in keeping with the occasion, a group of youths, whooping like puppy-dogs, were scaling the *bimah*, the podium at the front of the hall where the rabbis had once conducted services.

Miklós glanced up at the wall above the *bimah*. In the centre was a rectangular stained-glass window. Many of the coloured sections were broken and one complete panel was missing. The glass that remained was grimed and dusty, the colours faded into a neutral grey, the detail obscured. Miklós thought perhaps the scene depicted was of Samson in Gaza, but wasn't sure. Far more dramatic anyway was the setting sun through the tattered panes.

As he gazed upward, Miklós heard the doors clang shut. A sudden wailing resounded like a wave around the walls, broken by individual screams. The atmosphere was stifling. People stampeded for places to sit or lie down. Still the young men whooped, the girls giggled. Miklós tried to find Eva and her parents but they were nowhere to be seen. Perhaps they had been taken on an earlier transport.

Never before could this old synagogue have been required to accommodate so many souls. And now this scabrous, swarming crowd, striking a range of histrionic attitudes like figures in a Bosch painting, seemed to taunt the forgotten generations of Nagyvárad rabbis who had exhorted their flocks to gather for prayer and celebration in the House of God.

Rough, homespun tapestries were torn from the wall for bedding. As the evening wore on, alcoves bearing legends of praise and devotion, tributes to 'a man of learning', or 'a woman of worth', were smeared and stained; patches of old carpet grew rank and steaming as men and women scuttled into corners to relieve themselves.

Miklós and Ede found a place on the floor next to Weisz, their backs resting against a wooden pew. Although there was no room for them to stretch out, it was relatively cool and quiet. Some people around them dozed off but the three of them found it impossible to sleep.

The group of youths on the *bimah* kept up a high volume of noise. Nobody tried to stop them. Miklós could not settle and paced around restlessly. In the middle of the night he stumbled, and almost fell, over a couple murmuring together in the act of sex, one of several pairings strewn about the back of the room in a dark area in front of the locked doors.

Eventually he managed to sleep. Not in his chosen position next to Ede and Weisz, who remained awake in conversation, but at the back of the *bimah* once the rowdy youths had quietened down. He leaned his head against the splintered balustrade that ran around the *bimah*'s edge, and closed his eyes.

Visions and dreams accosted his brain as he twisted his body to get comfortable. The drone of sounds in the darkened synagogue, the coughs, screams, laughter, whispers and moans of despair, merged with impressions of the past and the future. Back with his parents in a Budapest street, one of his old schoolmasters accosting them and accusing Miklós of some terrible but unnamed crime. Then with the family, seated around a dinner table in the middle of the great Dohány Street synagogue, bare-breasted women singing provocatively to him over his father's shoulder. At the inn in Szeretfalva, debating with Molnár, the lawyer from the Jewish Hospital; reasoning with the Hungarian colonel of the ghetto – 'Come, we are all Hungarians, you have no need to ill-treat us.' And shouts of liberation amid gunfire and bombing – 'The Russians are here, the Russians!'

He was awoken soon after dawn by the crashing sound of a door flung open and a high-pitched, aggressive Hungarian voice.

8

Light flooded in. Nine or ten guards stood at the entrance, one slightly in front of the others. He it was who shouted the orders.

'Get up, all of you! Empty out your pockets. Remove your belts and any watches or rings. Leave them in a pile beside this door. Anyone who tries to hide anything will be shot. Form yourselves into an orderly column outside. Line up in threes. Come on, get moving.'

And so they emerged, these last ghetto prisoners, stooped and blinking, pouring out of the synagogue in their hundreds. They yawned and coughed in the fresh morning air. It was like a debased version of Yom Kippur, a grotesque parody of the close of the most crowded service of the year, the fasting worshippers departing for home and sustenance.

Miklós's head throbbed. His throat was parched, his mouth tasted foul and his limbs ached. Inside the synagogue, he felt himself choking on the malodorous and musty air. He dragged himself off the *bimah* and tried to pick out Ede from all the bodies rising amid the gloom.

Slowly, the huge, subdued crowd was marched to the railway sidings. As they drew nearer, Miklós was able to see black German uniforms for the first time. Scores of SS guards – each one carrying an automatic pistol – were busying themselves around a long convoy of cattle trucks. They paid no attention to the prisoners approaching under their Hungarian escort.

Eventually a long human chain coiled back from the edge of the tracks, beyond the sidings and into the street. Those at the head of the chain were ordered to the front of the convoy, which comprised some forty or fifty trucks. The SS guards then began to pack their human freight into the train, truck by truck.

It took two or three hours before Miklós and Ede's turn came to clamber up into one of the trucks. 'Just like the *Arbeitsdienst*, eh, Ede?' said Miklós, but neither of them smiled.

'*Los, los!*' The SS men urged old people to cram into the trucks with the young, the infirm with the fit and able-bodied, the women and children with the men.

'*Los, los!*'

Jammed together, eighty or more to a truck about twenty feet long and ten feet wide. All of them driven on by that strange, unfamiliar command: *Los!*

Miklós's shirt stuck to his back with sweat as he climbed up into the dank interior of his truck. In the middle of the floor was a large, empty barrel. A second barrel, half filled with water, was placed against one side of the truck, opposite the entrance.

Miklós and Ede made their way to the far corner of the truck, on the same side as the water barrel but at the other end. Here they became part of a young group including some of the boys who had been cavorting on the *bimah* the night before and a quartet of girls of around nineteen or twenty. And Zoltán Klein, the boy with the facial tic, the former butt of Weisz the tailor.

One of the young men, a tall, thin, red-haired youth, had spoken briefly to Miklós in the synagogue. He had described his recent and happy school days in the little country town of Kunmadaras.

Once the SS guards decided the truck was full, they closed the entrance by sliding a wooden panel across it and bolting it from the outside.

It became dark and hot, with only tiny slits of light and air from the four narrow, barred windows, two on each side of the truck, just above head height.

As the sliding doors were shut along the length of the train, people began to cry out in fear and panic. An SS officer outside succeeded in reducing the noise by shouting for silence and firing his pistol in the air. After that, a few isolated whimpers could be heard from the children but these were stifled by their parents or other adults around them. A baby in the next wagon persisted in crying and it was sought out by a guard and silenced with a bullet.

Despite the warning at the synagogue, Miklós had smuggled out a watch by hiding it in a blanket. As the door was slammed on his truck he produced the watch and held it out against a shaft of light from the window above him. Two minutes to noon – it was six hours since the Hungarian guards had burst into his sleep.

It was several hours more before the train began to move. In that time Miklós and Ede became acquainted with the young crowd in their corner, though Klein kept mostly to himself. Various other alliances were formed.

A number of people had the odd piece of bread or sausage with them, having stocked up as they left the ghetto, but hunger wasn't a problem in the heat and stench.

Miklós's group took turns to sit on the floor as they waited for the train to start. Miklós himself managed to hold out against making use of the water or the latrine barrel. But by the time the train did eventually crank its way out of the sidings, the majority of the truck's occupants had made at least one journey through the pack of bodies to the side wall to cup their hands into the water, or to the centre barrel to surrender to the demands of nature.

One or two had diarrhoea; a small child vomited over the wooden floor, another was constantly crying, 'Mummy, Mummy . . . Grandpa.' Everyone felt relief as the train got going. The rhythmic creaking noise overrode the sounds of the truck's occupants and a few wisps of breeze drifted in through the windows.

The high-spirited crowd from the *bimah* were full of escape talk.

'Where do you think this train's going then, Miklós?' asked the red-haired boy from Kunmadaras as they picked up speed to about twenty-five miles an hour.

'Certainly to the East. Possibly Poland,' Miklós replied.

'Well, it'll be going there without me.' The boy's defiant tone was picked up by one or two of his companions. 'Yeah, let's escape, get off this train.'

'How the hell will you escape?' Klein shrieked in a whisper. 'And even if you get off this train, where would you go?'

'The city. Budapest.' The red-haired youth fixed his challenging gaze on the nervous Klein much as Weisz had done in the ghetto apartment. 'I don't intend to slave for these Germans. I'll get back and take my chances in Budapest.'

'All right, but how?' Miklós's interjection took the sting away from Klein, who none the less froze with horror at the Kunmadaras boy's next words. 'Look,' he said, thrusting a red stubble-covered chin at Miklós. 'This floorboard where I'm sitting is broken.' And he moved aside to reveal a crack in the wood and a gap for leverage.

'What are you going to do?' Klein twitched furiously. 'You can't break out of there.'

'Of course I can. So can you. We'll break open this one and then we can tear up a couple of the planks next to it. Then we'll be able to drop through the floor when the train's not travelling too fast.'

The ginger boy covered up abruptly as an old man sitting nearby began to take an interest. Miklós and Ede exchanged sceptical, amused glances. Klein shuddered.

They were able to chart their journey by taking turns to be lifted up to the windows. After many miles of flat land they passed through the mountainous Tokaj wine-growing district. From here the countryside became more undulating; grassy hills fell steeply into valleys, narrow streams sparkled in the sunlight.

All the time the heat inside the truck grew more intense. The latrine barrel in the centre slid across the floor with the movement of the train. As it filled up, its fetid contents began to slop over the sides whenever the train lurched or suddenly picked up speed.

Two people fainted, a young man and an old woman, both quite near to Miklós. There wasn't enough room for them to be laid out comfortably on the floor, so they were propped up against the side of the truck. There happened to be a doctor somewhere in the pack but he could do nothing for either of them. Their faces were sprinkled with water and slapped and they eventually came round, though both promptly sank to the floor with exhaustion.

Darkness fell. The train continued north, through Sátoraljaujhely. By about midnight the ginger boy had succeeded in removing one board.

Then, while he collapsed from the physical effort, one of his friends, a small, wiry young fellow with tight black curly hair covering a mushroom-like head, began to beaver away at an adjoining plank.

Ede and Miklós formed part of the circle around this activity, shielding it from the other occupants of the truck, but otherwise played no part. They had long ago decided against attempting to get back to Budapest without money or contacts.

The young people in their corner slept by rota, most standing or sitting to allow four at a time to stretch out on the floor. Miklós's turn came at about one o'clock in the morning. He went off to sleep surprisingly easily but it was a fitful rest as the train went through a period of stopping and starting. After about an hour he was awoken by excited chatter: 'He did it. He did it.'

The ginger boy had dropped through the hole in the floor as the train slowed right down, and had been followed by three others. Except for Klein, who was covering his face with his hands, that corner of the truck was enjoying a small, vicarious triumph. And more space and ventilation into the bargain. Miklós was able to extend his shift. He fell into a deep sleep.

In the morning the train stopped at a station. One of the boys was hoisted up to peer through the window. Košice. They were in old Slovakia. Since the redhead and his three companions (one of them the curly-haired mushroom) had gone, the others had prevaricated about escaping, but now they all realized it was too late. They had gone too far. Budapest was too distant.

Noises were heard from outside. SS guards were shouting. Doors were being opened. Again that urgent command, '*Los, los!*' One guard had been stationed on the roof of the truck and they could hear his footsteps descending a ladder at the side. They heard him jump on to the station platform.

A minute or two later, the door was slid open and in the bright summer light Miklós was able to see that his truck had experienced its first fatality, an elderly man on the far side. His body had been leaned against the entrance and it fell forward as the guard opened the door. He ordered two of the occupants to carry out the corpse and two more to empty the latrine bucket and refill the water barrel at a cold-water tap.

All this took place without the hole in the floor being noticed. There was plenty of humanity to cover it.

The sunlight illuminated the shock and the shame on most faces. Some betrayed no emotion at all. Their eyes seemed dead. This was especially true of those unfortunate few forced into a position near the untethered latrine barrel, having lost the struggle for better locations.

One of these deadened souls now sat across from Miklós, the sleeves of his once elegant jacket stained with excrement. He had shuffled forward as the barrel was lifted out and, finding himself opposite Miklós, stared into his face before finally speaking. 'You, young man,' he said at last. 'What do you think of all this? Could you have imagined that such things could have happened?'

'At least we are not as badly off as him.' Miklós inclined his head towards the dead man, at that moment being carried from the truck.

'That is a matter of opinion,' answered this other man. He was probably in his forties, though a heavily lined face beneath neat, grey hair made him look older. 'What are you, a student?' he asked.

'I was a medical student,' Miklós replied. 'But I have been in the army – the labour battalion – for two years.'

'I am an accountant.' The stranger said this in a tone of self-reproach. 'I had a beautiful home, with servants. A wife and three fine children. I have advised members of the government on financial matters. I always wore well-tailored clothes. Went to the opera. Carried myself with pride. Now I can see I was a deluded fool. I don't care what happens to me now.'

'You must care,' Miklós said fervently. 'The war will soon be over. The Americans will invade. The British. The Russians. The Germans can't last out. We shall be free. All this talk of "falling back behind fortified lines". The Germans are on the run.'

'Freedom is up here, my young friend.' The accountant tapped the side of his head. 'You have the optimism of youth. They say you learn from experience. I have learned pessimism. I was a regular synagogue attender. Never did I imagine events inside a synagogue such as we have witnessed. And now this. Is this what my poor father sacrificed to have me trained for? Is this my real education? I fear that it is, young man. Make no mistake, we are being led into hell.'

Their conversation was ended by the return of the barrel. The accountant moved aside resignedly. The journey continued.

Ede nudged Miklós. 'Look at that poor woman,' he said, indicating a short, plump matron sitting near the door of the truck. Her face was round and smooth and bore traces of imperiousness, even though she was now sobbing with abandon.

She had no doubt been used to keeping up appearances, folding her layers of fat into a girdle, piling up her hair into plaits on top of her head.

At this moment, however, her hair hung down, twisted and matted, her white flesh spilled over the top of a torn velvet skirt. She was sitting with her head forward, refusing all comfort from her neighbours and making no attempt to stem the streaming flow from her eyes and nose.

'Ignore her. You must not even think about her. Or the man who died – or any of these snivelling children in here.' Ede winced at Miklós's reminder of the sad young faces almost hopelessly lost among the crush of bodies.

'Remember what Weisz used to tell us, Ede. Don't get involved. There are no luxuries here, and that includes the luxury of worrying about other people. Your best chance of getting through, of overcoming these terrible conditions, is to shed everything that is not part of yourself.'

A little later Miklós drew Ede's attention back to the plump woman. She was by then sleeping soundly, spread out on the floor, oblivious of two women standing on the hem of her skirt, conducting a loud dispute over a piece of sausage.

They gathered speed, carving their way rapidly through Slovakia. They passed through the town of Sabinov, near the old Hungarian border, trying all the time to guess their destination.

'Wherever it is,' said Miklós to one of his anxious companions, 'they need us to work. Especially us younger ones.'

Two more old people died during the night, one of them the woman who had fainted the day before.

As dawn broke for a second time, the train was moving at express speed. They entered Poland; recognized Polish names on road signs. Before long they saw Nowy Sącz and then Cracow. The train continued through Cracow station without stopping but, a mile or so beyond it, began to slow down. A few minutes later they came to a halt and the guards were again at the side of the train, opening doors.

There was no platform this time; just an expanse of rough grass and heath either side of the tracks. '*Toten! Toten!*' The call along the train was for dead bodies. The pair from Miklós's truck were carried out by the same men as before.

At the previous stop, they had been made to take their dead passengers on to a waiting cart. This time they were ordered to lay the bodies at the edge of a huge field. There was then a delay of an hour or so before they moved on once more.

Now they were in Poland, the desire to look outside intensified. They hoisted each other up to the window but the view remained much the same. Acres of green fields, small rural buildings, the occasional church. An hour or two past Cracow the train slowed down, sputtered along for a bit then squeezed to a stop. They could hear SS officers calling to each other, but could see nothing through the window except the sky.

Miklós's nostrils and mouth filled with the acrid air. His bowels tensed with fear. The noises outside grew louder, while inside the truck conversation dropped to a whisper. Ede stroked the stubble on his cheeks, Klein twitched feverishly. An old man groaned. All at once it seemed unbearably hot and damp.

The train remained stationary with the doors closed for about an hour. The din outside was incessant. The passengers became increasingly frightened and perplexed. 'Where do you think we are?' Miklós asked a man standing near him. 'Is it a factory?'

The man shrugged. 'Well, we're in Poland but the Germans seem to be running things judging from the sounds outside. Perhaps it's some sort of German military base or training camp.'

Klein suddenly stopped twitching and became eerily calm. His shoulders slumped and he lowered his eyelids in a heavy gesture of resignation. 'It is a camp,' he said. 'It must be a labour camp. We heard about them in Nagyvárad, these Polish labour camps.' His voice was husky, that of a much older man.

Suddenly, the door was flung open to the inevitable cry, 'Los, los!' In the foreground, in bright sunlight, stood an SS officer with a whip in his hand. Behind him was a wooden hut, its window open, two more SS men inside, bare-headed and shirt-sleeved. Around this focal point swarmed scores of people like ants in the shimmering heat.

As they stepped out they saw rows of disembarked passengers standing beside the train, most of them unsteady on their feet and shielding their eyes against the glare of the sun. Nipping among them like gadflies were thirty or so men in caps and striped uniforms. Some of the passengers asked about their blankets, coats and other items of luggage. 'We'll fetch it. Leave it,' the uniformed attendants replied tersely in German, urging the newcomers away from the train.

Hundreds of people seemed to be fanning out from the cattle trucks. Armed SS guards patrolled the area with dogs, shouting at the prisoners to hurry. Miklós pointed out to Ede a van with a red cross painted on it. 'They're taking the sick to hospital,' he said.

'Yes,' replied Ede, pointing beyond the van to a group of huts cordoned off with barbed wire. 'We've certainly arrived at our destination.'

A cacophony of languages assailed them. German, Hungarian, Polish and Slovak. And Yiddish! Miklós distinctly heard one of the men in striped uniform muttering oaths in Yiddish as he threaded his way through the crowd.

'Are you a Jew?' Miklós asked him. '*Jah, jah,*' the other replied indifferently. '*Kim schayn, kim schayn.*' 'Yes, yes, come along, hurry.'

The SS guards were trying to empty the train as quickly as possible. Some struck the passengers with whips and pistols in order to get them moving. Others, in contrast, were helping down old ladies and carrying children.

Amid the chaos, it was possible to make out signs of order. Passengers from the front trucks were already standing in some sort of formation. As the guards giving the orders drew nearer to Miklós's part of the train, he could see that the men were being put into one line, the women and children into another. Eventually, two huge columns of humanity stood in rows of five alongside the tracks. They shuffled slowly forward past a trio of SS officers.

In the middle, and the highest ranking, stood the man they had seen as the train door had been opened. Tall, dark, silent and severe, he indicated with a finger whether the Jews passing before him should be ordered off to his right or his left.

The rule seemed to be that older people went to the left, younger and middle-aged to the right.

The Red Cross van stood to his left. This seemed significant since, among the elderly trooping off in its direction, there were some young but obviously sick passengers. As the passengers from the truck in front of Miklós's awaited their turn for selection, he was struck by the sight of one young man wearing a handsome pair of black boots, despite the hot weather.

As this smart-looking youngster came alongside the dark SS man he was duly ordered to fall in with the right-hand section. However, he then approached the officer and said something to him, pointing in the direction of the Red Cross van.

Without changing expression the officer nodded and the young man went off with the sick and elderly. Only then did Miklós notice that he was limping, that his shiny black boots were surgically manufactured.

As Miklós came face-to-face with the SS officer he flinched, as numerous others must have done, from the German's cold, hard gaze. He and Ede were motioned to the right. Klein too. And Nagel, the gloomy accountant in the bespattered jacket.

They marched off in the direction of the barbed wire. More huts came into view. To one side of the barbed-wire barrier they noticed shaven-headed prisoners in striped uniforms, scurrying about like chickens in a coop. Only when they looked closely did they realize these dehumanized creatures were women.

The women prisoners' uniforms were similar to those worn by the strange band of escorts, among whom Miklós had encountered the Yiddish speaker. One of these now answered another question, the one on almost everyone's lips: 'Where are we?'

'*Birkenau. Du bist in Birkenau.*' Miklós and Ede looked at each other and shrugged. The name meant nothing to them.

A little further along they saw three large chimneys, all blowing out smoke. '*Was ist das?*' Miklós shouted to the nearest uniform. '*Himmelfahrt*' was the reply. 'Going to heaven.'

They came to a halt. '*Ausziehen! Bad!*' 'Strip! Bath!' The striped-uniformed attendants, whom by now they had learned to call *Häftlings,* were shouting the orders as an SS guard looked on.

They were standing before a rectangular brick building. The air was still warm, though freshened by a breeze which stroked the dazed passengers' bodies back to life as they slowly and mechanically pulled off their clothes. They filed inside the building and were told to leave their clothes and any other belongings in the room in which they found themselves – a cool, windowless ante-chamber. Everything except for their shoes, which they were told to carry with them into the bath-room.

As they lined up to go in for their baths, three *Häftlings* appeared with chairs and motioned three men from the crowd to sit down. The *Häftlings* then produced clippers and swiftly and expertly shaved the men's heads before sending them in to be washed. The others followed in the same fashion: a quick, radical haircut and into the bath-room.

Miklós, Ede, Klein, Nagel the accountant and the others from the truck stood naked and bemused in the same bath-house, holding their shoes, when scaldingly hot water suddenly sprayed over them from wall-mounted showers. The feeling of being cleansed outweighed the discomfort of the water temperature, and exuberant shouts and laughter roared out through the windows.

It lasted two or three minutes. Then the showers were turned off and the train passengers were led into another room where a *Häftling* handed out a striped cap, jacket and trousers to each man.

These were issued at random, with no regard for size. As they stepped into the open air, patting themselves dry with these new clothes, the men began to laugh as they held up trousers to themselves or tried on caps and jackets.

The tension of their journey gave way to unrestrained hilarity as they stumbled around in the sunshine, exchanging ill-fitting garments with each other.

There was almost a relaxed atmosphere now. The sun shone

in a cloudless sky and the men stretched, walked around and chatted. One or two of the *Häftlings* were surrounded by eager questioners.

Miklós could hear the words 'Birkenau' and 'crematorium' constantly repeated. A faint, slightly sweet smell pervaded the air. One or two of the newcomers remarked on it to the *Häftlings*, who shrugged and pointed in the direction of the tall chimneys.

While they waited, others went through the showers, all emerging pink and steaming with their odd assortments of caps, trousers and jackets. By the time there were about 500 grouped together, the *Häftlings* signalled for them to line up and move off, with the SS guard at their head, the *Häftlings* at the sides.

Again, the new arrivals peppered these *Häftlings* with questions: 'What next? What is happening to us? Where are we going now?' Again, the quick, terse replies: 'To work. To work.'

They were led to a barrack hut. The SS guard ushered them inside, two at a time. Each man was handed a crude metal dish and spoon. It soon became very crowded in the hut, which was a simple wooden structure with a mud floor.

Some people sat down, whereupon one of the accompanying *Häftlings* immediately ordered them up again. He lined them up in rough formation and told them to remove their caps.

The SS officer came into the hut and counted the new prisoners, tapping some of the shorter ones on their bare, shaven heads. He then stepped back a pace, announced in a loud voice, 'You will use the latrines in groups of ten,' turned on his heel and marched out of the hut.

Two men went up to the *Häftling* left in charge and began to speak to him. He was a lugubrious individual, tall, broad and rough-looking. As the first of the two prisoners approached him he sprang forward and slapped the man hard across the face. His companion began to protest but retreated when the *Häftling* held up an open hand and screamed at him: 'You want the same? Get back and shut up!'

The high spirits from the shower had completely disappeared. The *Häftling*'s morose features mirrored the mood of the hut. Several men were overcome by exhaustion and slumped down on the floor. Some gathered in small groups, quietly talking. Others stood, or leaned against the walls, their eyes registering shock or resignation.

9

'You. And you four there. You and you! You others!'

The sharp and strident voice of the *Häftling* rang in the air like an alarm. Those addressed by him scrambled to their feet. The rest stared as he waved his arms, beckoning the small group of men to follow him out of the hut.

This was the first 'latrine detail'. As it was leaving, a prisoner who hadn't been included rushed forward and asked permission to go outside. Contempt was probably the emotion most approximate to the *Häftling*'s expression as he heard this request, but even that was barely discernible in the hollow coldness of his face. His words – 'Wait your turn' – seemed disconnected from his person; he was like a machine.

The unfortunate prisoner continued to plead but was pushed to the ground as the *Häftling* went out and locked the door behind him.

The wretched fellow was included in the next batch, about fifteen minutes afterwards, but it was too late. He had soiled his newly acquired striped trousers. The *Häftling* hauled him away, closing the door on the others.

Miklós and Ede passed the time talking to some Hungarians whom they'd never seen before. Most had been separated from wives or families and were near to despair. One man wept as he described how his father had died in front of him in the transport truck. Another comforted him with an arm round the shoulders until his eyes, too, moistened at some painful, private memory.

Everybody discussed and tried to make sense of the new words and names they kept hearing: Birkenau, *Arbeitslager*, *Frauenlager*, *Zigeunerlager*, Auschwitz.

The *Häftling* returned without the disgraced prisoner and resumed his task of shuttling groups between the hut and the 'latrines'. These turned out to be open pits, dug into the earth, with planks thrown across for the prisoners to sit on. They were completely exposed, with neither wall nor fence around them.

Back in the hut, Miklós, Ede and Klein found themselves in a group with the young man who'd told them about his father dying, two other Hungarians and a Polish Jew who said he was a rabbi. They spoke in a mixture of German and Hungarian.

The man who'd lost his father, and one of the others, a short, fat extrovert, were former students who had served a mere few weeks in the *Arbeitsdienst*. The third Hungarian had been a pastrycook in Budapest.

Somebody remarked that the weather outside was 'glorious', at which the pastrycook spat on the floor. 'How can you talk in such a way?' he shouted. 'There is nothing glorious or even vaguely pleasant about our situation.'

But the weather remained a pressing topic. 'It will be stormy later anyway. I can feel it,' said Klein, who spoke now as if in a trance, slowly, deliberately but vacantly, his tic barely noticeable.

'Of course there won't be a storm,' scoffed the fat student.

'No, it's too hot. But it'll rain and we'll feel better,' said the boy whose father had died.

'Who cares about the storm or the heat or whatever happens to the weather?' glowered the pastrycook, by now in something of a storm himself. 'We are lost in any case.'

'No, no,' Miklós remonstrated. 'The war will soon be over. The Germans are losing. You must calm down.'

'What does it matter if the Germans are losing or winning? Nobody cares about us.'

'The English care. The rich Jews in America. The leaders in Palestine.'

'Of course they don't. They're safe. They've made it. They don't need us. We've had it. We'll die here.'

'You know, there *will* be a storm,' the Polish rabbi pronounced in a sombre, melodramatic voice. 'It will be a sign of the end of the world. Everything will perish. We will be the first.'

'Ach,' responded Ede, throwing up his hands. 'I think I'll cook myself a goulash.'

'A goulash!' The Polish rabbi was suddenly brought down to earth. 'What do you Hungarian boys know about cooking!' he cried dismissively. 'I learned how to cook at my mother's knee. Strudel. Cake.' A narrowing of the eyes, tip of thumb and forefinger pressed together. 'Delicacies.'

'Please,' interrupted the pastrycook, speaking directly to the Pole. 'You are talking about my trade. You think you know better how to make pastries? They teach you that at *yeshivah*?' This in German. Then in Hungarian: 'Superstitious imbecile!'

'Now, now, don't get excited,' the rabbi retorted, trying to soothe his aggressive adversary. 'I was just reminiscing. Like the others. Using my imagination. You think we get cake in *here*?'

The pastrycook made a gesture of surrender with his hands. 'All right, I'm sorry.'

Still they talked of food. Ede asked the pastrycook what constituted a proper goulash in his opinion. Miklós maintained that the meat had to be thoroughly prepared hours beforehand, soaked and cut and seasoned. The extrovert student elaborately mimed a cook selecting and mixing his ingredients.

They spoke of the vegetables that would accompany it, the wine with which they'd wash it down. But eventually the pastrycook had had enough. 'We are as likely to be eating such things again as we are to be caught in your end-of-the-world tempest,' he said to the rabbi. 'As likely as we are to be liberated by the Russians or the Americans. We will die squalid, miserable deaths. Ignored and forgotten.'

They talked until night overtook them. A hot, dry night; no storm. They sat and dozed and talked some more. The young man cried again for his father. The pastrycook wandered around the hut. Klein engaged the rabbi in conversation, desperate for solace. Ede and Miklós continued to concoct recipes. The fat student acted them out, miming and pulling faces, until they tired of him and pretended to sleep.

Within minutes of the light restoring them to the unreal reality of the hut, an SS officer arrived to conduct a roll-call. He asked for professionally qualified people – lawyers, doctors and dentists – to step forward. Ede cast a glance at Miklós, the erstwhile medic, but quite apart from his lack of full qualifications, Miklós had already learned from the *Arbeitsdienst* the merits of merging with the crowd. He had seen the risks of volunteering.

Such considerations did not prevent thirty or forty men coming forward, a mixture of compliance and enthusiasm, to be marched away by the officer. A second SS man, assisted by a quartet of *Häftlings*, then supervised the remainder of the hut's occupants into groups.

Miklós, Ede and Klein, still together, were in a group of twenty or so escorted out at around seven-thirty, the ground still moist, the air hazy with promise of heat.

As they marched off, Miklós happened to notice Nagel, the accountant, waiting in another group. For a second time in Birkenau, Miklós felt a surge of terror at the sight of a human face. But Nagel's expression, hideous in its abdication of life, of spirit, was much worse than that of the SS selecting officer.

A pale, moon-like apparition, it would haunt Miklós's imagination for days and nights to come. Dead still and downcast, the bloodshot eyes conveyed the most abject surrender.

It was the face of a corpse on which the worms had already begun their work but – and this was the horror that would never leave Miklós – as Nagel recognized him, those terrible, bloodshot eyes opened wide and the mouth split the cadaverous features into an obscene, sickly smile.

A short march and they arrived at another hut. Another mud floor. Another, smaller, group of prisoners. But this time there were bunk beds and the occupants had been in the camp a few days. There were no smiles of welcome for the newcomers. No greetings. Just stone-faced acceptance.

The existing occupants were hardly forthcoming, either, to the newcomers' questions. A single word would be enough to cover the most detailed or desperate inquiry. And, despite the fact that most of these prisoners were Hungarian, their brief replies were issued in the language of their captors: '*Gaskammer*,' and again, '*Himmelfahrt*.'

Miklós and most of the other newcomers had now gone without food for twenty-four hours. Water had been available in the other hut but its strong chemical taste and smell had put them off drinking it. Indeed, those who had drunk more than the odd cup had paid the penalty that morning, emerging with ashen faces and needle-like pains in the stomach and bowels. Fortunately they were allowed to use the latrines by request, without the allotted intervals of the night before.

For the most part, the men had quickly become accustomed to the primitive and exposed nature of the latrines. A few found leaves with which to wipe themselves but soon stopped bothering.

They had talked a lot about their dreams. Both the pastrycook and the fat student reported previously having dreamt of situations in which they were squatting in communal latrines exposed to public view. Now these nightmares were being enacted in their waking hours.

Miklós had been dreaming of the boy in the shiny black boots who'd limped away from the line of young and able-bodied prisoners. In his dream the boy had been accompanied by Nagel, still wearing the filthy jacket from the cattle truck. Nagel was urging Miklós to join them. 'Come with us, young man. I have influence here. I have done business with members of the Government. I know these people.' But Miklós had awoken before deciding whether or not to follow.

The morning of their arrival at the second hut was 1 June. Outside, the sun blazed. The heat took a little of the edge off their hunger but, for many, the gnawing sensation in the stomach was the only certainty amid the confusion, the one sharp point in their numbness.

Miklós and Ede were still together. They were given a bunk to share with a former schoolteacher named Gelb. It was just wide and long enough for them all to stretch out. They decided that Ede would sleep in the middle, his head flanked by the feet of the others.

Gelb was a taciturn man in his thirties. His face was constantly screwed into a frown beneath a surprising scrub of red hair. He rarely spoke without being spoken to first, something which both Miklós and Ede found extraordinary in an older man who was a teacher.

He had taught chemistry and biology at a good school in Budapest but had been removed from his post in 1938. His frown deepened considerably as he was relating this brief history, so that it was difficult to know whether his eyes were open.

They occupied a bunk at the end of a row. In the one next to theirs were three senior prisoners. One of these men, a stocky, muscular individual who looked like a torn teddy-bear, with hair sprouting thickly from his chest, wrist, ears and nose, leaned towards Miklós's bunk when he saw him pulling off his shoes. 'Don't lose sight of those,' he said. 'Keep your shoes or you're dead.'

'What do you mean?' asked Miklós. To this the teddy-bear simply waved a forefinger back and forth in front of him like a metronome. One of his companions took up the theme. 'No shoes,' he said, moving both hands in a wiping motion, '– dead.'

Some time in the middle of the morning they heard the hut door open. A quick flurry of footsteps was followed by the sounds of men scrambling to their feet. As Miklós and Ede peered from the edge of their bunk they saw a *Häftling* standing to attention and sniffing the air officiously, clearly waiting for something or somebody. After a moment or two, an SS officer came through the door and the *Häftling* shouted for the prisoners to line up alongside their bunks. Then '*Mützen ab*' – the order for caps to be removed. It was a roll-call. The German officer walked along the rows of men apparently concentrating hard on his task, teeth clenched, nodding silently like a tally clerk. Without a word he went on his way. '*Mützen auf*' – replace caps – and the *Häftling* was gone too.

An hour or so later another *Häftling* appeared. This time the cry was 'Soup!' He brought in a metal vat of a dirty-looking grey liquid which he spooned out to the prisoners standing in line with their bowls. Ede and Miklós appreciated its warmth and wetness. Otherwise it was tasteless. 'I don't think much of the catering at this hotel,' said Miklós. But they wolfed it down.

They quickly became hungry again, hungrier even than before. By the early evening, when another roll-call was followed by another plate of the grey soup, Ede was gripped by severe stomach cramp. This time they sipped the soup very slowly and made it last almost an hour.

Their bunk was quite near a window. At one point they saw the tall SS selection officer striding past. 'Who is that man?' Miklós asked his teddy-bear neighbour. 'Doctor Mengele,' was the reply, accompanied by more metronomic gestures. Twice they saw carts piled up with dead bodies, most in the striped uniforms but the odd few without any clothes.

'What things we are seeing, my friend,' said Miklós, shaking his head as he sat on his bunk with Ede. 'After all our learning, education, pride in our traditions. What was it all about, Ede?'

'I can remember,' Ede replied, 'your father lecturing us at synagogue. "Boys," he would say, "you are living in exciting times in one of the most exciting cities of the world. Soon you will have the opportunity to travel to other cities. But never forget that you are Jews. Nothing the new life can show you in all the great new cities of the world is as wonderful as the Torah, the ancient roots of your Judaism." He said it at my bar mitzvah. But it didn't have the desired effect. Quite the opposite. It filled me with longing for those foreign places.'

'My God, when I think of all the manners, all the decencies we had drummed into us. Look at it all now, Ede. Women shaven and herded together in degrading prison uniforms. This hut is not far from the women's camp, did you notice?'

'How the hell are they managing in such conditions?'

'Nothing seems real any more. At school, German lessons gave me such pleasure, I can't tell you. It was like paradise for me, a delight. I felt transported into a magical world. I used to run to the library to read Goethe and Schiller. I would dream of Beethoven. And here –' he spread open his arms, '*Los, los! Mützen ab, mützen auf!*'

After the pains of hunger came the discomforts of sleeping head to toe in the narrow confines of the hard wooden bunk. Each man's every movement disturbed the others. It was hot and noisy. From all parts of the hut came the screams of young boys and grown men alike.

A *Häftling* sat at a table at the end of the hut throughout the night. When one of the tormented sleepers cried out he would go over to him and hit him on the head. This sometimes succeeded in silencing the prisoner but when it didn't he dragged the unfortunate soul out of the hut and returned a few minutes later without him.

One boy of sixteen or seventeen, overwhelmed by some terrible nightmare, screamed so loudly and piteously that the *Häftling* did not even bother to try to stop him but pulled him off the bunk by his hair and took him away immediately.

In the morning Miklós and Ede were able to draw out Gelb a little as the three of them sat on their bunk and assessed their situation. 'When I first lost my job,' he told them, 'I was angry at the injustice of it. Then I looked at things in a more practical way. I began to give some of my former pupils private lessons in their homes, but then that came to a stop. I continued to read the scientific textbooks and keep up with new publications but that too became increasingly difficult.

'I no longer delude myself that I will teach again. My days of standing in front of a blackboard or of wearing my white coat in a laboratory are over. In fact, my whole life is over. As far as I am concerned, this place is a waiting-room for death. All contact with normal life has been severed.'

'But life cannot stop,' insisted Miklós. 'Perhaps things will never be the same as they were but there must be some kind of normal life to come. Things cannot carry on in this brutal way for ever. The war is not at a standstill. The Germans are finding it tough. The important thing is to survive this ordeal. Who is to say you won't be a teacher again some day?'

'Miki, you are the eternal optimist,' said Ede. 'I agree with you it is important to try to survive and that one day life will be back to normal, but we are at the mercy of brutes here. This is not the *Arbeitsdienst*. You've seen those emaciated walking corpses.'

'The shaved heads and uniforms make them look worse than they are. I think of myself as a realist rather than an optimist.'

'Ha!' Gelb suddenly laughed loudly. 'Realistically, we've had it. You, me, everyone in this hut.'

'No.' Miklós's tone was again insistent. 'All right, this is harder than the *Arbeitsdienst*. But the Germans have gathered us together for some purpose. They didn't just dump us or kill us. And they've started to feed us. They obviously need us to work. This is a labour camp. And like all work places and other institutions there will be tricks of the trade to help us get by. This fellow here told us how important it is to hang on to your shoes, for example. We'll learn. We'll speak to the old hands. We're all *Häftlings* now. We'll learn.'

The day continued with many similar conversations. Some of the 'old hands' relaxed their guard a little and provided snippets of information. Miklós learned that the orange glow that could be seen in the forests beyond the camp perimeters came from the burning of the dead bodies of prisoners.

This was visible two or three times a day from the compound surrounding their hut, around which they were allowed to wander. From here they could also see the chimneys with their regular plumes of smoke. Clearly, it seemed a lot of bodies had been unable to cope with the rigorous conditions.

They also learned that they should keep clear of the so-called 'number one' prisoners, hardened criminals from inside the Reich. And that they should never be caught stealing, the penalty for which was execution, but that they should know how to 'organize'.

'Organizing' meant getting hold of items like soap or cigarettes, which could be traded for bread or socks. A loaf of bread was worth twenty cigarettes; a long liver-sausage eighty or a hundred.

The distinction between stealing and organizing was very fine. It had something to do with planning, with negotiation and survival, but mostly it had to do with getting caught or not.

This information, along with the socializing, exercise and fresh air, gave them new heart. And when Ede found a spoon lying on the ground in the compound, they fought over it, laughing like excited schoolboys.

But the new mood was shattered when a young prisoner climbed through the barbed wire of the compound and ran the few yards to the outer fence, which was hung with posters warning of electrocution.

'How awful he looks,' said Miklós, thinking simply of the ungainly way in which the pallid, plump youth was running. And then how still more ungainly was the series of little jerks and spasms with which he embraced the wire.

Amid the din that followed, Miklós turned back towards the hut. As he did so he noticed a tall, elegant prisoner walking in his direction. The man's uniform looked well cut in comparison with most of the others. As he passed Miklós he smiled.

Miklós touched the man's arm and spoke to him. 'Excuse me.'

'Poor dog,' said the man, looking out towards the fence over the heads of the crowd chattering, panicking and pointing at the inert body of the fat youth.

'Yes,' Miklós shrugged. 'Desperate, or crazy . . . Excuse me,' he said again. 'You seem to be someone who knows the ropes here. And, well, to me you look like a sympathetic person. Lots of us here are new. Can you explain what this place is?'

The tall man's expression changed. He took on a brisk urgency. 'Do you understand Yiddish?' he asked.

Miklós replied that he did.

'I am from Bialystok,' he went on in the old language. 'We have been herded together here for nearly two years. My family went through the *Kamine*.'

'What do you mean, the *Kamine*?'

The stranger pointed to the chimneys. 'The smoke comes from the burning of human bodies. We have crematoria here, feeding those chimneys.'

'It is sad that so many people are dying,' said Miklós. 'It seems incredible that such a big and complicated operation can be organized in all this chaos.'

'You think this is chaos? You are naïve, my friend. Your eyes have not yet been opened. You and I are part of an extremely efficient, secret operation. People don't even know where they are and they disappear.'

'What do you mean, *disappear*?' Miklós was beginning to feel even more uneasy.

'Listen, you seem a bright enough young man. Look around. See if you can find anybody under the age of fifteen or sixteen. Or a white-haired person. When they came off the train with you they were taken straight to the crematoria. The ovens were kept warm for them.'

'This is some terrible joke.'

'Look, I shouldn't be talking to you, but I can see you have no idea of what is going on around you.'

Miklós had to catch his breath. He was looking at the other man but not focusing. Everything seemed silent and distant. 'There was a young man,' he said, 'wearing black boots. He could have come with us.'

The memory shocked him back into the present. He stared hard at the stranger from Bialystok; noticed that his uniform had a serial number stitched on to it, and a yellow triangle interwoven with a red one to make up a Star of David.

'How have you managed to keep going for two years?' he asked him.

'It's too long a story to tell and it's dangerous to stand here talking. Try to meet me here at the same time tomorrow and I'll tell you more.'

For the hundredth time, Miklós felt Mengele's cold stare upon him. Tasted again, even worse than the first time, the sour sickness of fear in his throat. 'Black boots,' he repeated. 'He could have come with us.'

The man squeezed Miklós's arm. 'I must go now,' he said. 'Keep your wits about you. See me tomorrow.'

As he turned away, Miklós saw that the crowd at the wire had largely dispersed. Ede was walking towards him at that moment signalling the arrival of a new, more pressing claim upon their attention. A *Häftling* was pulling a soup cauldron towards their hut.

They were more eager than ever for the soup and gulped it down rapidly. Miklós told Ede and Gelb what the prisoner from Bialystok had told him. Ede blew out through his mouth, puffing his cheeks. 'Well,' he said in a deep breath, 'this is not exactly the best trip away from home that I've ever taken.'

Miklós grabbed his arm. 'Ede, I'm serious. We must find out everything about this place as soon as possible. We *must* outlast them. It *can't* be long.'

Miklós looked more frightened and tired than Ede had ever seen him.

'What about that poor young fellow at the fence?' It was Gelb who had broken the silence. 'Dreadful suicide.'

'Yes,' said Miklós matter-of-factly, inwardly a little shocked at how casually he was ready to treat the death of a fellow prisoner.

Ede meanwhile was gazing into his empty soup bowl. He ignored Gelb's reference to the boy's suicide. Instead he looked up suddenly at the line of men with their bowls in their hands. 'He's still serving out the soup,' he said. 'The queue is enormous. I'm going to go round again. He'll never know. He doesn't even look at our faces.'

'Ede, be careful for God's sake.' Miklós was alarmed at his friend's bravado. 'Don't start any nonsense. This is not some ignorant Hungarian labour battalion sergeant we're dealing with. These people are dangerous.'

'Leave it to me,' said Ede. He wiped his bowl with his sleeve and went over to the back of the queue. Minutes later he was back with a second bowl of soup. He shared both the soup and his sense of triumph with Miklós and Gelb, producing for the occasion the spoon he had found outside earlier.

'Forty-eight hours,' he said, leaning forward conspiratorially 'Forty-eight hours and already we've tricked them.' Somehow the second bowl of soup tasted better than the first.

The next morning the steaming cauldron arrived much earlier. This time the liquid it contained was thinner and darker. 'Coffee,' announced the *Häftling* dishing it out. It tasted of grit but was hot and welcome to the prisoners. 'You see,' said Miklós to Gelb, 'they're giving us sustenance. They want to keep us alive, not kill us. We shall have to work soon. People have already lasted here for two years. The Germans will be defeated long before another two years pass.'

Miklós was impatient for his meeting with the prisoner from Bialystok. 'I'm determined to find out what is going on here,' he kept telling the others. He was outside well in advance of the appointed time. Then, as he made his way towards the meeting place, a mob of prisoners came rushing in his direction. Behind them were two SS officers brandishing whips. Miklós scattered with the rest of them and lost his opportunity of meeting his new informant. He never saw him again.

That day passed much as the previous one had done, as did the next. Long, drawn-out and hot. The big event was the arrival of the cauldron, in the morning with 'coffee' and in the afternoon with 'soup'.

They were allowed to walk around the compound more or less freely – it was wise to disappear whenever an SS man came along. Occasionally a prisoner would fail to get out of the way and suffer an assault with a whip or pistol butt.

They could also use the latrines and washing facilities as often as they wished. There were scores of taps set up adjacent to the latrine pits. The old *Häftlings* would keep telling the newcomers not to drink the water – 'Or you'll end up in the *Kamine*.'

This phrase, 'in the *Kamine*', quickly became part of the everyday slang used by the prisoners. If one prisoner asked another for a spoonful of soup, with the promise that he'd pay him back the next day, the other would reply, 'In the *Kamine*.' Ede's reaction to Miklós's repeated predictions that they would soon be out working together was always, 'Yes, in the *Kamine*.' Miklós's medical career, Gelb's teaching, these also were 'in the *Kamine*'.

They found that if they happened to splash water into their eyes when washing, it would sting quite painfully. Miklós couldn't imagine anybody needing to be warned off drinking it. But some did drink and most of these fell sick. A few were taken away to the hospital.

The places vacated by men who had gone to the hospital, or by those dragged off screaming during the night, were quickly filled by newcomers brought in by the attendant *Häftlings*. Almost all of these new arrivals were Hungarians. They included a couple of Gelb's former pupils.

Gelb himself had benefited considerably from the presence of Miklós and Ede. They had drawn him out. He was much less gloomy. He even joked occasionally, comparing the soup to the meals served at the school in Budapest, or their uniforms to the clothes worn by the schoolmasters. On the third afternoon he spent a couple of hours discussing science with Miklós.

The new prisoners and the serving *Häftlings* soon got to know each other. There would be no more chance of going round for a second portion of soup. In the compound, the new *Häftlings* were sometimes able to meet those of three or four months' standing and talk to them about camp routine. The surroundings became familiar and, along with them, certain key words, the most ominous of which was '*Vernichtungslager*' – extermination camp.

10

Zoltán Klein, together with the Polish rabbi and the pastrycook, had been taken to the same hut as Ede and Miklós. Klein and the rabbi had struck up a friendship and were often deep in conversation in some corner apart from the others. Klein's nervous tic appeared to have stabilized. It came on now only when emotion broke through the husky, deliberative way of speaking he had adopted since arriving in Birkenau. He also genuinely seemed to have found some comfort in the rabbi's presence.

One morning, there was a disturbance in the compound. The pastrycook grabbed the rabbi's nose between his knuckles and twisted it, half in mischief and half in malice. Klein reacted angrily. 'God will punish you, you ignorant swine,' he sniped at the offender, his tic now working violently.

'God will punish me?' The pastrycook's voice was loaded with menace. 'I haven't been punished enough in this place? You call on God and say *I* am ignorant, you idiotic bastard?'

He grabbed Klein by the collar of his uniform and punched him in the face, the blow landing on the bridge of his nose precisely at the point where the tic was most visible. A crowd gathered, most trying to pull the pastrycook off. Others, however, joined in the argument. Feelings against God were running high among some of the prisoners.

On the morning of 6 June, an old German *Häftling* came into the hut and announced to the prisoners that he was to be their supervisor – their *Blockschreiber*. He was accompanied by another *Häftling*, wearing a white coat and carrying a box.

Having introduced himself, the *Blockschreiber* then called for the prisoners to step forward — '*Antreten*' — and stand in line. The man in the white coat went to one end of the hut while the *Blockschreiber* told them all to 'wait quietly in an orderly and obedient fashion'. He walked along the line, inspecting it and pulling the odd prisoner into position, before going off to join his colleague.

Slowly, they edged towards the far end of the hut. Those at the back were unable to see what was happening at the front but gradually the news filtered through that they were having serial numbers tattooed on to their arms.

It was a long process. The prisoners became uncomfortably aware that the time for soup was passing. On previous days it had arrived regularly and punctually. Eventually it did come, with about half the men — including Miklós, Ede and Gelb — still awaiting their numbers and forbidden to leave their places.

Miklós arrived at the table where the two *Häftlings* were sitting at about two o'clock. For the first time since he'd been taken from the train at Nagyvárad he was asked his name. Then, where was he born? His father's occupation? His mother's name?

The *Blockschreiber* jotted down this information on a card while the tattooist asked Miklós to hold out his left arm. He was then indelibly etched with the number A-12152. Ede, following, was A-12153.

As they went about their business, the *Blockschreiber* and his assistant chatted to each other informally in German. 'Did you know,' asked the *Schreiber* as the tattooist pushed his needle into Miklós's forearm, 'they have landed?'

'No!' answered the tattooist without looking up. 'When was this? When did you hear?'

'Just before we came over here,' said the *Schreiber*, motioning Miklós away as he lingered at the table waiting for Ede and trying to catch some more of the conversation.

Miklós pulled his companion away hastily. 'Yes, yes, I know,' said Ede. 'We can still get some soup if we hurry. Come on then, let's grab our bowls.'

'No, Ede, that is not why I am excited.'

'What then? What do you mean?'

'Ede, that *Häftling*, that *Blockschreiber* – he said, "They've landed."'

'What do you mean?' Ede repeated. 'Who has landed?'

'Ede, don't you understand? There's obviously a radio in this camp somewhere and this old fellow has got to hear the news. The Allies. The British and the Americans. *They* have landed. The Germans really are on the run. It really can't last much longer.'

Two days later, the men in Miklós's hut were sitting on their bunks, trying to make their portions of soup last, when they were surprised by a visit from the *Lagerältester*. This was the most senior prisoner in the camp – or the *Lager* as it was known to them all by now. A German Gentile, dressed in a well-tailored uniform with a black cap, he was at the top of the dung-heap hierarchy the SS operated in Birkenau.

He summoned a few stragglers from outside into the hut and stood in front of the door. He cleared his throat and produced a document from his pocket which he held up close to his face. From this he read out a series of numbers in groups of five. As he concluded the reading of each group, the prisoners bearing those numbers were sent outside and told to line up in formation.

The compound quickly filled up as they were joined by men from other blocks. They stood for about an hour in the heat of the late afternoon. A buzz of expectant chatter passed through their ranks. They were going somewhere! They had been given serial numbers and put on lists. This was more like it. This was proper organization. They were going at last! They were going to serve some purpose.

They moved forward under the escort of a gang of veteran *Häftlings*, slowly, steadily; united in their desire to be doing something.

They went out of the compound and before long arrived at a gate none of them recognized. Here, an SS squad took over from the accompanying *Häftlings*. Miklós was in a body of about 100 prisoners. A pair of armed SS men walked at their head, another couple followed at the rear. Several more, with dogs, flanked them to the left and right.

They were led through the gate. At the end of a gravel path, they turned into a country road and passed fields, cottages and farmhouses. Their pace quickened under the direction of the SS men in front. Miklós felt weak. His uniform was sticky with sweat. But he was pleased and relieved to have left behind the harsh uncertainties of Birkenau.

After a time, the rural scenery gave way to an estate of warehouses and dingy, grey industrial buildings. The road became uneven and muddy. The prisoners felt their limbs beginning to stiffen and ache.

They had been walking for forty-five minutes and had encountered nobody. Then half a dozen women emerged from a yard in front of one of the warehouses. These were some of the cropped-haired creatures previously seen only through a barbed-wire fence. Their heads were uncovered but they wore jackets similar to those of the male prisoners. Beneath rough cotton skirts each one's legs were bare and bony.

They were staggering from the weight of huge slabs of stone which they carried under the direction of a female SS officer, who held a whip in one hand and the lead of a ferocious, noisy dog in the other. Other batches of women followed, attended in the same fashion. If any individual happened to cast a glance at the men marching before them, or slackened in her task of moving her stone burden to its destination, she would be struck across the head with a whip handle.

Such were the only signs of human life seen by Miklós's detachment in their hour-long march, at the end of which they came to a halt in front of an iron gate bearing an inscription above it in German. Miklós translated for Ede: 'Work makes you free.'

Clearly, they were at the entrance of another *Lager*. Through the gates they could see neat, two-storey brick buildings. The place had an air of permanence which Birkenau had lacked.

The SS officer at their head turned to inspect them before calling them to attention and leading them inside to an assembly point just beyond the gates.

As they approached this they heard the sound of an orchestra playing a march. Their amazement grew as the orchestra came into view. Twenty or thirty men, *Häftlings* like themselves in striped uniforms, stood in a formal group playing a full range of instruments.

They came to a halt in the assembly area. Hundreds of other prisoners were already there, lined up and waiting. The orchestra carried on playing while the SS officers who had accompanied the new arrivals took up positions around the edge of the columns of *Häftlings*.

Miklós, Ede and the others took in their new surroundings. 'No chimneys,' Ede remarked.

'Look over there,' said Miklós. In a single-storey building to their right a number of men were visible through the windows. They wore aprons and carried cooking pots. A stale, steamy vegetable smell floated out.

To the left was a building housing women. Leaning out of the windows, laughing and pointing, they presented a sight as incredible as the orchestra. Most of them were fair-complexioned with blonde hair. They were young and good-looking.

As the last strains of the music died away, a number of SS officers stepped forward and led groups of prisoners off in different directions. Miklós's group was taken to one of the more distant buildings. As they entered at one end they could see more prisoners leaving at the other. The same sweet smell filled the air as in Birkenau, though here it was fainter.

They were in a bath-house. This time they were not given a haircut but otherwise the procedure was the same as on their first day in Birkenau. They were told to leave their clothes in an ante-room and take their shoes with them into the showers.

Once again the water was scalding hot, though this time they were given soap. When they had finished they were issued with new uniforms. This was better organized than it had been in

Birkenau. The *Häftling* responsible was able to select different sizes from various shelves. The design was the same but the new uniforms felt cleaner and more comfortable. 'Now we look like the old hands in Birkenau,' Miklós commented. 'Fully-fledged *Häftlings*.'

Their new home was to be in Block 6. As they were led over to it, still in ranks of five, they noticed that the barbed-wire fences were much higher and thicker in this *Lager*. The same electrification warning notices hung on them, but they were additionally punctuated with observation towers, manned by armed guards.

Block 6 had two floors; Miklós and Ede were led to the upper. It was better equipped than their last hut had been. There were narrow, single bunks of polished wood, each covered with a sheet and a straw mattress. Miklós was given a top bunk with Ede below him.

'Ede, this is luxury. I am in the János Hegyi Sanatorium,' said Miklós, referring to a spa favoured by the rich in pre-war Budapest. This brought a laugh from a man in an opposite bunk, one of the existing residents of Block 6 and, like most of them, a Hungarian.

Miklós shouted a greeting at the man and asked him where they were. '*Auschwitz Eins*,' was the reply. 'Auschwitz One.'

'Guttman's the name,' he went on, coming over to Miklós and extending a hand. 'David Guttman. I've been in here three weeks and I can tell you it's not János Hegyi.' He was short and wiry, very dark, with eyes that still contained the vestige of a twinkle.

From Guttman they soon learned the layout and organization of the block. The newcomers were filling up recently vacated places to keep it fully occupied, 300 to each floor. On the ground floor there was a small office occupied by the *Block-ältester*, the senior administrator. This was an old Gentile prisoner responsible to the SS for the cleanliness and order of his block.

Miklós was delighted by the improved conditions. Even the dish issued to each man in here was clean and new, unlike the crude implements of Birkenau. And when they were ordered to line up by their bunks for their first food ration, the new *Häftlings* were astonished to receive a thick piece of bread with liver sausage and marmalade.

Ede and Miklós devoured their rations with frantic hunger. The marmalade was a dark lilac colour and contained pieces of grit. The liver sausage was bitter and the bread had an artificial, unnatural taste. But it was a banquet.

As they were stuffing in their last mouthfuls, Guttman came over to them. 'Boys,' he said, his hands patting the air in a restraining gesture. 'Never do that again. This is your ration for a whole day. You won't get any more until tomorrow evening. You are going to work and if you eat it up in one go you'll be sorry.' He smiled. 'You're green, yet. You've got a lot to learn.'

In addition to the *Blockältester* downstairs, each floor had its *Stubenältester*. The one in charge of Miklós's dormitory was a German prisoner with sallow skin, a long scraggy neck, hooded eyes and a bulbous nose. A triangle of pink cloth was stitched to his uniform. The men called him 'the tortoise'. He came into the room while Miklós and Ede were still talking to Guttman and turned out the lights. 'Sleep now,' he called out. 'Work tomorrow.'

As he had learned to do in Birkenau, Miklós made a pillow out of his uniform by wrapping it around his shoes. He put his head back, closed his eyes and wallowed in the luxury of the sheet and mattress. The day had brought a satisfying change of circumstances. His breathing soon assumed a relaxed, regular pattern.

It was a shock to be woken from such a deep, disorientating sleep. The lights in the hut glowed against the darkness outside. The tortoise was calling them up, the veins in his neck tightening like twisted chords; men all around were muttering, coughing, breaking wind.

Miklós took a few seconds to adjust to his surroundings. At first he thought he was still on the train. He could sense its rhythm in his ears. It was as though he had come to a halt on his back in the bunk. His breathing was shallow and rapid. For a moment he felt completely alone and in despair. Then he became calm as he heard Guttman's voice and remembered that they would be starting work, that proper German organization was taking over.

He followed the lead of the others and quickly slipped on his trousers and shoes. He picked up his jacket and cap and joined the line of bodies picking their way downstairs. They entered a large wash-room. A pipe ran along the length of one wall, taps jutting out from it at intervals over basins. At the far end were about twenty proper lavatories.

Prisoners were washing themselves busily. Ede came alongside Miklós and leaned on the pipe, thrusting himself almost joyfully under the tap. 'Better than that other place, eh, Miki?' he said as he shook his head like a dog to flick the moisture from his hair.

'Ede, look,' said Miklós, grabbing his friend's arm and pointing to a couple of men who were using soap. 'Ha!' Ede responded with an incredulous shout. 'And, hey, look over there!' Miklós had now spotted two more men with toothbrushes and another drying himself with a towel. He found Guttman at a nearby tap. 'How did these men get those things?' he asked him. Guttman spat out some water before replying. 'God knows,' he answered blearily. 'They *organized*.' And he turned back to his basin.

On the wall was an enormous notice written in Gothic script: '*Eine Laus dein Tod*.' 'One louse – your death.' Guttman saw Miklós and Ede reading it. 'The German way of telling you to keep clean,' he said, lifting his eyes scornfully in the direction of the notice. 'Oh, don't drink the water, by the way, or you'll be carried out. You see, young Hammer,' he added, smiling, 'it's not quite the same as János Hegyi in here.'

When they returned upstairs they were met by two *Häftlings* lugging a huge, steaming vat to the centre of the room. This contained 'coffee' similar in appearance to the stuff they had become accustomed to in Birkenau. It was less gritty, however, and tasted slightly better.

Everything was happening rapidly now. They were ordered outside and lined up in ranks of five. By this time the birds were noisily announcing the dawn. The sun rose spectacularly over a squad of dark-olive-uniformed guards marching into the street where Miklós and his colleagues waited expectantly in the fresh air.

The tortoise was there, looking pained and weary as he always did. When the guards stopped a few feet from the prisoners he ambled forward and reported in a slang sort of German peculiar to the *Lager* that they were all present and correct. Then he turned his sallow face back to the men and ordered them to remove their caps

Roll-call followed. As usual, a serious business, the grim-faced SS guard counting heads with a severe concentration. '*Mützen ab*,' yelled the tortoise, his face almost as pink as the triangle on his breast. And then a new order was heard: '*Arbeitskommando abtreten*', at which a group of men standing next to those from Miklós's hut marched off in the direction of the *Lager* entrance. At their head was a *Häftling* wearing a yellow armband with the word '*Kapo*' written on it in black letters.

Other groups immediately followed, each led by a *Kapo*. The orchestra began to play. SS men joined the *Kapos* at the main gate. Some of the groups were counted once more before filing smartly through the gate and away in different directions as the music receded behind them.

This activity continued for an hour or more, the orchestra keeping up an unrelenting programme of military marches, until the assembly area was clear except for Miklós's group of new arrivals from Birkenau.

Finally, with the last notes of the orchestra fading into the summer breeze, they were ordered back to their block.

As they trooped through the door, the *Blockschreiber* awaited them. In his hand was a list of their serial numbers, which he ticked as each individual passed him in strict numerical order, forearms bared. Behind him stood another *Häftling* who handed each man a strip of white cloth with his serial number on it and a downward-pointing yellow triangle combined with an upward-pointing red one to form the Star of David. These were to be sewn on to the left breasts of their jackets.

The tortoise had already given a needle and cotton to one young prisoner, a sixteen-year-old schoolboy whom he seemed to have befriended. One or two of Guttman's contemporaries had also managed to stow some in their bunks – enough for the newcomers to do their sewing.

As Ede sat stitching on his star, Miklós pointed to his own, already sewn on. 'So now we have badges of identity. You know, Ede, I believe that each new stage here confirms our survival. The more involved we become in the routine, the more necessary we are to them. It is up to us to stay alert and stay alive.'

'You notice,' said Ede, 'that the Jews are the only ones with two triangles? I wonder what they mean, all these different colours.'

Miklós shrugged. 'It's obviously some chain of command. The *Lagerältester* wore a black triangle, the *Blockschreiber* has a red one. These Germans have to grade everything precisely, even their prisoners. One thing is for sure, Ede, we're at the bottom of the pile. But at least we're included.'

Around midday they were given soup, of a similar taste and texture to that in Birkenau. Afterwards Miklós lay on his bunk and slept for an hour or two. Ede and Gelb played children's spelling and guessing games.

Towards the end of the afternoon they heard the orchestra again. They rushed to the window and watched the working parties returning. Most of the men looked tired, though they maintained a brisk pace to the music. At the rear of some groups the odd pair of *Häftlings* could be seen carrying dead bodies.

The tortoise appeared in the room as if from nowhere and called them away from the window and out on to the parade ground.

They fell in alongside the returning workers from Block 6,

were counted with them and dismissed with them. Together they were issued with the daily food ration: a third of a loaf, margarine, marmalade, liver sausage and coffee. This time Miklós and Ede were careful to eat only half and save the remainder under their pillows.

The tortoise woke them at five the next morning, switching on the lights, clapping his hands and shouting furiously. His face looked even more downcast than normal and he became irritated with anybody who didn't get out of bed quickly. But he kissed his sixteen-year-old friend on the lips before moving on to yell at the man in the next bunk.

It was the same routine as the day before.

In the wash-room, several cakes of soap were laid out. 'These are brought over from Birkenau by the SS,' Guttman informed Miklós. 'A luxury denied those poor creatures over there.'

But this new soap had a peculiar, sticky texture and failed to produce any lather.

'What's the matter with this soap?' Miklós asked. 'Why doesn't it lather?'

'Don't you realize?' Guttman laughed. 'It's made from human fat and bones.'

After using the washing and latrine facilities they were given coffee and taken to the assembly point. Once again the music struck up and they watched the working parties follow their *Kapos* towards the gate.

This time, however, they were not sent back to their block. The *Blockschreiber* appeared, carrying a set of printed forms, and divided the men into separate working parties, or *Kommandos*. As always, they were lined up numerically, Ede next to Miklós. But now they were to be split up. The *Blockschreiber*'s hand carved the air between them as he finished counting one *Kommando* with Miklós, the SS *Unterkunft*, and began another, the *Bäckerei* – bakery – with Ede.

Each *Kommando* was housed in its own block. The members of the *Unterkunft* were taken to Block 23, those of the *Bäckerei* to Block 25, at the opposite end of the *Lager*.

Block 23 looked exactly the same as Block 6. A *Blockältester* stood at the door awaiting them. He was considerably fatter than anyone Miklós had so far seen in Auschwitz and his bloated features made him appear older than his probably thirty-odd years. Like the tortoise, he wore a pink triangle. A young boy stood with him, vacantly staring at the new intake.

As the new members of the *Unterkunft* approached the building, the *Blockältester* called inside to an elderly *Stubenältester* who came out to receive them and direct them to their quarters.

Miklós was again given an upper bunk on the upper floor. This was a bare board covered with a blanket; no sheet or mattress this time. And it was shared, with a middle-aged lawyer with protruding teeth. There were about thirty of the recent arrivals from Birkenau in the upper room, including Klein, who seemed to be haunting Miklós wherever he went. Otherwise, he was continually having to adjust. Not only had he lost the immediate companionship of Ede but Guttman and Gelb were also in different *Kommandos*.

Miklós consumed the rest of the previous day's ration and washed it down with the soup that came at lunchtime just like before. He pretended to sleep to avoid the attentions of Klein, and after a while did in fact drift off.

He dreamed that he was marching with a group of other prisoners along a country lane. Ede appeared at the head of another group, marching past them in the opposite direction. In Ede's group were some of the shaven-headed women they'd encountered on the road to Auschwitz, along with Rosa and Ibolya. Miklós waved but couldn't attract their attention. He called out to them as they marched away but his voice was drowned by the sound of the Auschwitz orchestra playing a stirring military piece.

As he tried to break away from his party and run towards his mother and sister, he sat up in his bunk with a start and realized that the orchestra was in reality playing at that moment. The workers were back. The evening ration would be served and he hadn't even developed an appetite. He would be able to save most of it for the next day, his first working day in Auschwitz.

He had a disturbed night. This was partly because he'd already rested and partly because he was anxious and excited about the day ahead. It was also difficult to sleep amid so much noise. Several men were shouting in their sleep. The man in the bunk below cried out, '*Du, mein Brot!*' – 'You, my bread!' Miklós stuffed his own, uneaten rations deeper into the pockets of his trousers, at that moment rolled into a pillow beneath his head.

In the morning they were awoken and led to the assembly point in the usual way. A few minutes passed and then a refined-looking man in an impeccable prisoner's uniform, the *Kapo* band on his sleeve, walked over to them '*Unterkunft, antreten,*' he commanded in a firm, educated Viennese voice.

He was a slim, handsome man of about thirty or so, with large brown eyes above a sharp, well-proportioned nose, along-side which was a three-inch duelling scar. He wore a red triangle and a neat black cap. His shoes were polished and his fingernails were manicured.

'Who is that man?' Miklós asked one of the veteran *Kommando* members. 'What's he like? He seems like an aristocrat.'

'Don't worry,' was the answer. 'He's OK.'

Now the music thrilled Miklós, knowing that he would be among the thousands marching out to it. He looked around him intently. The condition of the prisoners varied greatly between the *Kommandos*. Some were like *Muselmänner*, all skin and bone, while others seemed reasonably well built.

Those in his own *Kommando*, which numbered around 100 men, looked healthy enough. Whenever he asked one of the veterans about the work, they simply told him not to worry. 'You are lucky,' they said. 'It's a good *Kommando*. The best *Kapo*.'

As they marched under the *Arbeit macht frei* emblem they picked up their detachment of SS guards. After half a mile or so they arrived at a yard surrounded by a number of large storage buildings. The *Kapo* and the accompanying SS men stopped. A senior SS officer emerged from one of the buildings and the

Kapo saluted him and ordered the prisoners to remove their caps.

'Reporting for duty, *Oberscharführer* Hoffmayer.'

'Thank you,' replied the officer, a tall, thin man with an Austrian accent. And then, more quietly and informally: 'OK, Heinz, take them away.'

The *Kapo* led them into the building and down some stairs into a huge warehouse area containing piles of suitcases and other, smaller items such as brushes, combs and soap dishes.

At this point the *Kapo* left them in charge of another red-triangle prisoner, a bald-headed Pole who spoke broken German. 'Who is this?' Miklós whispered to his neighbour. 'He is Mjetek, the foreman,' the other replied. 'A crazy Pole. Keep away from him as much as possible.'

Mjetek gave them their duties, which basically consisted of sorting items from suitcases into separate piles – soap, tooth-brushes, glasses, handkerchieves, shirts, socks and so on. He then divided them into groups of twenty, directed them to different parts of the storeroom and left them to get on with it.

It was about seven when they began. Miklós noticed that many of the suitcases had names and addresses on them. Some were from Holland, others from Hungary, France and Poland. He became absorbed, wondering what had happened to the owner of a beautifully hand-painted spectacle case, or where now was the little girl whose knitted hat he found in a suitcase with an Amsterdam address stamped on it.

At nine, Mjetek went on his rounds. When he reached Miklós's section he clapped his hands together for attention.

'I want to inform all new people here that any theft will be punished by death,' he announced. 'You are expected to keep the oven filled with wood,' he went on, indicating a large stove in the centre of the room, 'and you may use this to cook during your midday break, and to make coffee.

'There are mincing machines on the table over there, through which you must put all soap that you find. You must also open up all toothpaste tubes and throw them away after examining them. Remember, theft is punishable by death. Any of you can be taken to the *Kamine*.'

After that, Mjetek left them alone and they worked at their own pace. The *Kapo* appeared at noon and announced the lunch break, for which they were allowed out into the yard. Outside, some *Häftlings* had arrived from the *Lager* with a cauldron of soup.

'How long is the break?' Miklós spoke to the *Kapo* for the first time.

'An hour.' Miklós couldn't believe it.

'Is it always like this?' he asked one of his group.

'Ha, you greener. You don't know how lucky you are. This is a wonderful *Kommando*. Look over there in that building.'

Miklós turned to where the man was pointing. A window was open and he was able to see young women working inside. He turned back to the man, his mouth open in astonishment.

'Slovak girls,' his informant revealed. 'Lovely. Greener, you've got more luck than sense, let me tell you.'

When they arrived back at the *Lager* gates at five-thirty, they were stopped and subjected to a token search by SS guards before they were allowed through for a head count and a musical march to Block 23 for coffee and provisions.

There was a free hour before lights-out. Miklós went to look for Ede at the bakery. After a while he gave up and returned to chew over the day's events with his new working colleagues. By the time he put his head down he was exhausted and, despite having to share a bunk with the toothy lawyer, sank easily into sleep.

'You want *Himmelfahrt* before your time?'

The *Blockältester* was smiling. Miklós was trembling.

The offence had been minor. Miklós had failed to acknowledge the delegated authority of the fat official's *Piepel*, his fifteen-year-old servant, when the boy had asked him to hand over a book that Miklós had been reading, a tattered copy of a cheap romance that had unaccountably been circulating in the block.

The *Blockältester* had struck him in the face. That was nothing. Even the threat was nothing. It was routine. But now, as the *Blockältester* laughed through greasy lips, hugging his young boy to him, Miklós suddenly felt the implication of the words. '*Before your time.*'

'You see what this means,' he said later to his bunkmate, Dr Révész, the lawyer. 'We are all destined to end up there eventually. And nobody will know. This whole thing is secret. Nobody knows about Auschwitz. Had you heard of Auschwitz or Birkenau before you came here?'

'No,' answered Révész, 'and the old *Häftlings* can't remember a single soul escaping. Hardly surprising with all that electrified wire and watchtowers. You are right. We are sentenced to death. It's just a question of when.'

'You know, until I heard that slob, that homosexual, saying those words to me, I'd always believed in survival. Right up to that very moment. If we could stay fit, carry on working. After all, they've organized us, kept records, tattooed us with numbers.'

'Six months,' said Révész. 'That's what I heard the SS say. Most men here are useful to the Nazi machine for six months and then they're disposable. There's always a fresh supply of workers.'

'I've met people who've been in here for two, two-and-a-half years,' said Miklós.

'Rare exceptions. Mostly criminal types,' said Révész gravely. 'Six months is what I heard. From the Germans themselves.'

Most of Miklós's discussions with Révész were shrouded in bitterness or despair. The lawyer had left his wife and children in Birkenau. He craved darkness; his only hope was for a quick death. He was only too willing to assent to Miklós's new understanding of their situation.

For his part, Miklós continued to work hard at survival. The *Blockältester*'s chance remark had rocked him but he was too committed to beating the system to submit to it now. He was still in sound physical condition and he continued to believe in the Germans' defeat, perhaps inside his own 'six months'.

He linked up with Ede after a couple of days. Working where he did, Ede was well placed to 'organize' for himself and others, including Miklós. Bread was a matter of life and death. Liverwurst, marmalade and margarine were also constant goals of 'organization'. A square of margarine, known as a *kocka*, could be organized at a cost of forty cigarettes.

On his fourth day with the *Unterkunft*, Miklós found himself alone in a secluded corner of the storeroom deliberating over a large bar of soap. He knew that inside the *Lager* he could get twenty or thirty cigarettes for it. He sat there for ten minutes or more, his head pounding, turning the soap over in his hands, feeling its shape.

He tried to place it under his armpit but remembered having been searched there. He thought of breaking it in half and placing the two halves inside his shoes. But this would have diminished its value and might not have worked.

Then he tried placing the soap high up between his legs. He found that if he walked very slowly, as they invariably did on their return to the *Lager*, he could hold the soap firmly in position.

He decided to risk it. The searches so far had been quite superficial. Certainly, none of them had been searched between the legs.

As they neared the gate, Miklós broke into a sweat. He began to worry that the perspiration would cause the soap to slip down his leg. He was tempted to let it drop on the road but decided that was even more dangerous since it might easily be spotted by the SS escort.

They stopped at the gate. As usual the waiting guards came into their ranks, asking the odd prisoner to raise his arms or roll up his sleeves. One of the guards stopped in front of Miklós. 'You look uncomfortable, Jew,' he said. 'You're sweating. Not hiding anything, I hope.'

Miklós shook his head without speaking.

'Open your mouth,' said the guard, a rough-looking youth of no more than twenty. Miklós complied. 'Wider,' said the youth. 'God what a revolting sight. You'd better close it again, you're putting me off my dinner. And I think you need something to wash away that sweat.'

Had he guessed? Miklós stood rigid. Surely not? How could he know?

The youth took one more look at Miklós's face and moved on. A senior officer dismissed the *Kapo*, who led the *Unterkunft* back across the *Appellplatz* to Block 23. Miklós raced Révész to the bunk and pushed the soap into a corner underneath the blanket.

I I

Business was conducted during the hour preceding curfew. Having put the soap into his pocket, along with the greater part of the evening's food ration, Miklós went straight to a man in Ede's hut whom he knew would be willing to trade. They agreed on twenty-five cigarettes, which Miklós then gave to Ede in exchange for a chunk of bread and a small piece of liver sausage.

On his way back to Block 23 he called in at Gelb's hut. The teacher was in a much tougher *Kommando* than his two former companions, and spent hours each day digging in a quarry and carrying huge slabs of stone. Gelb looked drained. His shock of red hair was almost white with quarry dust. His frown was etched deeper than ever into his face. He was thin and bent. He sat silently for a few moments before speaking.

'Miklós,' he said, lifting a hand in greeting. 'The man next to me died today. It was horrible. He was hacking away with a pick and suddenly sank to the ground, still holding the pick. He hadn't been working particularly hard. In fact, he always used to take a rest when the *Kapo* was out of sight.

'Yesterday the *Kapo* caught him and kicked him hard in the stomach. I don't know whether that had anything to do with it. He seemed to have recovered last night and was well enough this morning. He'd been chatting to me about his father, who was also a schoolteacher apparently. The *Kapo* had to prise the pick from his hands. He was carried back at the end of the day and counted with the rest of us.'

Miklós remained silent. Gelb attempted a smile. 'How does our realist see things now?' he asked. 'Will we all be free men

125

next month? Next year? You are a bit like the Germans, Miklós. "Work makes us free." *Arbeit macht frei.*'

Gelb's chest wheezed when he spoke. Miklós shrugged, his hands plunged into his bulging pockets. He returned, with relief, to his own hut.

All kinds of treasures were discovered on the *Unterkunft*. Gold dollar pieces, dollar notes, items of jewellery, even bottles of perfume and spirits were packed away in suitcases. Miklós never came across any perfume or spirits but Révész once found a miniature bottle of brandy which he immediately handed in to Mjetek. Révész would never organize. 'My face would give me away,' he said.

Some *Häftlings* were in *Kommandos* which lay beyond the *Kette*, the outer limit of Auschwitz. They worked side by side with local Polish civilians. Whenever they could, these *Häftlings* smuggled money out to the civilians in exchange for jewellery or spirits. With jewellery, it was said, you could even bribe the SS. And spirits were the highest currency in the *Lager*. A bottle of vodka would fetch between 150 and 200 cigarettes.

Miklós often saw small pieces of jewellery, wrapped inside a dress or a piece of newspaper. He handed most of these in, but once or twice levered individual stones out of bracelets or necklaces before surrendering them to Mjetek. Coins were plentiful, too. One day he brought a Swiss twenty-franc piece into the *Lager*, concealed between his toes.

The place where the *Unterkunft* worked was known as *Kanada*. It was an overflow building from another *Kanada* in Birkenau, to which suitcases were taken directly off the trains. Miklós and the other *Häftlings* worked as slowly as possible, not only to conserve energy but because they feared the supply might run out. If *Kanada* ceased they would have to go to a harder *Kommando*, they reasoned, or even 'in the *Kamine*'.

Neither Hoffmayer, the SS officer in charge of the *Unterkunft*, nor Heinz Dürmayer, the *Kapo*, seemed to care at what pace the prisoners worked. Only Mjetek gave them any trouble, throwing his weight around every so often, but he too had a vested interest in staying in *Kanada*.

One of the men with whom Miklós worked closest on the *Unterkunft* was a large, friendly fellow in his thirties called Tadek Halter, a former actor. He seemed to be perpetually on the point of laughter, his lips pursed, his eyes wide open. And when he did laugh he made a lot of noise and included others in the joke by slapping them on the arm or shoulder.

Tadek appeared to have no worries about *Kanada* closing: 'The supply is endless, my friends. All the Jews left in Budapest will be coming soon. We'll have all their belongings to sort through.'

'Have you heard this?' Miklós asked him, steeling himself from thinking about his parents and his sisters.

'Sure, I heard Hoffmayer talking about it to the *Kapo*. And one of the SS guards boasted of it to a Hungarian boy I know in the kitchens.'

'Tadek,' asked Miklós, 'how do you stop yourself worrying about your wife and children?'

'I just don't think about them. There's no point. What good would it do me? Look at Dr Révész – worrying himself sick. He gets thinner and thinner. He'll probably never see his family again, so what's the use in worrying about them? He can't help them and they can't help him. I can't help my wife and kids, wherever they are, but I can help *me*. And when you think about it, that's the best way that I have of helping them, the only way. Looking after myself. Worrying is useless.'

'You are right. It isn't easy, even without a wife and children. But it *is* the only way.'

Tadek was from Bialystok. Miklós told him about the stranger from Bialystok whom he had met in Birkenau and asked if he knew who the man might have been.

'How should I know?' he boomed at Miklós as they sat together in front of a suitcase brimming with the dark brown clothing, photographs and handkerchiefs of an old lady from Warsaw. 'But if he managed to keep going for two years he had the right idea. No sentimentality. Look after oneself.'

Sometimes Miklós wondered if Tadek Halter protested too much. At all events he was a colourful character; quick-witted and amusing. He'd been a member of the Yiddish Theatre Company of Bialystok and was fluent in Yiddish. He gave Miklós lessons in Yiddish literature.

He was also a connoisseur of Polish folk-songs, which he would sing lustily and expertly to his workmates as they ransacked the personal effects misguidedly hoarded by all those passengers on the trains to hell.

After that first time with the soap, Miklós smuggled items into the *Lager* most days. He strapped tubes of toothpaste to his leg, put coins under his tongue, razor blades in his shoes, banknotes in the shoulders of his jacket. Normally he would go off by himself to the latrine to hide these things. It was a rule not to trust anybody. 'Who knows what could be blurted out under duress?' he explained one night to Dr Révész.

Miklós kept himself occupied in the pre-curfew hour, usually meeting his contacts on the streets of the *Lager*. More or less standard rates of exchange were established; little negotiation was involved. Aside from the risks taken in organizing the various items in the first place, most transactions were uncomplicated. Inside the *Lager* no questions were asked of a man using soap or smoking cigarettes.

Häftlings were seldom caught stealing. Since the guards who counted them back into the *Lager* in the evening were the same ones who'd seen them out in the morning, it was possible to gauge the danger.

Occasionally a guard on search duty might even laugh indulgently at a group of prisoners and ask them, 'What have you been organizing today, eh?' And when a thorough search was to take place, the older *Häftlings* were often tipped off beforehand.

But it did happen. That was how Miklós heard about Block 10.

A man from the *Unterkunft* was discovered with a pair of socks stuffed inside his trousers. Two guards immediately seized him and announced they were taking him to Block 10. Miklós had heard the phrase 'Block 10' used, a little like 'in the *Kamine*', as a kind of curse. He had paid scant attention to the actual block itself, which was fenced off and under guard most of the time. Like most *Häftlings*, he avoided walking near it.

Now, with the arrest of a man from his *Kommando*, he heard more about the shadowy Block 10. He learned about the tiny, damp cells; the torture; the shootings. Most who entered Block 10, including the man from Miklós's *Kommando*, were never seen again.

Sometimes *Häftlings* stole from each other. One evening, while Miklós was visiting Ede, a young Dutch boy ran out of the hut clutching a loaf of bread and pursued by an older man. Miklós recognized the latter as one of the barbers who came round every three weeks to shave the heads of the men in his block.

Amused and curious, Miklós and Ede followed the two men out of the hut to see if the barber could catch his thief. The boy had already disappeared, however, while his victim shouted after him down one of Auschwitz's darker streets.

At that moment an SS guard turned the corner and stopped as he saw the irate barber a yard or two in front of him. By now the barber's anger was turning to tears and he looked as if he would collapse on the spot.

Without warning, Miklós and Ede shivered at the barber's sudden, appalling cry of anguish. The SS guard hadn't seemed to move and yet he was on top of his prey, the base of his whip handle rammed into the barber's eye.

Ede and Miklós recovered themselves in time to turn back from the crunching and gasping sounds of a broken man being beaten to death. And from the brief glimpse of hatred in the crossed eyes of the SS guard.

This was their first sight of Kadouk.

Révész had heard of Kadouk. Klein had heard of him. Tadek had mentioned his name. Now Miklós too, shivering in his bunk with horror and fear, knew about this brutal, cross-eyed executioner.

Tadek supplied the details: 'Kadouk is from Silesia. A Polish *Volksdeutscher*. Huge. A savage. He has killed hundreds, possibly thousands. You did the right thing, keeping your distance. Don't ever get within fifty yards of him.'

Besides Tadek and Dr Révész, Miklós grew friendly with a number of other men in his *Kommando*. They were mostly Hungarian Jews but in his regular set of twenty there were also a Belgian, a Dutchman and a Ukrainian called Vanya who taught him how to swear in Russian.

Miklós worked closest with Tadek and a man called Erdös – though 'work' was hardly the word to describe their activity most of the time. This consisted of idle talk, jokes and elaborate word games.

One week, Erdös and Miklós were jointly deputed by Mjetek to fold and pile blankets. Erdös, a thirty-five-year-old cloth merchant, was of Jewish origin but had been baptized at the age of twelve, along with the rest of his family. In recent years he had become a respected member of his local church in the central Hungarian town of Cegléd. But none of this had saved him from the *Arbeitsdienst* and subsequent deportation to Auschwitz.

'You must feel especially bitter about all this,' Miklós remarked to him one day.

Erdös at first tried to deflect this observation with a joke. 'What do you mean?' he exclaimed. 'I'm a cloth merchant, after all. Folding blankets comes naturally to me.'

Miklós persisted. 'I mean, you are a Christian. And yet you are in here with the rest of us.'

'I do consider myself a Christian, yes.'

'They don't.'

'I know ... Yes, I am bitter, bitter at the whole business. Why arrest the Jews? Jews fought for them in the last war. But, yes, if I am honest I am more bitter about my own situation. I had no Jewish upbringing at all. I don't know a word of

Hebrew. I've no Jewish friends, just one or two business associates, none of whom knows of my Jewish blood. It makes me wonder how they knew. When the papers came for the *Arbeitsdienst* I immediately contacted the authorities. Surely it was a mistake? My father protested. My mother protested that I was too old to be enlisted, that I'd already done my army service. We just couldn't believe it. And now this.'

'Do you feel bitter towards us?' Miklós asked.

'No, of course not. That would be succumbing to *their* ignorance – condemning Jews just because they are Jews. Jew, Christian, what does it matter? All I know, Miklós, is that you and I, Tadek, even the *Kapo*, we are decent human beings. Men who persecute decent humanity are simply evil, whatever labels are attached. In a way it is better to be their prisoner than to pretend to be their friend. Better for one's conscience, at least. As for me, yes, I do consider myself a Christian, even though not a single voice from my own church spoke up for me when I was drafted. But look, I was born a Jew and it very much looks like I'll die a Jew. Whether I like it or not. That's the essence of it.'

'I can't help feeling the irony, though,' said Miklós. 'Look at me. I went to a Jewish school. My father is a rabbi. I come from a kosher home with every religious duty and festival observed to the letter. All my friends are Jewish. And you – from another world! For all that, here we are lumped together, the same work, the same place, the same system, the same fate – a Jewish fate. It must be tough for you.'

'It isn't tough for you?'

Miklós laughed. 'You know, Erdös, you are more Jewish than you realize.'

Their discussion was interrupted by the lunch break, and the cherished access to the stove. Here they were given coffee and were occasionally able to use the water from it to cook onions or eggs.

Even Mjetek relaxed at lunch time. He was a non-Jew, a former chocolate manufacturer from Warsaw. Generally, he kept aloof from the Jewish *Häftlings* but now and again he reminisced to them over the coffee, describing the peasant girls who'd worked in his factory and the lavish, sugary treats he'd prepare every year on his wife's birthday.

After coffee, the rest of the break was taken outside in the yard. Sometimes the Slovak girls in the next building would lean out of their window and wave. If the SS guards were around they usually prevented the men from responding. But there were days when the *Häftlings* would blow kisses and shout greetings without interference.

One such day, Miklós caught the smile of a pink-cheeked blonde girl, craning her face above the ledge of the open window. He waved at her enthusiastically. She laughed and waved back. The window was too high up for them to communicate properly but Miklós stepped forward, cupped one hand to his mouth and shouted, 'This is for you, my angel,' as with his other hand he lobbed up a bar of soap.

She caught it gleefully and made signs for him to wait while she turned back into the building. She reappeared a moment later and, laughing loudly, tossed out a pair of men's underpants to him, a forbidden luxury. Miklós looked around to check there were no guards in the vicinity, held the underpants up to his lips and blew the girl a kiss before putting them in his jacket.

Such an amorous interlude was an extreme rarity. But the lack of sexual contact was of little consequence. Constant hunger and fatigue curbed the desires of most *Häftlings*, and one of the more important ingredients of the soup and coffee was bromide.

If the Slovak girls offered a brief hint of pleasure, the other group of women seen regularly by the members of the *Unterkunft* provoked altogether different emotions.

Each day at arrival and departure time Miklós and his colleagues could see other *Kommandos* passing outside their yard, en route to or from some more distant work detail. One of these was a women's *Kommando*, similar to the one they'd encountered on the road to Auschwitz from Birkenau. The physical appearance of these women was dreadful. Some of them were so thin it seemed incredible they could still stand.

Their eyes protruded dully from dark, hollowed faces. Their heads were shaved much closer than the men's, exposing scars and bruises on their scalps. They wore wooden clogs and appeared to drag themselves along rather than walk.

Those unable to keep up were whipped by their German female escorts or bitten by the Alsatian dogs snapping from their leashes. Miklós frequently saw women prisoners collapse on the road, immediately to be dragged, driven or carried away.

Another working party which passed by *Kanada* was a tailoring *Kommando*. This was a large group which, in addition to its *Kapo*, had an *Unterkapo* – a Yugoslavian Jew named Schultz, a former professional footballer. A crude, violent man, he was forever shoving, kicking or abusing the prisoners in his control.

The nature of Schultz's *Kommando* was in marked contrast to that of the *Unterkunft*. Thefts and murders between the tailoring workers were commonplace. Schultz's bullying set the tone. They would kill for food and fight over each other's rations At the *Unterkunft*, Miklós, Révész and the rest could safely leave a piece of bread in one place overnight and collect it untouched the next morning.

Even some of the SS guards assigned to them were reasonably tolerant, or at least restrained. Hoffmayer largely ignored them while one man, Lemelsen, a *Volksdeutscher* from Hungary, was quite humane and sympathetic. Lemelsen even had the occasional friendly chat with Miklós and let him know how the war was going, particularly with regard to Hungary.

On Sundays they finished work at one o'clock. Once back in the *Lager* they were free to roam as they pleased. The orchestra played Beethoven, Bach, Mozart and Wagner on the *Appellplatz*. Appreciative *Häftlings* strolled the *Lagerstrassen* listening and chatting.

The orchestra was a hand-picked *Kommando*, carefully

cultivated by the Germans and kept supplied with musical instruments from *Kanada*. Even the Polish girls from the entrance block would come out to hear them play, though all contact between them and the *Häftlings* was forbidden. The girls' services were reserved for SS officers and a privileged handful of 'high-ranking' Gentile prisoners.

On Sunday afternoons, Miklós and Ede spent hours together talking, as they had in Nagyvárad. Ede was increasingly concerned about his family in Budapest. 'What do you think has become of them?' he would ask. 'Can they still be safe with the Germans running the city? Don't you worry about *your* parents, Miki?'

Miklós's line was always the same. 'Ede, we must not think of them. Even if we were able to find out what is happening to them, there's nothing we can do. Our minds will only go round in circles. Far better to consider *ourselves*, where we can see what's happening.'

With Ede, Miklós talked of the business and family life of former days in Budapest. Or they told each other about events in the bakery or the *Unterkunft*. Ede envied the greater comradeship Miklós enjoyed with his workmates. Miklós in turn envied Ede's ability to organize profitably with minimal risk.

There was a kind of shop near the bakery, manned by a *Häftling*, where coins and paper currency could be exchanged for small items such as pencils or playing cards. The money was issued to the *Häftlings* every Sunday as 'payment' for their work in the *Kommandos*.

One Sunday Miklós bought a pencil, having organized himself some envelopes from a suitcase. He wrote puzzles and arithmetical calculations on some and attempted drawings of fellow inmates on others. Vanya, the Ukrainian, even posed for him, holding his head in profile as he leaned against his bunk. When the *Stubenältester* saw this, he confiscated the pencil and the drawings.

Some Sundays, Miklós played chess with Révész. Tadek and others would stand round, urging advice. Or they would challenge each other to intellectual debate. One day they argued over Plato; another day over Maimonides. They discussed their literary and musical interests; recalled visits to the theatre or concert hall.

Religion was a perennial topic.

'I have lost my faith,' Klein announced one day. He was barely recognizable from the nervous boy of Nagyvárad. His movements were much slower and no longer jerky.

'Did you ever really have faith to lose?' inquired a still-devout Hungarian Jew.

'Of course,' said Klein. 'My prayers in Birkenau were the most intensely sincere of my whole life. But here, now, how can one continue to believe in God?'

'How can one not believe in God?' countered the devout Jew. 'Our history and our tradition are full of the most arduous trials pulling us away from the complacency of worldly luxury. And what is this,' he asked, extending both arms figuratively to embrace the whole of Auschwitz, 'if not just such a trial?'

'You think Kadouk is an instrument of God?' This from Tadek, who always made his points in forceful, dramatic style.

'Kadouk is a force of evil. Just as Amalek was. Just as Haman was,' said the devout Hungarian.

'But what about those Jews who have kept all the *mitzvot*? Remained observant? Like you, perhaps? They're all suffering with the rest of us. Do they deserve such a trial?' said Tadek.

'The motives of the Almighty are not mine to know or explain,' the spokesman for faith replied grandly.

Miklós remembered the dinner-table arguments at home between his father and Ibolya. 'Look,' he said, turning to the religious Jew, 'what good has it done us to obey all the rules? To the exclusion of the world outside. A real world, whose ground we walk upon and whose air we breathe. Our heads have been buried in the sand and now the rest of our bodies will follow. You people are too bound up with rules. Tradition also teaches that the Merciful One desires the *heart*. Mercy. Heart. You are like the Germans – all rules and no heart.'

'And,' added Tadek, 'where is the mercy, I'd like to know?'

The SS simply let all this recreation happen. The senior officers went home to their villas on Sunday afternoons to be with their families. The lower ranks went out to get drunk. They were to be avoided on their return. Many, when drunk, killed *Häftlings* for sport.

In the dusk of one Sunday evening, Miklós saw through the window of his hut two SS men stop a *Häftling* careless enough to have strayed in their path. They stood either side of him, about a yard apart. First, one punched him in the head and then the other did the same. As the unfortunate *Häftling* staggered from one blow, he'd be knocked back in the opposite direction by another.

The two guards seemed to be playing a grisly form of tennis, using the man's head as a ball. 'Stinking Jew!' yelled one as his fist hammered into the *Häftling*'s temple. 'Scum!' volleyed the other.

After a few minutes the prisoner fell down. The two sportsmen finished off their afternoon's leisure by switching from 'tennis' to football practice and kicking the remaining breath out of the *Häftling*.

Another violent incident which Miklós witnessed on a Sunday took place in Block 23 itself. A *Häftling* at the far end of Miklós's room had worn out his shoes. Not having managed to organize himself a pair, he tried to take those belonging to another man who was sleeping.

The victim of the intended theft was known to be a quiet, mild man, who took everything that happened to him with stoic resignation. But when he awoke and saw his shoes being taken he exploded. He leapt upon the culprit and scratched, bit and kicked him.

The other man fought back and swung a punch to his adversary's head which knocked him against his bunk. This stung the victim into still more violent retaliation and he rushed forward with his head down, butting the other *Häftling* in the stomach and bundling him to the floor.

He then grabbed one of the prized shoes and smacked it into the would-be thief's face. Finally, he stood up and kicked him in the testicles, spat at him and left him on the floor, groaning in pain.

One night early in July, just as the *Stubenältester* in Block 23 was calling lights-out, a loud, wailing noise echoed round the *Lager*. The *Häftlings* ran to the windows in alarm.

'Calm down! Back to your beds!' the *Stubenältester* shouted above the din. 'It's the siren. Probably some fool trying to escape.'

'Escape?' Tadek, whose bed the *Stubenältester* was alongside, was incredulous.

'Oh yes,' their supervisor gleefully informed them, 'it has been tried. Not so long ago a dozen prisoners broke out together. They were all recaptured and shot.'

'Doesn't anybody ever get away?' asked another *Häftling*.

'I don't think so,' the *Stubenältester* answered with an unctuous grin. 'In fact, the siren went off once when somebody was missing from a *Kommando* roll-call. But he was just late. He ran to try to catch up. They shot him just the same. Now, all of you, heads down. You'll never be beautiful if you don't get your sleep.' And he switched off the light.

The following evening, when the *Unterkunftkommando* arrived back from *Kanada*, they found the *Lager* streets crowded. Everybody, it seemed, was outside.

'A prisoner has been caught trying to escape,' one of the guards at the gate told them. 'He will be executed, as an example.'

'The siren!' said Erdös. 'That's what the siren was for last night!'

'The *Stubie* was right,' said Tadek. 'And now we are to have a public execution.'

They were made to take their places on the *Appellplatz*. The two or three remaining *Kommandos* filtered in shortly afterwards and the entire *Lager* stood in eerie anticipation as an SS officer

137

mounted a gallows rostrum in the centre of the square. Behind him came a boy of sixteen or seventeen with a placard around his neck bearing the words: 'Back again.'

'Tonight we have an important lesson for all inmates,' declared the SS officer. 'It is that any escape attempt is doomed to failure. You cannot get away. Anyone stupid enough to try will pay with his life. Like this person here. He thought he could get back to Hungary. As if he was wanted there!'

At this point the officer turned to face the boy and called forward a tall, broad individual with bushy eyebrows overhanging a craggy face.

'That's Jakub, the Jewish hangman,' the *Stubenältester* whispered to Tadek and Miklós, who happened to be standing next to him. 'And that,' he said in an even lower tone, indicating a short, red-haired man with pinched features, standing at one corner of the rostrum, 'is Hoessler, the commandant.'

Jakub was ready. The noose was placed over the boy's head. The last words he heard were those of the SS officer: 'Hungary is a long way off.'

It was plain the boy had already been severely beaten. His body was left hanging for twenty minutes or so while the *Lager* got itself back to normal.

During the lunch break on 20 July, one of the *Unterkunfthäftlings* came into the yard carrying a football. Miklós was talking to Vanya at the time. They were both leaning against a wall, their eyes closed, their faces turned up to the sun. Hearing shouts, they opened their eyes.

'Hey, Miki, look!' Vanya slapped Miklós exuberantly and galloped across the yard to join the mêlée of *Häftlings* striving to wrest the ball from its possessor's grasp.

Miklós ran in pursuit and most of the *Häftlings* in the yard joined in the free-for-all. The ball was punted up in the air, caught, and carried a few yards until the person with it released it or was tackled. One or two cuts and bruises appeared and the noise grew louder.

Some of the Slovak girls had come to their window and

were themselves laughing loudly. The SS stayed inside, however, although the gathering crescendo did bring Mjetek running.

Red-faced, he screamed to make himself heard before charging towards the football, which had rolled loose at that moment. The *Häftlings* nearest to it stopped when they saw Mjetek and he was enabled to gather the ball, but only at the second attempt after slipping slightly. Nobody laughed. Nevertheless, this indignity added to his fury and he roared at the men to go back inside the building.

Just as they were doing so, an SS guard came running into the yard from the lane outside. He slowed down a little when he saw the prisoners. When he passed Mjetek, still holding the ball, he said, 'Ah, football. Good healthy sport. Well done,' and strode on into the building.

'All right,' said Mjetek. 'There is half an hour to go. Form yourselves into teams.'

No sooner had the *Häftlings* started to play again in earnest than the same SS guard came out again, followed by one of the regular *Unterkunft* escorts. The footballers slowed to a halt but the SS men ignored them, racing across the yard to another part of the building where Lemelsen and two of his colleagues were having lunch.

Miklós watched this activity with fascination. He saw Lemelsen come out of the building and respond with an uncharacteristically angry snarl to something the other guards were telling him. He mouthed the words, '*Ach Scheisse!*'

The SS were coming and going in a kind of frenzy. At one point, they all gathered in Hoffmayer's office. Hoffmayer himself looked like thunder.

Meanwhile, the football proceeded. A little less frenziedly than before but still with great energy and high spirits. The mood was festive when the *Kapo* came out and called the men back to work.

When the *Kommando* returned to the *Lager* that evening, there was no search and they were dispatched immediately to their block. After the supper ration, Miklós went out on the street. He hadn't smuggled anything in that day but wanted to find out why the SS guards had been so preoccupied.

He met one of his contacts, Roman Levitzky, a Jew from Warsaw. Levitzky had told Miklós about the existence of a *Häftlings'* 'underground' group. This was made up of non-Jewish prisoners, mainly Poles, who had contacts among the civilians who worked in the outer *Kommandos* and among the secretaries who did the typing for the SS.

This group held their meetings in Levitzky's hut and he sometimes picked up items of gossip from them. Today's news was more than gossip, however. 'There's been an attempt on Hitler's life,' Levitzky informed Miklós, 'but it failed.' He shook his head and went on, 'Bloody hell. Oh God, if only! The "underground" say that the SS would have run away from Auschwitz and abandoned us here.'

'How do they know?' asked Miklós.

'That's what they said,' replied Levitzky with a shrug. 'They have connections. They know these things. They don't usually tell me.'

'Oh God,' Miklós sighed. He shook Levitzky's hand, thanked him, and quickly returned to his hut to spread the news. But he wasn't the first. As he got back Tadek greeted him, one hand held aloft.

'We know already,' he said before Miklós had a chance to utter a word. 'The hut is buzzing. The whole *Lager* must be buzzing.'

'Now we know why Lemelsen and Hoffmayer were so put out this afternoon,' said Miklós. 'Levitzky said the SS would have left Auschwitz if Hitler had been killed. It's probably true. Those at the *Unterkunft* would have gone, that's for sure.'

'I'm not so certain,' said Tadek. 'That Hoessler looks like a mean piece of work to me. Would they defy him just like that?'

'Maybe he'd want to go himself. After all, he's answerable to the Führer. But what's the use of talking about it? It didn't work.'

'Yes. Things will probably get worse now.'

'Not necessarily. At least it shows there's a strong feeling against Hitler in his own ranks. Perhaps the Germans' defeat is not so far off, now.'

'Ask your friend Levitzky. Tell him to keep his ear to the "underground".'

The SS continued to look distracted for the next few days. In some ways life grew more tense; in others, more lax. At the gate, the guards only went through the motions of searching. Scores of unlikely items were smuggled through.

Two *Häftlings* tried to take advantage of this new mood to escape. Both members of the tailors' *Kommando*, they hid when the others lined up to return to the *Lager*. They were reported missing almost immediately and the siren sounded. They made a run for it across a field. But this simply led to another part of the *Lager* boundary and they ran virtually into the arms of waiting SS officers.

The ceremonial execution restored normality. One of the men was given a placard to wear which bore the legend: 'I am a stupid Jew.' Both were subjected to a beating on the gallows platform by the same SS officer who'd seen off the Hungarian boy. Then Jakub stepped up as before for the final act. Miklós watched the men die with considerably less emotion than he experienced during the *Unterkunft*'s lunchtime football matches, which had now become part of the daily routine.

One afternoon the temperature dropped. Klein seemed to feel it keenly. He was shivering as they marched back to the *Lager*. By the time they arrived at the gate, his whole body was shaking violently. One of the guards looked at him with suspicion. Klein turned away and coughed. He was promptly searched, the guard taking a malicious pleasure in the nervous boy's discomfort. He put a hand inside Klein's trousers and laughed. Klein looked as if he would faint, and swayed unsteadily back to the block after dismissal.

He barely touched his ration. Tadek tried to jolly him out of it. 'Hey there, Klein. *Zoltele*.' Tadek was the only one who used the affectionate diminutive of Klein's first name. 'Been working too hard? I didn't notice. Why not come and join me in a song, eh? Teach me something Hungarian. Or we'll sing in Yiddish. "*Oifen pripetchik*", eh?'

Klein shook his head feebly. He pulled the blanket up and closed his eyes, the tic between them once more a regular pulse. Tadek shrugged and left him. That night Klein developed a cough, which kept him and some of the other inmates from sleep. At one point the *Stubenältester* shouted for him to stop. By the morning the cough was tearing his throat and rattling his ribs.

Klein's companions forced him to dress for the morning parade. His body was convulsed with coughing. As they assembled, waiting for the *Kapo*, he could barely stand and held on to the sleeve of the *Häftling* next to him. This man brushed him off and he rocked forward into the person in front. His face was grey and his eyes were by now streaming.

The *Blockältester* came over and pulled Klein from the ranks. 'Sir, this man is unwell,' he said to a nearby SS officer. The officer looked at Klein disinterestedly and called two guards. 'Take him to the *Revier*,' he ordered, and Klein's slight, vulnerable frame was dragged away in the direction of the *Lager* hospital.

Later that morning, Miklós asked one of the old hands at the *Unterkunft* about the hospital. 'Ah, the *Revier*,' the old hand replied. 'Let me just give you a piece of advice, my friend. Don't get ill. Don't *ever* get ill. That place is like Block 10. Hospital! Ha! Nobody ever comes out.'

'Is it true about the experiments?' Miklós had heard about the experiments from the pastrycook in Birkenau. 'Are they done in the *Revier* here too?'

'I've heard of such things, yes. They have women in there, you know. They experimented on some Dutch women's eye colours.'

'Is it true that they have Jewish doctors?'

'Yes, but under the control of the SS of course. All their patients finish up in the crematorium in any case.'

Miklós thought of Klein and shuddered. 'The thing is not that he has come to an early end,' he said to himself. 'What is remarkable is that he lasted this long.' And the face of the nervous, twitching boy, whose eyes so clearly revealed his inner feelings, and who had clung on pitifully to the imaginary guarantee of his late father's position in the Hungarian state police, crowded in with those – Eva, Mengele, Nagel, and that other boy, the one in the shiny black boots – which already invaded Miklós's sleep and mocked his determination to survive.

There was no possibility of insulating the mind against the presence and purpose of the crematoria. They were part of the daily conversation of the *Lager*; part, indeed, of its routine. Work parties – the *Sonderkommandos* – were employed to service them, to transfer the human debris from their nauseous ante-chambers.

Moreover, new arrivals from Birkenau, at the rate of a couple of hundred a week, acted as constant reminders that the Nazis seemed bent on eliminating the Jews.

From Birkenau came the regular re-enactment of the bewildered journey in the infernal heat and stench of the cattle trucks, the clinical selection process, the conditions of utter deprivation. From Birkenau, too, and from the *Sonderkommandos*, came news of the war's progress and rumours of its next effects within the microcosm of Auschwitz.

The first Sunday evening after Klein's departure for the *Revier* brought further talk of the imminent arrival of the Jews of Budapest. 'So, your family too, now, eh, Miklós?' said Révész, as if picking at an old wound.

'Who knows?' Miklós stared into the air beyond Révész as he replied.

Both men were in the bunk, ready for lights-out. Miklós lay on his back, hands tucked behind his head. Révész sat on the edge, sideways on to Miklós. The lawyer was pale and shrivelled. His teeth were more prominent than ever, jutting out between his hollow cheeks like stone slabs about to slide down over his lower lip.

He realized he'd said enough and fluttered his stick-like legs beneath the blanket. Miklós ignored him and listened to the conversation about Budapest. Tadek was reassuring. 'How many times have we heard this?' he said. 'And,' turning directly to Miklós, 'how many times has it been wrong?'

In the manner of Sunday evenings the talk rambled on to other topics. Believers in Communism, with their great faith in the Russians, contended with the diminishing band of religious believers.

'I've been saying this all along,' crowed one man. 'The party has been saying it all along. But you kept on going to your synagogues and your churches. Now all your beliefs lie in ruins.'

'How can God Almighty allow the destruction in this way of so many people, so many children?' asked one waverer of the still-faithful Jew who had remonstrated with Klein in that previous discussion.

Once more Miklós was spurred by memories to join in, memories this time of his own rebelliousness in a home in which God had been a significant presence.

'There is no answer to such a question,' he cried out. He felt sorry for the devout believer in the neighbouring bunk. He felt sorry for his father. His thoughts drifted back to Budapest as the lights went out.

By now Miklós was fully initiated into camp life. He and the other *Häftlings* at his stage now took on, for newcomers, the role which Guttman had once performed for Ede and himself.

There was widespread commerce between the different blocks and *Kommandos*. Little that happened in the *Lager* could be kept hidden for long. When a batch of Gentile prisoners was brought in from Warsaw and immediately dispatched to Block 10 and shot, Miklós knew about it that same afternoon.

One morning, as the *Häftlings* filed into the assembly area, they could see that the reception block, number 7, was filled with gypsies. Men, women and children, crowded in together, were leaning out of the windows and screaming for food. They wore ragged jackets of the Birkenau kind, with numbers taped on to the pockets alongside the letter 'Z'.

Two days later Miklós heard they had all been gassed.

'God bless Sundays!' Miklós felt almost exhilarated as the sounds of the orchestra ushered them through the gate.

'It's too late to turn Christian,' said Erdös, marching alongside him. 'And, as you know, it doesn't help.' He too was in a lighthearted mood.

The two men had spent the morning on their own, building fantasies around objects removed from the solitary suitcase to which they had devoted their energies that day. Miklós had kept Erdös entertained with a child's rattle. Erdös had found a woman's velvet hat, with which he'd imitated the sweeping flourishes of a minor courtier to some grand Habsburg monarch.

It was a warm afternoon and the two of them joined Ede and Gelb in the sun on the *Appellplatz*. After about half an hour, the drone of conversation which augmented the music was itself broken by an eruption of noise. A crowd was gathering in a corner of the square, from where a kind of wild incantation was issuing.

The orchestra played on, indifferent to this distraction. They were performing the last movement of Beethoven's Fourth Symphony and seemed carried away in their own intensity. Everyone else's attention was focused on that one corner of the square.

'There is no God in this earth! There is no God in this earth!'

SS men plunged into the crowd to restore order. Still the profane phrase carried repeatedly above the commotion: '*Es is nit da a Gott in der Welt.*' Plumbing the depths of his brain, some demented soul was screaming forth his blasphemy in Yiddish.

As the crowd parted to allow a pair of guards to drag away the offender, a slight, grey, gaunt figure was revealed, scooped up between his captors like a struggling insect, his eyes popping and his throat straining with the terrible, unstoppable cry.

Blasphemy, indeed. The man was one of France's leading rabbis. Respected for his knowledge, urbane and scholarly. Author of learned books; commentator on holy scriptures. Now all this had fallen away like dead leaves. His faith had become inverted and distilled into one simple, annihilating denial.

The incident subsided as quickly as it had arisen. The French rabbi's yells and pain were ended somewhere out of sight. Beethoven's Fourth was concluded with a flourish, and the *Häftlings* drifted back to their huts.

As the summer wore on, life in the *Lager* became harsher. The intake from Birkenau fell. News and rumours of the outside world abounded. Guards and *Häftlings* grew edgier, more apprehensive. Incidents constantly occurred to prevent anybody slipping into the security of predictable routine.

A couple of weeks after the French rabbi's outburst, a seventeen-year-old from Łódź, who had been occupying the bunk beneath Miklós's, gave up hope and walked out towards the electrified fence. Still his death came to him sooner than anticipated. When he failed to answer a guard's order to halt, he was a simple target for the machine-guns.

By now Miklós was inured to the death around him. He felt no emotion at the loss of a young bunkmate other than brief anger that such a young boy had given in so easily.

But then came a confrontation with Kadouk.

Miklós was walking one evening with Guttman and Levitzky. Levitzky was describing how he'd tried to eavesdrop on a meeting of the 'underground' and how his every attempt had been rebuffed. His antics had made Guttman laugh aloud. Then Kadouk appeared.

'Laughing, eh, Jew?' Kadouk's sneer silenced Guttman.

'You find it funny here?' With his second question Kadouk prodded Guttman with the stick he was carrying. Guttman shook his head, his face white with fear. His two friends stood by, frozen. Kadouk cast his eyes towards them and decided it was his turn to laugh, his crossed eyes meeting in a hideous gleam. 'Crawl back into your holes,' he snorted. 'Not you!' Guttman was hauled back. 'Get down!'

Miklós knew what would happen next and felt helpless and sick, even as he made his escape. It would have been unwise to look back. He didn't need to, anyway. His mental picture was accurate enough. Kadouk would be placing the stick across Guttman's neck as he lay on the ground. He would spit and shout insults at him. Then he would jump up and down on the stick until the prisoner's last breath was forced out of his body.

Back in his hut, Miklós fell on to his bed, the taste of vomit in his mouth. He closed his eyes and tried not to see Guttman's face. Tried to dislodge the inner gallery of Mengele, Klein, Nagel and the others.

He imagined himself back at the Jewish Hospital in Budapest, laughing with Theresa and baiting Molnár. He took himself further back, to his adolescent years, his bar mitzvah, his father in full, energetic flow at the dinner table, the girls teasing Julia, his mother smiling with pride.

But he couldn't inhabit these memories in the first person. The present reality was too harsh. He seemed now to be standing and walking alongside the boy that he'd been, another person entirely.

He opened his eyes and looked around the hut. Erdös. Tadek Halter, loafing amiably with Vanya the Ukrainian. Révész, bent and bucktoothed, looking like a diseased rabbit. The reality. Klein and Guttman, cracked, discarded, were as unreal as Hammer the medical student, Miki the bar mitzvah boy.

12

The condition of each *Häftling* was affected by his attitude to his situation. Those, like Révész, whose minds dwelt on their losses, deteriorated rapidly. The same was true of those torn by a sense of injustice, especially if they were in a tough *Kommando*. Those who gave vent to their feelings were simply crushed by the SS. Those desperate enough to attempt escape were invariably brought back with a bullet in the skull or to face the humiliation of the execution ritual, the bland silence of Jakub in place of the mourners' *kaddish*.

Miklós's group at the *Unterkunft* forged a kind of community and were able to keep each other going. Tadek's humour and Vanya's earthy solidity were invaluable.

For some, the heat of that summer was the final oppression. They allowed the sun to burn away their resistance and passively succumbed to the inevitable, at the hands of the guards or at the hospital.

Miklós, Tadek, Erdös and even Révész coped more easily with the summer. They rested in the shade during their lunch breaks at the *Unterkunft* or stripped off in the sun's glare, rinsing themselves and their uniforms in cold water at every opportunity.

Only once did Miklós allow his spirit to become agitated, to emerge from the steady, everyday containment necessary to keep a stride or two ahead of death.

He'd managed to find a prisoner in Block 4 who worked on an 'outside' *Kommando* with Polish civilians through whom he would be able to trade the Swiss twenty-franc coin he'd smuggled in and sewn into his blanket. This could command five loaves of bread or a full sausage.

The man from Block 4 took the coin but never paid Miklós. There was no authority to complain to and Miklós ranted impotently at the thief, who showed his contempt in a smile. This in itself was a lesson for Miklós. He settled back into his regular calmness with an increased determination to maintain it as steadfastly as possible.

On the morning of 13 September, at around eleven, they heard the siren. '*Fliegeralarm! Fliegeralarm!*' The SS were scurrying like mice.

'I can't believe it.' Erdös looked at Miklós as their basement filled with *Häftlings* and guards streaming down the stairs. 'Are the Americans or the British here?'

The thud rocked them violently. Miklós was thrown against the wall. A suitcase Erdös was holding fell to pieces in front of him. The alarm continued for a few minutes. An SS guard crouching alongside them audibly held his breath before screaming and running back up the steps.

A building two blocks away had been ripped in half. Scores of those inside it had died. The SS barracks had also been hit. The 'all-clear' signal brought relief but there had been the thrill of seeing the fear in the eyes of the guards.

Through clouds of dust and smoke, men were running in all directions, some of them bleeding badly. As they wandered out together to survey the damage, Miklós put a hand on Erdös's shoulder. 'You know, Erdös, of all things, the Bible comes into my mind, looking at all this. Samson, praying to God for strength – just once more – so that he can push away the columns and destroy the Philistines along with himself.'

But this was not yet the destruction of the Philistines, though the mood of expectancy created by that sole American raid, striking at a nearby oil refinery, lasted for several days.

The twenty-sixth of September 1944 was the eve of Yom Kippur – Kol Nidrei, the most sacred night of the Jewish calendar. The SS decided to mark it accordingly. Upon their return from their *Kommandos*, the *Häftlings* were assembled on the *Appellplatz*. The siren was sounded. They were then taken in strict formation to Block 1, where the main bath-house was situated. They were ordered to undress and run through the showers.

As they emerged they were confronted by a pair of SS officers and a knot of *Blockschreibers*. The latter were taking note of the serial numbers of the men passing before them. This was a 'selection'. As on the day of arrival in Birkenau, the 'able-bodied' were to be separated from those deemed unfit to work.

Most of the *Unterkunfthäftlings* still had flesh on their bones and were able to walk upright. They were ushered quickly past the *Schreibers* until the bent form of Dr Révész appeared, damp and feeble-looking from the shower. An SS officer stepped forward, nodded his head and the old lawyer was lost to them.

'Mjetek, can't you do something? Speak to Hoffmayer.' This abrupt removal of one of their number shocked them into a desperate solidarity. 'I can do nothing. You know that.' The former chocolate manufacturer was pained to admit his own helplessness to Miklós, Tadek and Erdös.

'What about the *Kapo*? What about that Heinz?' Tadek's entreaty was a token. Even as they spoke, the trucks were on their way from Birkenau to pick up the thousand or so men, among them Dr Révész, who had been ordered to wait alongside Block 7 by the selecting officers.

The next morning, on his way to the wash-room, Miklós passed a still-observant Jew at his devotions. As the man uttered a blessing to God, Miklós slapped him heartily on the back, saying, 'God is on holiday, my friend,' and laughed loudly and briefly. The man called after him: 'I have kept my faith! What are you? You are a low-life. Crazy political rabble. I have kept my faith!'

Miklós continued walking to his ablutions. He washed himself abstractedly, plunging his head under the tap. As usual, he did not use soap. He avoided the 'official' kind from Birkenau and any that he managed to organize from *Kanada* was always traded for food.

He walked slowly to the *Appellplatz*, muttering to himself the phrase he'd used to taunt the man at prayer – 'God is on holiday. God is on holiday.'

Though death was all around them, most of the men in Miklós's block were deeply affected by Révész's 'selection'. The mood on the *Unterkunft* was subdued, though work proceeded as usual. Football was played at lunchtime, Mjetek threw his weight around and Vanya mouthed his Russian curses.

Towards the end of the morning, Miklós was cutting up a tube of toothpaste when his knife struck something hard. He probed inside the tube and found a gemstone. He quickly put this in his shoe and, while outside in the lunch break, buried the stone beside a tree, intending to come back for it.

Later, in the *Lager*, Miklós went to visit Ede and exchanged some toothpaste for bread. Normally they would chat for half an hour or so but this evening Miklós remained only a few minutes.

He told Ede about Dr Révész.

'Your chess partner? The lawyer, with the teeth?'

'That's right. He was the only one taken away.'

'Miki, there's a Hungarian in my block who has organized himself a chessboard. Just this week. He's looking for someone to play with. You can meet him on Sunday. Give him a game.'

And so the gap left by Dr Révész in Miklós's social life was partially filled when he met his new chess partner, a morose youngster called Imre from a town called Beregszász.

Imre was even more gloomy an opponent than Révész had been. 'Miklós,' he asked during their first game, 'do you think we'll ever again have daylight? I don't. Look out of the window at that bird there, sitting on the roof of that building. How lucky to be able to fly over the electric wire. Why couldn't we have been born birds? Do you know about the *Sonderkommandos*?' There was no stopping him.

'I know about them,' replied Miklós, trying to concentrate on his next move, rolling the crudely carved knight between his fingers.

'They pull out the gold teeth before they clear away the bodies. Did you know that? They get the best food in Auschwitz. They live as well as the guards. They even have access to the prostitutes, I heard. Then every three or four months the SS push them into the ovens and a new *Sonderkommando* takes over.'

'Yes, Imre, I've heard about it. There, it's your move.'

On 6 October, a cool, dry day, the lunch break was disturbed by what sounded like a bomb going off somewhere near the edge of the *Lager*.

Miklós was talking to Tadek. They both stopped and exchanged looks which mixed fear and longing.

On the *Lager* streets that evening, all was excitement. Ede came running to meet Miklós outside Block 23.

'Did you hear what happened?' Ede's face was more alive than at any time since the *Arbeitsdienst*.

'What was it?' asked Miklós. 'An air raid?'

'No. One of the crematoria was blown up. Number 4, I think.'

'What! But how come? Who did it – the guards?'

'No – the *Sonderkommandos*.'

'The *Sonderkommandos*?'

'That's right. The "underground" are going around looking very pleased with themselves. Everybody in here is talking about it. Some of the girls working in the office had been smuggling in sticks of dynamite from outside. Can you believe it? They say some of the men in the *Sonderkommando* broke out in all the confusion. The crematorium is wrecked, the fence is down, everything!'

'Oh, please God they got away.'

The smoke and ruin of the crematorium explosion did not relieve the nightmare but became part of it. Several of the men from the *Sonderkommando* break-out were seen being brought back. Nobody knew of a single one who had got away. Some were hanged and some were shot. The part played by the women working in the office was discovered and some of them were hanged too.

That same week two boys from the tailors' *Kommando* tried to steal from the kitchens. One of the cooks caught them and immediately called his colleagues. All of them rounded on the two intruders. Each of the cooks took down any instrument he could quickly lay his hands on from the kitchen shelves and beat the two boys with extreme force.

One of the pair managed to run out into the courtyard but two cooks pursued and overpowered him without any mercy while his accomplice was being finished off inside.

At least a dozen people – including some SS guards – witnessed the killing in the courtyard, but nobody intervened. The loss of a man was no more than routine, especially on that particular *Kommando*. Both the tailors' *Kapo* and his *Unterkapo*, Schultz, the footballer, had contributed to the depletion of what had formerly been a large *Kommando*. Most other *Kapos* behaved in the same way. Heinz Dürmayer at the *Unterkunft* was a singular exception.

As the autumn wore on, still more *Häftlings* caught cold or pneumonia and died. With the intake diminishing, the *Lager*'s population was thinning out perceptibly. News filtered through that transports were leaving Birkenau for the Reich rather than Auschwitz. On a couple of occasions volunteers were requested for transfer to 'the Fatherland'. Nobody from the *Unterkunft* block volunteered.

The working schedules remained exactly the same for the shorter winter days. The men rose at the same hour and went off and returned in darkness. A few were issued with thin cotton coats to wear over their uniforms. The orchestra played as before. However, the physical burden of living from day to day was appreciably heavier, even on 'soft' *Kommandos* like the *Unterkunft*.

All the *Häftlings* were thinner, though Miklós, for one, remained at a reasonably healthy weight. He was also free of the skin diseases that plagued many prisoners. Erdös's face had become blotchy, his cheeks sunken. Tadek and Vanya had both lost teeth and suffered from bleeding gums. And young Imre's eyes now bulged fiercely over the chessboard.

But Ede, like Miklós, was still in relatively good condition, benefiting from the warmth of the bakery. Their old companion Gelb, on the other hand, whom they still visited, was fading. His eyes had become glazed and his cheeks hollow. His ribs jutted through his papery, yellow skin. The last time Ede and Miklós saw him he was coughing in slow, painful rhythm, his shrunken head lolling from side to side like that of a newborn child.

One November Sunday afternoon, all the *Häftlings* were summoned to a surprise roll-call. A sharp wind tore at their faces and whirled icy sleet around them, insidiously soaking their uniforms.

SS men came among them and announced they were to have a bath. They were made to strip off in preparation, each man carrying his uniform and shoes under his arm. The wind dropped a little as the sleet thickened to snow. Their hair whitened under the fall and their feet gradually became covered as they stood there for hours.

Scores of men dropped to the ground, fainting suddenly or sliding on to the icy surface with a sigh. Some were promptly dragged off by *Kapos* or *Blockschreibers*; others were left to freeze under a slow, gentle coating of snow.

After almost six hours' waiting, the *Häftlings* in Miklós's column were ordered to run to the bath-house. The hot steam hit them with a gigantic slap as they came in from the cold, taking their breath away until they raced through the scalding water yelling exultantly.

In *Kanada* there was no sign of the intake of belongings slowing down. The men of the *Unterkunft* sorted their way through the usual mixture of suitcases, looking out for sweaters or other garments they could slip on under their uniforms.

There was still plenty of profit to be had from the range of items passing through their hands, even on the basis of 'organizing' less than five per cent of it. Most of the stuff was handed to Mjetek, who then passed on to the SS whatever he felt appropriate. The SS were especially interested in jewellery and money and were satisfied so long as Mjetek kept a regular supply coming. By the time the pickings from *Kanada* reached Berlin, they had been eaten into substantially.

The football came to an end with the onset of winter. Lunch was taken inside, the ovens offering welcome heat. There was no more waving at the Slovak girls, no more high-spirited singing from Tadek. Everything had slowed down. Then one day a young Hungarian went berserk.

This was Blau, who had entered Auschwitz a fat and heavy youth but who was now stooped and matchstick-thin. Folds of skin flapped around his bony frame. He hardly ever spoke. Then, while sorting through a suitcase, he began to make a low, breathy sound and to rock back and forth as if in prayer or ecstasy.

The noises became louder and turned to sobs. Eventually he screamed aloud, 'No! No!', pulling a photograph from a wallet and holding it high above his head. Tadek and Erdös, who were a few yards away, rushed forward to try to pacify him. But he was screaming inconsolably: 'It's her! It's her! Oh my God, it's her.'

The thin, mottled skin on his arms swung to and fro as he continued to shout and wave the photograph, which showed a girl of sixteen or seventeen wearing a cloche hat and an uncertain expression.

Mjetek came running out of his little room, red-faced and puffing. He slapped Blau's face and the boy dropped his head and cried like a child. 'Quiet,' ordered Mjetek, but it was too late.

The nearest SS guard was a young fellow about the same age as Blau. The small gathering of men looked round to see him standing there. He hauled Blau away, ripping the picture from his grasp and curling it into a ball which he stuffed into the young Hungarian's mouth.

That evening, Miklós met Ede and Levitzky. He told them about Blau and they introduced him to a Gentile prisoner with a bald head and strong, commanding features.

'This is Josef Cyrankiewicz, Miklós,' said Ede, announcing the name of the Polish Communist leader of the 'underground', whom Levitzky had so often mentioned in admiring tones. Ede, too, had met him before and boasted of it to his friends.

Miklós felt exalted to shake the man's hand.

'Which block are you from?' Cyrankiewicz asked him.

'Block 23.'

'Ah, you lucky devil. Give my regards to your *Kapo*, Heinz Dürmayer. You are Hungarian?'

Miklós nodded.

Cyrankiewicz lightly tapped his elbow. 'Don't worry,' he said, 'it won't last much longer,' and walked off.

'It won't last much longer, can't last much longer.' These were the sentiments the *Häftlings* constantly exchanged among themselves, like passwords in a society dedicated to survival. Their ears were attuned to the slightest crumb of information from the outside. They noted any sudden changes in the behaviour of their captors.

Miklós's *Volksdeutsche* confidant, Lemelsen, spoke more and more freely as the winter wore on. A few days before Christmas he seemed almost as dejected as Miklós at the news he was passing on about Hitler's 'renewed vigour' in pursuing the war.

'You know, Hammer, they executed von Hofacker in Berlin. He was a big businessman and he'd been involved in the July plot against the Führer. This execution is a sign that the Führer is flexing his muscles again. He has scored a notable victory against the British and the Americans in the Ardennes. Your Allies have been beaten back. The Americans are surrounded in the town of Bastogne. They will surrender.'

But when Cyrankiewicz told Miklós, 'It won't last much longer,' he felt reassured. As if to confirm this, after Cyrankiewicz had left them, Levitzky told Ede and Miklós that the 'underground' had seemed much more active in recent days.

'They're no longer so careful to stop talking when a Jew appears,' he said. 'They are huddled together a lot, and they look confident and organized. They smuggle in schnapps and vodka from outside the *Kette*. They are buying human lives with schnapps.'

'The Russians are on their way,' said Miklós. 'The Germans are fighting hard on their West flank. The Ardennes. But the Russians are rolling forward from the East. It really can't last much longer. This man Cyrankiewicz knows.'

'You know what I heard from a man in our *Kommando*?' said Ede. 'It seems that a Russian officer came into the *Lager*, dressed as a general in SS uniform. Then when the commandant contacted Berlin to ask why he hadn't been warned of the general's visit, they said to him: "What general?"'

'The SS are thinking more about their escape than about us,' said Miklós. 'They're not so arrogant any more. They're laying off the beatings and killings. We are seeing the wolf shed his coat.'

'But if they are going to run, what about us?' Ede asked in some consternation. 'They won't just leave us here as witnesses. They'll kill us.'

'How will they have time to kill us all? To dispose of our bodies and cover all the traces? Ede, the Russians are closing in and these bastards will run.'

Josef Cyrankiewicz's presence on the *Lager* streets was much more visible during the ensuing days. When he saw Miklós he acknowledged him with a warm smile and a nod. It symbolized the mood of many of the *Häftlings*, including those in Block 23. They were thinner, weaker, slower. The freezing weather penetrated their bones. Even their leisure activities were curtailed; Miklós and Imre no longer had the energy for their chess games. But they felt defiant and believed the future would bring some sort of victory.

On the evening of 24 December 1944, Miklós, Tadek and Ede went to visit Levitzky. Miklós also hoped to have a few words with Cyrankiewicz.

When they arrived at Levitzky's hut, three of the Polish prisoners were quietly singing a carol – 'Silent Night' – in German. This was under the eye of not only the *Stubenältester* but also the *Blockältester* standing in the doorway. Both men were smiling benignly.

Others joined in slowly, including some of the Jewish prisoners. Cyrankiewicz waved to Miklós, signalling him to sing with them.

> *Stille Nacht, heilige Nacht.*
> *Alles schläft, einsam wacht.*

Miklós, Ede and Tadek added their voices, as did Levitzky. The *Blockältester*, the *Stubenältester* and all the *Häftlings*, Jews and Gentiles, joined in with gusto. Several men were crying. Outside, the *Lager* seemed deathly quiet as the music swelled and soared.

> *Nur das traute hochheilige Paar.*
> *Holder Knabe mit lockigem Haar.*

Miklós and Ede stared into each other's faces as they sang. Two Jewish childhood friends singing these Christian verses without any inhibition. But there was no religious doctrine in this. The singers were part of the song. A song of fervent defiance.

> *Schlaf in himmlischer Ruh'.*
> *Schlaf in himmlischer Ruh'!*

13

January was painfully cold. Their cotton coats afforded little protection against driving snow and strong winds. The walk to and from the workplaces was icy, dark and bitter. The *Lager* population continued to fall. The intake had long since dried up, while death inside Auschwitz remained common enough.

Miklós's chess partner Imre died of a fever. This at least kept him from the clutches of Kadouk, who took to stalking around the bakery in those early days of 1945 and making individual *Häftlings* stand naked in the snow for hours.

One day he called out a father and son who worked together at the bakery. He made them face each other and told them that at least one of them was about to die.

'One of you can save yourself by killing the other for me,' he announced. 'If this fails I will kill both of you with my bare hands.' Kadouk pointed his whip at the father. 'You! Punch him – hard.'

The father closed his eyes, swung a punch at his son's shoulder and fell into his arms, whispering to him in Hungarian, 'Kill me, son. You must kill me. It's your duty to save yourself. Don't worry about hurting me. Strike hard. God bless.'

'Come on, come on.' Kadouk separated them and ordered the son to hit his father. 'Hard this time. And in the face.'

The young man gazed fully into Kadouk's bilious eyes then turned back to his father and struck him with full force on the nose. The older man fell to the ground and, to Kadouk's excited exhortations, the son rained blows on to his father's head. Soon he was swinging wildly and screaming to cover up his father's moans.

When it was over, Kadouk laughed: 'You killed your father, Jew.'

Kadouk was an exception. Most of the guards seemed to be self-absorbed and largely ignored the *Häftlings* during those first January weeks.

On 17 January they were sent back to their bunks after they'd used the wash-room. They were kept in all day. There was no midday food ration but the normal provisions were issued in the evening.

That night Miklós dreamed of Dr Révész, his teeth protruding so grotesquely that it was impossible for him to speak clearly. He was eagerly trying to board a cattle truck at the Birkenau siding and Miklós was attempting to stop him. Kadouk and Mengele intervened and threw Miklós aside, leaving Révész free to scamper on board spluttering the word 'goodbye' over and over through interlocking and bleeding teeth.

He was awoken in the morning by the light being switched on and the *Stubenältester* shouting and clapping his hands as usual. Once the men had completed their ablutions a cauldron of coffee was brought in and an SS guard entered to make a brief announcement: 'Nobody will go to work today. Wait for further orders.'

The *Lager* streets were bristling with activity and the men from Miklós's hut quickly went out to add to it. Everybody was in a frenzy. Many were devastated, expecting death. Nobody seemed to know what was happening, except that irregular and muffled bangs in the distance told them that the Russian artillery was moving within range.

Ede was certain the SS would kill them all that day. Then came Levitzky, out of breath with running: 'We are going to be taken away today. The rumour is that they are planning to evacuate the *Lager*.'

'Are you sure?' asked Ede anxiously.

'This is what is being said,' replied Levitzky.

'What will they do with us?' Ede's fears were growing.

'Some people are talking of hiding,' said Levitzky.

'Ah, that would be easy enough if we were at the *Unterkunft*,' said Miklós. 'But it's unrealistic to think of hiding in the *Lager* itself.'

'There is a place where coal is kept where someone in my block said it would be possible to hide,' revealed Levitzky.

'Ah, this is just rumour. Where can that be?' Miklós was growing sceptical.

'Miki, it surely must be possible.' Ede was almost pleading. 'We can't leave ourselves to the mercy of these bastards. Come on, Miklós, this is not like you. Don't let them get you now, after everything.'

'Ede, I said to you before. They can't kill everybody here in the time available to them. The *Häftlings* will be part of the evacuation. You can count on it.'

'So what are they going to do? Take us back to the Reich? No thank you, I'll take my chances here. I'm for hiding.'

As he walked back to his own hut, Miklós could see SS men running from block to block. The formerly cool, ruthless organization seemed to have broken down. 'This is it,' he said to himself, realizing that a roll-call was to take place.

In his pocket was a small coin he'd taken a few days earlier from a suitcase inside which a Dutch name and address had been written in proud, artistic handwriting. He took out the coin now, turning it round in his fingers as he considered Ede's insistence on remaining in the *Lager* and Levitzky's suggestion that there might be a secure hiding place among the coal.

He and Ede had consistently stuck together. They had grown extremely close. Could they take different paths now? Miklós looked at the coin in his hand and suddenly flipped it into the air. He caught it in his right palm and slapped it on to the back of his left hand. 'Heads,' he said, determinedly. 'I go with the evacuation.'

He was soon caught up in the roll-call. Guards were rushing in every direction, shouting. The dogs were making a noise too, and even the Polish women from the prostitutes' block could be heard shrieking.

Miklós felt like a man who'd been rescued from drowning.

Repeatedly, he had heard that the only way out of Auschwitz was to be through the *Kamine*, the chimneys, and now he was on the point of walking out through the gates. Having made his decision, he was eager to be among the first to leave.

As he stood there, in one of the rows of five the SS were hastily arranging, a ration of bread in his hand, the fateful coin in one pocket and a bar of soap in the other, he looked around calmly at the newly frenetic urgency of the guards. 'In spite of everything,' he thought, 'I'm still here.' Like others alongside him, he experienced a small note of victory in his soul.

He was standing with Vanya and Tadek, no longer the expansive, extrovert actor, but a frail and prematurely aged man. None the less, he smiled now at Miklós and gripped his arm affectionately.

Most of his companions from the *Unterkunft* could be accounted for, though Erdös was nowhere to be seen. 'And what about the *Kapo*?' Miklós asked Tadek. Tadek shrugged, his eyes large and expressive in his bony face. 'He will probably go with the SS. I heard that's what other *Kapos* are doing.'

'But aren't we going with the SS?'

'We are being led by them. We are not *with* them, Miklós.'

'I somehow don't think our *Kapo* will enjoy their company.'

'No, he's a good man.' Tadek nodded like an old *tzaddik*.

'You know, Tadek, I buried a gemstone in the yard at the *Unterkunft*.'

'Ah, shrewd!'

'It was just after Révész was taken. I wanted to go back for it. I suppose I wanted to smuggle it out of the *Lager* one day.'

'Yeah, holiday souvenir. Well, you're not going to be able to get it now.'

Now it was Miklós who shrugged.

The SS wore greatcoats and carried rucksacks and submachine-guns. They stamped their feet to keep warm while they waited for the order to get going. Their dogs, too, seemed impatient, growling and leaping restlessly. As the hours passed and the sky began to darken, Miklós's calmness gave way to anxiety.

At shortly after five o'clock, through a gathering blizzard, they could see that the columns lined up far ahead of them were beginning to move. The sound built up steadily of hundreds of men marching. 'No music,' Tadek mouthed to Miklós. The orchestra's absence was unsettling.

Miklós's column was on its way by six o'clock. As they passed under the main gate he turned his head for a last look at that mocking emblem, stark and ironic in the growing darkness.

As they reached the open road, the wind cut into them, freezing their faces and hands. The guards goaded them urgently – 'Los, los!' – forcibly pushing any stragglers

They moved forward in a great mass. Miklós could see rows of prisoners stretching in front and behind him for at least 500 yards in each direction. Vanya was already lost to sight, though Tadek still stood next to Miklós. The packed snow at the roadside almost glowed in the darkness. The SS men and their dogs stood out against it like figures in a stark, Flemish landscape painting.

The marching columns had gone a short way when Tadek tapped Miklós's arm. 'Look,' he said, lifting his head in front of him. 'Women.'

Miklós peered forward and saw hundreds of female heads bobbing up and down amid the forest of Häftlings. 'They are clearing everybody out,' he said. 'From Birkenau and all of Auschwitz. I wonder what has happened to Ede and Levitzky.'

The prisoners continued to chatter among themselves. The SS, fifteen or twenty yards to the sides of the main column, ignored them. The sound was no more than a murmur, muffled by the snow.

After a quarter of an hour a couple of men in the row in front of Miklós stepped out to the side and relieved themselves at the roadside. A guard quickly came and pushed them back into the main body of marchers, some nine or ten rows behind the one they had left.

The next time somebody broke away from the mass, he was

knocked to the ground. A couple of hours later the monotony was broken when a *Häftling* as thin as a reed stopped at the side of the main column. An SS guard took two purposeful steps towards the man and shot him in the side of the head as he stood urinating.

Others stopped from time to time, often from sheer exhaustion. If they were in the middle of a row they could be pulled up by their fellow *Häftlings* and drawn back into the pack. But those who stopped at the edges were picked off by the vigilant SS guards.

Occasionally a casualty in the middle of the crowd was too far gone for rescue. Miklós passed by one such man, a pale, whiskery Polish Jew, who was on his knees in the snow with the marching columns flowing round him like a stream around a rock. He looked as though he might be praying. But the brief, harsh sounds he uttered were those of death.

As the night wore on and they tried to work out where they were going – the road signs indicated they were passing through Upper Silesia – the odd person whispered about making a dash for it. Miklós saw one man try. They were walking alongside farmland when the man ran towards a tree in a field. He was brought down by a gunshot about ten yards short of it. Even in the dark Miklós could make out the blood trickling into the snow. The man's body, like all the others, was left where it fell.

The faces along the row kept changing as individuals fell back or changed pace, but Miklós and Tadek were still together. Tadek looked weak.

'Are you all right, Tadek?' Miklós held out his hand to help his friend as he expressed his concern.

'Yes, thank you, Miki. I was just thinking that, in all my career, this is the hardest part I've had to play.'

'This is no play. This is real, Tadek, desperately real.'

'Maybe. But I can only deal with this exhaustion and cold and boredom by acting. You see, I pretend that I'm all right. A contented man taking a little exercise in the night air.'

'That's one way to keep going.'

'For me it's the only way.'

'It must be marvellous to be on the stage.'

'It is, but it is hard work. We used to do three different plays in one week's repertoire. You had to prepare yourself thoroughly. But once you had mastered your part and you could control that audience as one person ... Oh, Miklós, it was magical! I could always make them laugh, you know; sometimes even weep – with my singing. Those old Yiddish songs. The feeling between the actors and the audience was like a wedding. I felt like a bridegroom wooing his bride.'

'I'm sure you are a great actor, Tadek.'

'I am a journeyman, Miki. No more. Except now, perhaps. Here, I am acting with all my strength.'

Shortly before dawn, with the snow easing, they were ordered to halt. The SS announced this was to be a rest and everybody sank to the ground, many falling asleep almost instantly on the cold, wet surface.

Miklós curled up and dozed. His head and limbs ached and his feet throbbed. The relief was immeasurable but he fought against sleeping. Next to him, Tadek's head fell forward on to his chest.

They rested for a couple of hours during which the new day broke, giving a clear view of the farm buildings around them. Everything was still. There was no sign of life on the farms. It was as if the inhabitants had suspended normal activity while these abnormal creatures passed by.

When the order came to rise, some of them could not get up. Their comrades shook and even kicked them but a few would still not be roused. The shots dispatching these stragglers could be heard as soon as the last row of the huge column had moved a few yards.

On and on through the day they went. The roads were icy and the wind got up again but by mid-afternoon Miklós felt as though his feet were on fire. By that time he had only a corner of his bread left. Tadek's acting was not standing up too well to the prolonged encore imposed upon him by his German 'audience'. He twisted his head round and round to remain awake and to prevent his neck from stiffening, but even this was a strain.

More and more fell by the wayside. Some of the stronger ones still tried to urge on their weaker colleagues and to give them a hand when they stopped or stumbled. But each individual increasingly had to save his strength for himself. Or herself – a number of women were visibly struggling. Miklós stopped to try to pull up one young girl who had rolled herself into a ball on the freezing road. But his promptings were useless and eventually he had to leave her there.

As the sun began to set at the end of the afternoon, the marching column was broken up into sections by those leading it. The section that Miklós was in was steered into a farmyard. The officers commandeered the farmhouse while a handful of guards were posted outside to supervise the *Häftlings*, most of whom were ushered into a barn piled high with hay.

Miklós sank gratefully into the soft, aromatic mass. He didn't know how long he had been sleeping when Tadek whispered into his ear. 'Did you hear, Miki? Some of the men are not going to rejoin the march.'

'Not going?' Miklós was sleepy, uncomprehending. 'Yes, it would be lovely to stay here and sleep.'

'Some *are* staying here. Burying themselves in the hay as a way to hide from the guards. They didn't count us. Others have decided to make a break for it. What do you think?'

Miklós was alert now. 'No, Tadek. This is not the time. How far will they get? A few miles if they're lucky. And then what? Do they expect the Polish farmers to take them in, give them a meal and hide them?'

Tadek shrugged. 'I don't know. Some are desperate.'

'As for me,' said Miklós, 'I don't even speak Polish. I wouldn't have a hope. Are you going?'

Tadek shook his head. 'No. He is, though,' he said, pointing to a dark young Polish Jew who'd spent the past few hours marching alongside them. The young man nodded in confirmation. 'Goodbye,' he said, shaking both Tadek and Miklós by the hand before slipping off between the bales of hay. 'Victory to the people!'

'So, Tadek,' Miklós smiled as his friend frowned. 'Let us get some sleep now, while we can. You need to refresh yourself for your next performance.'

Three hours later they were on the move. Their ears grew accustomed to the sporadic gunshots. And now they stepped over dead and dying bodies without a second glance.

'I wonder what happened to the Polish boy Communist,' Miklós remarked to Tadek after a mile or so. Tadek raised his eyebrows and pursed his lips in answer.

A tall, pock-marked and talkative youth joined their line. He asked Miklós and Tadek where they were from and introduced himself. 'My name is Imre Katz. I come from Ungvár,' he said, naming a town in north-eastern Hungary. 'I have lost everyone in that place. I'm pleased to be out of there. I don't care if we march round in circles for a hundred miles.'

'We've got a long way to go before we've done that,' said Miklós. 'I don't think we've covered much distance. I can still smell Auschwitz.'

'That's because we all smell of it,' said Imre.

'I don't think we're going round in circles,' put in Tadek.

'No, of course not,' said Miklós. 'These fellows are on the run. They must be taking us somewhere. They have maps. They've got a definite destination in mind.'

By now the prisoners were in an appalling state. Exhaustion dragged at them like a heavy weight. Some were delirious. It was still very cold, with a sprinkling of snow, but this could not obliterate the fetid odours issuing from the mass of bodies. Most kept walking while urinating or defecating, partly because they were too numbed to stop but also because the SS had ceased to show any mercy to those who lagged behind or strayed from the column.

'My family kept a bookshop in Ungvár,' announced Katz. 'I grew up with books. I became familiar with their feel and their

167

smell. And I loved it. I devoured them. Not only Hungarian books but Hebrew – my father was a self-taught but pious man – German, Russian, French . . .'

'You were lucky,' interrupted Tadek, who was limiting his dialogue to single sentences.

'Yes, I was lucky.' Katz sighed heavily before continuing. 'My father and mother were in the truck with me to that place. My last day with my mother is one I would wipe from my memory if I could. But of course it's the one most indelibly printed there. Sometimes it's the only one. I forget what her face was like when I was a child. I can't remember her taking me to school, what words she used to calm me when I woke in the night, how she scolded me when I misbehaved. But how she was in the truck, I'll never forget. In that truck, on that day, I saw her nakedness for the first time. Saw her without any of the authority I relied upon all my life. And I looked into her face, as close as I am to you, and she stared out without seeing me. I swear it.' He turned abruptly to Miklós. 'And your family?'

'No, they were not there. They were left in Budapest.'

Just then a shot was fired near them. Imre Katz cried out, 'My God, he shot me!'

'Don't be stupid,' said Miklós. 'He shot that fellow over there. The one who fell at the end of the line. Look.'

'I'm hurt,' insisted Imre. 'I can't walk.'

'Don't be a fool,' said Tadek, suddenly animated. 'You know what it means if you can't walk. Keep going!'

'I can't,' repeated Katz. 'He shot me. My left foot.'

'It must have rebounded,' said Miklós. 'Here, put your arm around my shoulder and just keep going.'

Miklós supported him for half an hour then Tadek took over, the great effort apparent on his face. Then two others in the row, Hungarian boys of eighteen or nineteen, took their turns too.

'I'm sure he wasn't hit,' Miklós whispered to Tadek while one of the others was shouldering the burden.

'Perhaps it's in his mind,' suggested Tadek. 'Maybe he's crazy.'

'He's a decent lad,' said Miklós. 'Could be he's an actor, too,' he added, grinning at Tadek, who refused to see the joke.

And so they proceeded through the rest of the night and into the day, shifting along the row to support Katz. Every time they asked him if his foot was feeling better he shook his head and complained of the pain preventing him from walking.

They talked little and their movements became mechanical. Some people around them carried on conversations, others simply groaned. They came across a girl of about fifteen standing facing the back of the column with the mass of weary *Häftlings* picking their way past her. She was crying, 'Mummy, mummy.'

Miklós and one of the Hungarian boys tried to turn her around and urge her forward but she resisted – 'I can't, I'm tired, I want my mummy.' So they trudged on, heads down, without looking back and without uttering a word to each other for an hour or more.

'We are no longer human beings. We are just cattle.' It was Tadek who eventually broke the silence.

'Heading for the slaughterhouse, eh, Tadek,' said Imre Katz.

'That proves we're not cattle,' said Miklós. 'Cattle don't think about the slaughterhouse.'

At that moment a woman three or four rows ahead of them fainted and was immediately shot by a nearby guard.

Tadek looked into Miklós's face, closed his eyes and turned away again. 'Cattle don't think about the slaughterhouse,' Miklós repeated. Tadek began to hum a Yiddish lullaby to himself.

They could see the outlines of a town on the horizon. As they drew nearer to it, along neat, tree-lined avenues, Miklós turned to the Hungarian youth on his right, who was at that point supporting the limping Imre Katz. 'This is the industrialized part of Upper Silesia,' he told him. 'We have left the countryside behind. They cannot parade us through a town without feeding us.'

The youth had hardly spoken during the hours he had marched alongside Miklós and Tadek, except to complain of hunger. For the past two or three miles he'd sustained himself – as had many others – by eating snow. Now he hung on Miklós's words. 'God, I pray so,' he cried.

They could see lights behind shuttered windows. 'I wonder what they make of all this,' said Miklós, inclining his head upwards. The youth smiled cautiously, saying nothing.

But Imre Katz did reply. 'They will just say to each other, "There go the Jews." Those who notice us, that is. To them also we are cattle, eh, Tadek? Their hearts won't bleed for us. "There go the Jews on their way to market." That's what they'll be saying.'

As they came towards the main part of the town, they were led down a road which deviated from the centre, to the right. It led to a railway station where a sign told them they were in Loslau.

They were formed into groups in the goods yard and given half a loaf each and a freezing cold mug of water. They were then directed into waiting cattle trucks, similar to those in which they had arrived at Birkenau. In the scramble aboard, Miklós and Tadek stayed together but became separated from Imre Katz and the two Hungarian lads.

There were about 100 prisoners to each truck. As soon as they were inside they squashed up together on the floor, exhausted and desperate for sleep.

Miklós was barely aware of the train moving off. Its rhythm was that of his dreams. He had no idea how long they had been travelling when the train came to a halt and the prisoners were ordered out.

They found themselves at an enormous *Lager*. The guards informed them that they were at Gross-Rosen concentration camp, near Breslau. The name of the camp was familiar. In recent weeks a number of *Häftlings* had been transferred there from Auschwitz. It was known to be a major labour camp.

Miklós was in a batch of 1,000 or more men being marched

towards the barracks. As they passed the few stray, curious inmates watching their arrival, they called out to them: 'Do you have gas chambers and crematoria here?'

'Crematoria, we have. Gas chambers? No.'

Their destination was a large hut with a concrete floor. Once inside, almost all of them sank to the floor to rest. Miklós quickly fell asleep.

In the morning they were allowed to roam around outside. Among the hundreds of lost and frightened faces Miklós spotted his mother's cousin, Szender, fifteen years his senior, a tailor from a small eastern Hungarian town. They hadn't seen each other for ten years and yet they exchanged only a word or two of greeting. Anything more would have required too much energy.

At midday, a *Häftling* brought them a cauldron of warm, bitter 'coffee'. It settled immediately and uncomfortably in the gut.

Everybody had lost weight dramatically. Miklós felt weaker than at any previous time. He kept stroking his skin where it felt like a fine tissue through which his bones could protrude. Tadek was barely recognizable, so stooped he could hardly lift his head. But still he insisted on maintaining his performance, and sang old tunes under his breath.

They were ignored for the rest of the day. At four the next morning they were awoken by a guard and ordered to the wash-house. This lay behind their hut and housed a few primitive and rusty sinks with taps dribbling out thin trails of cold water. There was also a row of wooden latrines, each one broken, soiled and foul-smelling.

Later that morning, Miklós went out again to the latrines. On his way back he decided to walk around behind the wash-house. As he did so, he stopped short, with an involuntary intake of breath. Laid out against the rear wall were rows of naked corpses. They appeared to be lined up for counting. Many of them had had the centre of their heads shaved in a wide channel running from front to back.

Miklós was about to turn away when his attention was caught by one of the bodies furthest away from where he stood. He walked over to it. It was Imre Katz. Miklós stared down at the bent, lifeless shape, and could feel almost physically the burden of Katz's body which he and the others had shared right up to Loslau station.

'No more books for you, my friend,' Miklós muttered. 'This is the end of your learning.' And walked back to his hut.

Later in the day he got together with his cousin Szender. Seated on the ground, they talked of other cousins and grand-parents, and of their own families, in a flat, unsentimental manner.

'So you are not married, Miklós?'

'No. And you? You have children, I believe?'

'Yes.'

After Szender had softly uttered that one word, neither man could speak further. Miklós sighed, stood, nodded to his cousin and walked off. Szender remained sitting, staring hard at the ground.

14

In the middle of the afternoon, soup and bread arrived. There was not enough to go round and some *Häftlings* went without. While Miklós ate his, making it last as long as he could, he stared through the window of the hut. Outside, hundreds of new prisoners were being herded into the *Lager*.

Many of the new arrivals were brought into Miklós's hut. As the snow dried on their clothes they gave off a dank smell which added to the unpleasantness of the grossly overcrowded area. Night fell with people fighting for space. Miklós lay down against a wall and slept fitfully while around him others chattered, complained, coughed, sneezed and hawked up from diseased lungs.

Gross-Rosen appeared to be a repository for *Häftlings* gathered up from various camps by the Germans in their retreat from the Eastern front. Each day the trains disgorged scores of weary, emaciated men, including many Gentiles. The women had been taken elsewhere.

Organization was much less disciplined than in Auschwitz. Some *Kommandos* were established but the later arrivals were left alone for the most part and were free to mingle.

Miklós wanted to find out what had happened to Imre Katz. He spoke to a *Häftling* employed in the hospital. This man told him that very few of the patients were released. Those who didn't oblige the authorities by dying were dispatched by other *Häftlings* injecting them with petrol. He also explained that the prisoners with lines shaved across their heads were captured Russian soldiers.

After a week, the Auschwitz intake began to resemble one

another in that they all still had their heads shaved, their bodies were bent and wasted and their eyes appeared deeply set in their skull-like faces. They all felt weak and dispirited in the stinking, overcrowded hut. Several died and were gratefully ejected for collection by the regular death carts.

By this time Miklós limited his conversation to brief exchanges with Szender or Tadek. Szender maintained a fixed expression, his lips drawn tightly together, his brows held in a frown. Tadek was mostly silent. He no longer sang, even to himself.

Their days were broken only by the unpredictable arrival of soup and bread – the former a thin, watery substance, the latter gritty and hard – or by SS officers calling for volunteers for work detachments.

Eventually Miklós decided to volunteer. An officer had come into the hut and announced that he needed men for an outer *Kommando* on a small *Lager* 'a few miles away'. Miklós didn't consult Tadek or Szender, neither of whom volunteered. He'd simply had enough.

The officer led out about 250 men, Miklós among them. The SS man was an enlisted *Volksdeutscher* rather than a professional soldier, white-haired, loud-mouthed and corpulent. His figure made a bizarre contrast with those of his charges, each of whom was issued with a piece of bread before departure.

As they set off along the road, two lower-ranking SS men brought up the rear. Miklós felt cleansed and uplifted by the crisp, cold air. He took pleasure in the sight of the countryside, contrasting dramatically as it did with the unsavoury atmosphere of the hut in Gross-Rosen.

After a couple of hours' marching, they were allowed to rest in a clearing by the roadside. The ice and snow were receding before expanding patches of grass and gravel. The prisoners basked in the high, bright sunlight, while the white-haired officer stood by and relieved himself.

They didn't feel as isolated as they had on the trek out of Auschwitz. They had encountered a little traffic this time. The business of farm and village life seemed to be continuing normally. Local people stared at them curiously from bicycles or over fences. And conversations and written signs told them this was no longer Poland, but Germany proper.

When they were ordered to restart, a couple of *Häftlings* who had been sitting at the back of the clearing ran off towards a nearby copse. The commander sent one of his guards after them while the rest of the prisoners were made to wait at attention.

Both were recaptured within minutes and led back with their hands on their heads. The white-haired *Stahrführer* ordered them to the edge of the road and shot them both in the head from close range. He replaced his pistol, cleared his throat and yelled at the men to start moving.

Several more prisoners tried to escape throughout the day, running off into woods, down alleys or across fields. Some were shot, others got away. Miklós had no intention other than to stay with the march. He spoke to nobody and just kept going.

In the evening they arrived at a farmhouse and barn. Both buildings were clean and orderly. Miklós felt comforted by the square of yellow light glowing from the farmhouse door and by the fresh, earthy smell of the animal fodder.

The two junior SS men took up posts at the entrance to the barn as the *Volksdeutsche* commander ushered in the prisoners. 'All right,' he shouted. 'Sleep. You must build up your strength for work.' With a nod towards each of his two men, he turned and made his way to the farmhouse.

The two guards sat down. Everyone relaxed. The hay offered them all a luxurious night's sleep.

Morning came to the barn in sharp, bright needles of light. Three men alongside Miklós were talking of escape. One of the guards had gone; the other stood at the entrance, yawning.

The missing guard reappeared after a few moments, followed by the white-haired *Stahrführer*. All three men roused the *Häftlings* and lined them up in single file. The *Stahrführer* told them to march out of the barn and, as they did so, he singled out the odd individual to stand aside.

When the main group, including Miklós, had assembled outside, they were left under the charge of the two guards while the old *Volksdeutscher* led those he'd picked out into a field at the back of the barn. After about ten minutes there was a peal of shots. It seemed that not all the volunteers were needed.

Towards the end of that day they reached their destination. This was a small camp with only a handful of buildings, the most prominent of which were the kitchen and bath-house. There was no sign to tell them where they were.

Two SS officers met them at the gate. One of them made a joke with the white-haired *Stahrführer*, who laughed a loud, vulgar laugh causing his large stomach to shake and shift grotesquely.

A few minutes later the new prisoners were led in and taken to the bath-house. After an unexpectedly long and hot shower they were taken to an adjoining hut where a team of *Häftlings* shaved the hair not only from their heads but from all over their bodies.

A *Kapo* standing by the exit told them what was happening. 'Delousing!' he shouted. 'Take your clothes now and soak them in the stream outside here.'

This *Kapo* was a German Gentile, wearing a dark cotton prisoner's uniform. He was a big man, tall and gangling, with a huge head that was emphasized by his shaven scalp. Beneath a wide expanse of forehead he had small eyes, a large, scabbed nose and a narrow slit of a mouth with no sign of any lips.

Once they had cleaned their uniforms, the *Kapo* led them to what seemed to be a large, private house, rather than a barrack hut. He took them inside, into a large hall. 'These are your quarters,' he announced. 'You will sleep on the floor. This is a former military establishment and we run things ourselves, more or less, with very little interference from the SS. So make sure you all keep your noses clean. Now, do we have any lawyers here? Lawyers who can understand me, who can speak German.'

One man stepped forward. 'And what is your name?' asked the *Kapo*.

'Imre Friedman,' was the reply. He was a Hungarian from the town of Satmár.

'Good. You, Friedman, are now the *Blockschreiber* here. Collect everybody's numbers for the daily roll-call.'

He left them where they were and returned an hour or so later with another *Häftling* and a cauldron of soup. When he departed a second time he sought out Imre Friedman. 'Remember, *Blockschreiber*,' he told him. 'Roll-call tomorrow morning. Everybody's number.'

The next few days passed relatively easily. A roll-call was held each dawn but only once were volunteers requested for work. Six men were given shovels and taken outside the camp. They returned after a few hours and said they had been made to bury six bodies.

One morning Friedman unaccountably forgot Miklós's number for the roll-call. Once the omission was rectified, the *Kapo* stepped up to Miklós and punched him hard in the mouth, splitting his lip.

After eight days the camp was evacuated. Approximately 400 men were marched out by four SS guards, the pair who had accompanied the *Volksdeutscher* from Gross-Rosen and the two who'd greeted him at the gate. The *Stabführer* himself had returned to Gross-Rosen.

The *Kapo* was at the head of the march, just behind two of the SS men. The two others were positioned at the rear.

They proceeded more rapidly than before. The weather was milder and they were refreshed by their stay in the small military camp. Looking round, Miklós could recognize nobody whom he'd known in Auschwitz.

They continued for two days in a south-westerly direction, stopping off at barns to sleep and obtaining meagre rations from farmers. Miklós heard the occasional gunshot but saw no one die.

On the second evening they entered a *Lager* at the edge of a town. Protected by watchtowers and barbed wire, it was considerably smaller than Auschwitz or Gross-Rosen but larger than the place they had just left. It and the town were called Hirschberg.

The leading SS officers took them through the gate and straight into the shower. As at their previous camp, they were left in there long enough to clean themselves thoroughly. The showers were primitive constructions, rubber hoses dangling from wooden frames.

While Miklós was wallowing in the warm, wet flow over his face and chest, he noticed a *Häftling*, a Czech Jew, steal up on another prisoner and grab him from behind in a stranglehold around his neck. He then took hold of the rubber hose hanging above the man's head and forced it into his mouth.

The rest of the men carried on washing themselves as the mysterious victim submitted to the assault and died, choking, before their eyes. Miklós looked at his neighbour, who shrugged. 'Revenge?' he speculated. 'Some old score settled.'

They were taken to a proper barrack hut, where each man had his own bunk. There was a roll-call and they were given soup and, later, coffee. Both tasted better than in any of the previous *Lagers*.

Miklós became friendly with Imre Friedman and a tall, bespectacled young man from Budapest who introduced himself as Imre Löwy. On their second or third morning in Hirschberg, the three of them approached a group of the older hands among the *Häftlings* and asked them if they had been able to keep track of developments in the war.

A brief conversation followed, cut short by the German *Kapo* who had split Miklós's lip, but it was long enough to inform the newcomers of the meeting of 'the Big Three' at Yalta and of Turkey's entry into the war on the Allies' side.

They remained in Hirschberg only a week. Miklós regretted leaving such comfortable surroundings for the open road once more but took heart from the fact that the Germans were now retreating further and quicker.

As they made their way towards the mountainous region of the Erz Gebirge in Moravia, Miklós walked alongside Löwy and talked with him about the plays and concerts they'd seen in Budapest.

Löwy asked him what he thought of their prospects.

'I feel the worst is over,' he replied. 'I know we are moving further into Germany but they no longer have time to torture us.'

'But they could still kill us?'

'Yes, but a quick death would be a sort of victory after Birkenau and Auschwitz. Besides, I don't think they want to kill us. They still have need of us. Otherwise, why keep taking us with them?'

'They didn't have much need of us in Hirschberg. We weren't exactly busy in there.'

'Perhaps not, but as far as I'm concerned I'm still here and I intend to keep going.'

'Miklós, I want you to do something for me. You know where I live in Budapest. Please, when the war is over, go and see my family and tell them you saw me here. I'm certain *you* will survive.'

'Ah, you will be in Budapest yet. The German defeat is not far off.'

The pace gradually slackened as they continued on and upwards towards the mountains. The temperature dropped and light snow began to brush their faces. Miklós recognized some of the place names – Teplice, Chemnitz – from his school geography lessons. They were moving along the border with Czechoslovakia.

One or two prisoners, too weak to manage the ascent, were shot, but generally the conditions were better than on the march from Auschwitz. If anybody wanted to relieve himself the SS allowed him to stand aside from the column for a minute or so.

Miklós benefited from a pair of sturdy shoes he'd organized from the *Unterkunft* and, underneath his uniform, a sweater from the same source. But he still felt the sharpness of the wind, burning his ears and nagging at his ribs.

It was almost the end of February 1945. The snow and wind contested for supremacy for the three days and nights of their march, broken by occasional stops at farms for rest and bread.

From one farm they took away a cart, loaded with horsemeat. Volunteers pushed it along in shifts. Miklós and Löwy were among the first to volunteer and secretly tore off pieces of the raw flesh to stuff into their mouths.

On the morning of the fourth day they arrived at a railway goods siding. They were allowed to rest in the cobblestoned courtyard. Some men, including Löwy, had brought blankets with them, in which they wrapped themselves to try to keep warm and sleep. Löwy spread his on the ground and let Miklós share it.

They were kept there for most of the day, without food or water, until, around nightfall, a goods train pulled in. This consisted of a long line of open trucks that had once contained coal. The men were ordered into the trucks, where those who had blankets used them to shelter from the snow. Once again Miklós shared Löwy's blanket. They remained there all night.

They awoke to a smooth coating of snow. The tracks were barely visible and the cobblestones in the yard not at all. The white deposit around the edges of the trucks and on the blankets and prisoners' heads made a striking contrast with the coal dust at the bottom of the wagons.

Shortly after dawn the train began to move. Löwy and Miklós massaged each other's feet to restore some feeling and warmth. Others around them did the same as the train continued at a slow, even pace through stations – Zittau, Bautzen – without stopping.

Many of them had carried utensils with them from Hirschberg; cups, pots and pans. They collected snow in these and ate it as slowly as they could. The train clattered along relentlessly. The afternoon passed, and the evening. By the time night fell, with their journey continuing, the snow had ceased. The wind tore at their bodies from the outside while hunger gnawed at them from within.

Some of the men urinated in the utensils. Others didn't bother and made watery channels in the coal dust. Excrement accumulated in corners. Miklós felt almost delirious with hunger. His eyes burned, his head reeled, and his intestines seemed to be on fire. An acute physical pain cut through him like a sword.

Still the train continued on its way. There was a stop in the night, presumably to refuel, but otherwise no let-up. By the time the second morning broke, several men had died. They were pushed aside like bundles, but this didn't prevent the lice migrating from the dead to the living.

Miklós and Löwy hadn't the strength to talk to each other. They sat against the side of the truck, the blanket wrapped around them, intermittently sleeping. The agony and chaos in front of him seemed to Miklós like an illusion. His mouth hung open as if he could release through it some of the fire from inside his body. He closed his eyes to try to blot out the pain but his consciousness held on. He opened his eyes again and two men were drinking urine from their cooking pots. The long day – and the journey – ground on.

One man near him was shivering and sweating with fever. Another was suffering from a racking cough. More died in the course of the morning. Eventually Miklós fell into a more prolonged sleep.

He was surprised by the silence when he awoke. The train was still rumbling its way along the track but the cold air was still, the sky heavy with impending snow, and nobody was talking.

He blinked, yawned and swallowed hard, trying to produce saliva to dampen his parched throat. Then he turned his head and saw, about five feet to his right, a man bent over one of the corpses like a pathologist conducting an autopsy.

Miklós blinked again, fascinated by the man's strange movements and posture. He saw that Löwy was also staring at this strange sight. Then Löwy retched and turned his eyes away, clutching his stomach. Miklós turned back to the other man and saw he was holding a knife. His hand shook as he sliced small pieces of flesh from the dead man's buttocks. Old Rozenberg the butcher used to slice off meat for Miklós's mother in much the same way. A few drops of snow gently landed on the back of the man's head as he leaned over the body, oblivious of Miklós and Löwy watching him.

'Look what we have come to.' Löwy spoke for the first time in hours.

'One day we will talk about it,' Miklós whispered in reply.

On the morning of 5 March, the train pulled into Buchenwald.

'Thank God,' breathed Imre Löwy through dry, cracked lips.

About half the men in Miklós's wagon had survived the journey. Most of these shared Löwy's relief at arriving at this huge, well-established *Lager*. Buchenwald was well known since before the war as a concentration camp for political enemies of the Reich. The prospect of another fixed routine, as in Auschwitz, cheered them.

The survivors were peeled off the train and taken to be showered and de-loused. Their clothes, which were crawling, were destroyed. Even after the showers, the barbers brought along to shave off the prisoners' body hair approached them with cringing reluctance.

For days afterwards, Miklós would recount the experience of that first-day shower. 'This was an orgasm,' he said to Löwy. 'I became a new man when that hot water poured over me. I could have stayed and stayed and stayed. You know, Imre, the pleasure of crossing over from barbaric degeneracy into the basic human decencies is every bit as strong as that to be had from sex or from eating the most exquisite food.'

They occupied a dismal, wooden barrack with no windows. Such light as there was came from a couple of dim bulbs at either end of the hut. It was filled with prisoners of various nationalities, though most of those around Miklós were Hungarian. They slept two or three to a bunk in an arrangement of three-tiered bunks. Their new uniforms were similar to the old ones from Auschwitz, except there were no triangles or numbers sewn on to them. They were given half a loaf of bread each day, as well as one cup each of soup and coffee, and were warned not to drink the water.

Miklós and Löwy fell in with a serious-looking prisoner in his early forties. This was Josef Stern, a former headmaster of a Jewish high school in Volóc, near to where Miklós had been stationed with the *Arbeitsdienst*.

'You boys from Auschwitz?' Stern asked them on the first day.

Miklós nodded.

'Me too. I've been in this place a week. Where are you from originally?'

'Budapest.' Again Miklós was the one to answer, waving an open palm between himself and Löwy as he did so.

'My sister married a teacher at a school in Budapest,' said Stern, naming Miklós's old school. Miklós remembered well the teacher in question, a dour pedagogue who never smiled.

'Ah, that was just his professional face,' said Josef Stern. 'He really does have a wicked sense of humour. He used to do a brilliant impersonation of the headmaster.'

They spoke a great deal about the city of Budapest, its streets, its shops and its people, about school life and about the abiding fantasy of the *Lager* – food. They endlessly conjured up dishes in their minds, meticulously weighing measures of salt, pepper, paprika and onions. Sometimes it helped them almost to relish the insipid, watery abstraction served to them in the middle of each day.

On the second or third arrival of the soup, Miklós stared with shocked recognition at the *Häftling* distributing it. Dr Frigyes! The Hammers' family physician; the man who with great kindness and patience had attended Rosa during long bouts of illness, always with a smiling word for her young son.

Miklós bounded up to him. 'Dr Frigyes, it's me – Miki Hammer.'

Frigyes responded with a stony, indifferent expression.

'Rabbi and Rosa Hammer's son. From the flat on Murányi Street. Don't you remember?'

'If you want soup,' said Frigyes curtly, 'join the queue.'

'Dr Frigyes! For God's sake. You treated my mother a hundred times. Miki Hammer!'

Frigyes turned his head away and spat.

At the back of the queue, Miklós met up with Löwy and Josef Stern. The latter addressed him anxiously. 'Hammer, you should beware of that man. He is a monster.'

'But he was my family doctor. He has visited our home, drunk tea with us, more times than I can count.'

'That may be, but in here he is a monster.'

'He took care of my mother. He was always so considerate. I can't believe it. I've known him for something like fifteen years.'

'Let me repeat' – Stern dropped his voice as they neared the head of the queue – 'Frigyes is a monster. A complete brute.'

Miklós attempted to look into Frigyes's face as he received his soup but could elicit no glimmer of recognition. In Buchenwald there was no place for the niceties of professional life or the manners of social tea-drinking. Frigyes was now simply a cold, calculating human being. Part of a small gang of functionaries who cruelly exploited their miserable advantage over the mass of prisoners.

Here, the erstwhile caring medical man was a singularly uncaring individual. He would, for his own ends, contrive punishments for others by falsely informing on them to a *Blockältester* or *Kapo* for some trivial offence or other. These, in the Buchenwald system, merited 'exercises' – the lugging of heavy stones back and forth across a yard – and the surrender of food rations to Frigyes or one of his friends.

As time passed, more and more prisoners were admitted to the camp. Food rations became irregular and hunger a constant companion. Miklós steeled himself as best he could against the pain and tried to take comfort from the Nazis' withdrawal into Germany and, more immediately, from the agreeable presence of Josef Stern and Imre Löwy. Imre Friedman was in a separate hut, but Miklós saw him quite often too.

The SS were hardly seen. The organization of the prisoners was left to the hierarchy of *Häftlings*. Much of this was conducted with the utmost cruelty. There were no work *Kommandos* for the growing number of new inmates; they were simply ordered about in a random way, often as a form of sport for Frigyes and his colleagues.

Severe beatings were commonplace. Skulls, necks and limbs were broken, to the mild satisfaction of the authorities, ever happy to delegate the task of elimination.

After a day or two, the men of Miklós's intake were allowed to walk outside the hut. He and Löwy explored as much of the *Lager*'s vast area as they could. They discovered several blocks which housed single nationalities. There was one barrack exclusively of Russians, another of Italians, a French block, a Belgian.

There were many non-Jewish prisoners as well as Jews, most of them staggering rather than walking, ribs and joints visible through anaemic skin, eyes hauntingly large in hollowed sockets. On the other hand, some of the longer-serving prisoners, notably those employed on work *Kommandos* around the camp perimeter, appeared more robust.

Miklós mingled freely among many different groups of *Häftlings*. He spoke to chief rabbis and labourers; bankers, butchers and craftsmen. The main topic of conversation for all of them was the possibility of liberation by the Americans, awaited here as fervently as the Russians had been in Auschwitz.

'*Wann werden die Amerikaner ankommen?*' – 'When will the Americans come?' – became the heartfelt cry of the Hungarians, Czechs, Russians, Poles, Yugoslavs, Norwegians, Italians and others, united by the Germans in bondage and language.

During Miklós's second week in Buchenwald, an outbreak of diarrhoea occurred, killing most of the sufferers. Miklós and the others in his and the surrounding bunks managed to avoid the illness until, on the fifth or sixth day of the epidemic, Stern went down with it.

Miklós was deeply distressed when he heard of this. 'We must help him,' he urged Löwy.

'Of course, but how?'

'I remember from my days as a medical student that carbon is effective against diarrhoea. If we can slice up his bread and toast the pieces at the stove it might help.'

Miklós borrowed a knife from a Hungarian student whom he had known in Hirschberg and each day painstakingly cut and toasted Stern's bread.

At first, Stern protested. 'Please, don't do this. I don't want it. Please, I can't eat. I'm too weak.'

'That is exactly why you must eat,' Miklós would reply insistently, patiently waiting to put the charred pieces into Josef's mouth. Eventually the older man relented and slowly chewed the rough-edged bread held before him.

Except when Frigyes was handing out the provisions, the 'healthy' *Häftlings* were allowed to collect the ration for those too weak to move. Unlike in Auschwitz, such people were ignored while they remained alive. The authorities simply removed their bodies when they died.

After two weeks of Miklós's treatment, with assistance from Löwy, Josef Stern took up his spectacles, which he'd laid aside at the onset of his illness, and began to hold the toasted bread in his own hands. Over the next few days he became more animated and was able to count himself among the few survivors of the diarrhoea epidemic.

Time passed slowly. Only once was there any real sign that the agony might soon be over. This was towards the end of March with the cancellation of a *Kommando* that had been travelling to a workplace some ten miles outside the *Lager*. The enemy was too close for this to continue. The *Amerikaner* were coming at last.

Miklós spent his days exploring the camp. Walking tired him out very quickly and he needed to rest frequently, but he persisted, talking to as many people as he could.

He met an old schoolfriend, Lajos Grünfeld; heard that a cousin, Berti Teitelbaum, had died in Buchenwald a week or so before his arrival. He had long conversations with several Gentile prisoners. They asked about Auschwitz. What was the extent there of human depravity?

'I have seen the lowest depths,' said Miklós, 'beneath which it is impossible for man to sink.'

'But when you were in Auschwitz,' pressed his interlocutor, 'did the commandant's wife have lampshades in her home made out of human skin? That's what happens here.'

'What do you mean?' asked Miklós.

'In the workshop the skin of prisoners is turned into lampshades to decorate the fine home of our commandant's good lady.'

'But Buchenwald is a detention camp,' protested Miklós, 'not a *Vernichtungslager*.'

'Ah, but people die all the same. And this lady is quite persuasive when it comes to having the odd *Häftling* eliminated. Particularly if he has an ornate tattoo on his body. It's a kind of memorial, the light shining after you through your skin.'

One morning, a group of former Auschwitz inmates arrived. Among them was the notorious Schultz, the footballer from the tailors' *Kommando*. He was barely recognizable, his muscles having wasted away and the flesh having dropped from his face.

These new arrivals were placed in Miklós's block. As soon as it became known that Schultz was there, he was cornered in the yard by a young Polish Jew and a couple of friends.

The Pole, a squat youth of eighteen or nineteen with a large brow and closely set eyes, began to taunt Schultz. 'In here you are not a *Kapo*. Here, Schultz, you are rubbish!'

At that, he grabbed the one-time full-back by his collar and forced him against the wall of the hut. The Polish boy was thin but wiry and in much better physical condition than the broken-down Schultz, who was unable to offer any resistance.

This happened within a few feet of where Miklós was standing. There was a sprinkling of other *Häftlings* around but nobody seemed to be taking any notice.

The Polish youth then bodily tipped Schultz into a rainwater barrel that stood outside the entrance to the block. Miklós watched spellbound and powerless in the face of this cruelty. The Pole forced Schultz's head under the water and held it there. Just before he did so, Schultz's eyes met Miklós's in an imploring gaze.

But in a moment it was over. 'The bastard is dead,' proclaimed one of the young Pole's friends and the three of them walked away, leaving Schultz's body in the barrel.

Miklós was interrupted by Stern as he wandered aimlessly about the *Lager*.

'Hammer! Miklós, are you all right?'

'I have just witnessed a murder. Schultz, the terrible *Unterkapo* from Auschwitz. I will always remember the last look in his eyes. I did nothing. If I had tried to intervene I would probably have been the next victim. I asked no questions. I know Schultz was a swine, but he was a *Häftling* like the rest of us.

'This is not the first time I've seen this happen,' Miklós continued. 'There was a similar killing in the showers at Hirschberg. Someone I'd never seen before. An act of revenge. What have we come to, Josef? They just walked away. One of them said, "The bastard is dead." What have we come to?'

15

In the days that followed, as more people died from hunger, some of the prisoners tried to stave off death by eating a powdered-down form of leaf. This was traded throughout the *Lager*. It had a strong chlorophyll taste but seemed to afford some nourishment. One small pack of it was rated at the value of a quarter of a loaf.

The weather was beginning to improve and the *Häftlings* spent more time in the open air. One afternoon, a couple of the veteran prisoners from the central blocks noticed Miklós on one of his exploratory walks and invited him into their compound for a couple of hours, until one of the men advised him to leave before he was caught in there.

Rumours spread of a special section for important political prisoners. It was said that Admiral Horthy, the former Hungarian head of state, was being held in Buchenwald, along with the former Austrian chancellor, Schuschnigg. Among other illustrious names mentioned were Léon Blum, the former prime minister of France; Telemann, the leader of the German Communist party; and various members of the Italian royal family.

On 1 or 2 April, the camp siren sounded. A round-up was taking place. SS guards in unprecedented numbers surrounded Miklós's barracks and others nearby. A cry went up of '*Juden antreten!*' Jews were being summoned.

Miklós felt a chill of apprehension pass through him. His was an entirely Jewish block. Some of the occupants, including both Stern and Löwy, were at that moment in another part of the *Lager* and since the barrack was so overcrowded and disorganized their absence would probably not be noticed. But none of those present would be able to slip through the net.

It took little more than a few minutes to gather together the Jewish prisoners and assemble them in the yard. They were marched off under guard for some considerable distance until they found themselves approaching a kind of annexe to the main camp. Here, behind a tattered barrier of barbed wire, was a huge, run-down warehouse and a number of workshops and other buildings.

The prisoners filed into the clearing, where they were joined by hundreds more Jewish *Häftlings* from other parts of the *Lager*. There were about 2,000 in all and the SS were having difficulty in sorting them into orderly ranks. There was a great deal of noise and the scene bordered on chaos.

Various individuals were running up to SS officers and protesting that they weren't Jewish, there'd been a mistake, they'd somehow got caught up. The officers rejected all such entreaties and manhandled the protestors back into the throng.

It was about ten o'clock in the morning when they arrived at the clearing, and well into the afternoon by the time the columns started shifting forward towards the main warehouse. In the intervening time, Miklós threaded his way backwards and forwards through the crowd, trying to assess the situation. He teamed up with two other Hungarian Jews. Between them they had two packs of leaf powder to eat.

As the first prisoners began to enter the warehouse, Miklós noticed the building had a cellar. 'I'm going to investigate,' he told the others. 'Nobody will notice me in this pandemonium.'

He stealthily made his way round the side of the building and went through the cellar entrance. Despite the bright daylight outside, the cellar was dark. He could faintly make out a number of barrels, shovels and various items of working gear which had been dumped there.

He returned to his two associates, both of whom shared his unease about the *Häftlings'* intended fate. 'It seems to be about five yards by four,' he told them. 'I think we could hide there until the round-up is completed.'

It was now about four o'clock. An SS guard was patrolling that side of the building. The three men waited for him to pass and then ran towards the cellar. Once inside, each man found himself a barrel and climbed into it.

The darkness was penetrated by a shaft of light coming through the doorway. Every so often the patrolling guard's shadow fell across this, so they could estimate his pace and position.

They were able to whisper to each other as they waited for the *Häftlings* upstairs to depart. They intended to stay there until the operation was concluded and then make their way back to the main *Lager*.

'They're all going to be killed, you know,' said one of the Hungarians. 'We did the right thing, running away.'

'I just wish they would go,' said the other.

'Yes,' thought Miklós to himself. 'Hundreds of men going to their deaths and all we can do is urge them to get on with it. What a world we are living in.'

It grew darker and the sounds above them showed no sign of abating. They could hear a constant rhythm of footsteps, voices, comings and goings. After a while there was a general shuffling and scraping.

'I think they're settling in for the night,' said Miklós excitedly.

'My God, I can't stand it in here all night,' said one of the others.

'At least those poor bastards might have some bread and water up there,' said his companion. 'I know they are probably going to die but if we are caught here we will definitely be shot. No bread, no ceremony. Just a bullet in the head.'

'The longer we stay here, the more danger we are in,' said the first man. 'Let's pray they move off at daybreak at least.'

'But it would be easier to escape at night,' said the other.

'Not while the guards are outside,' Miklós reminded him, before taking his first nibble that day of his portion of leaf powder.

All became silent upstairs. The prisoners were sleeping. Miklós and his fellow truants passed an uncomfortable night.

He awoke to the sound of movement above his head.

'They are going,' hissed one of his two companions.

'Thank God!' exclaimed the other.

But no. The sounds intensified – scraping, stamping and murmuring.

'What is going on?' The younger of the two Hungarians was becoming distraught.

'There is certainly some activity,' said Miklós. 'But it doesn't sound like a mass evacuation. Perhaps some more prisoners are being brought in, or possibly they are taking away just a few. Perhaps they are evacuating in stages.'

'My God, why don't they go?' The young Hungarian was almost hysterical. 'There's no way out now. It's either them or the three of us. Very soon someone's going to be killed. Oh God, let it be them. Soon.'

Hours dragged by. Light streamed into the cellar and gradually diminished into the same narrow shaft of the day before. And still the muffled hubbub went on over their heads.

As the afternoon wore on, Miklós's younger companion announced that he was going to make a break for it. 'Tonight, I'm going. I'm running back to the *Lager* come what may.'

'Are you crazy?' said Miklós. 'The guard is outside.'

'I don't care. I can't take it any longer. I'm going. I'll wait until dark and then I'll make a dash for it whether or not those bastards upstairs have gone.'

'He's right, you know,' said the other man. 'Without food or water, we shall die anyway if we stay here much longer.'

'They'll be on the move soon,' said Miklós. 'They must be.'

At about eight or nine that evening, it began to rain. Within minutes it had become torrential. The young Hungarian reacted to this as if it was a signal. 'I'm going,' he cried, and scrambled out of his barrel and away through the doorway.

Miklós and the other man held their breath. A minute passed, five, ten, nothing. About twenty minutes after the youngster's departure they heard heavy, military boot steps at the entrance. Miklós crouched down in his barrel, sweating and praying. The footsteps slowed down. He could hear a man breathing.

'*Jemand da?*' The guard's voice shattered the tense silence. 'Is anybody there?' Miklós held himself rigid, not daring to breathe. He could hear the guard moving slowly round the cellar, kicking aside the odd box, pulling planks away from walls against which they were leaning and then letting them go with a smack that raised little puffs of dust.

The man's boots scraped the ground a foot or two from Miklós's barrel, grew fainter and then were gone.

Miklós was shaking. The blood in his head and chest was pounding so loudly it seemed to drown out the footsteps above him, which had suddenly resumed in earnest.

'That's it,' whispered the voice from the other barrel. 'I've had it. I can't spend another night like this. I'm leaving.'

'You mustn't,' pleaded Miklós. 'Listen. There's movement upstairs. They'll be away soon.'

'I've had enough. I've been here a night and a day already,' said his companion, and he was gone.

Miklós waited for what seemed hours. The rain came down unremittingly and the cellar began to feel damp. He ached in every part of his body. The top of his head felt as though it was on fire.

When he heard bedding-down sounds above him, similar to those of the previous night, his heart sank. He sat in the barrel wondering what to do; wondering if his two colleagues had got away.

At about midnight, he pulled himself out of his barrel. He listened intently for any noises, but all he could hear was the pounding in his head, echoing the rain outside. He stuck his head out of the doorway. The rain seemed to invigorate him and he ran as straight and as fast as he could towards the *Lager*.

A voice burst through the rain behind him. '*Halt!*' He kept running, somehow finding the strength to increase his pace.

Again the order, '*Halt!*' Then a gunshot, which pinged past his head, stinging the outer skin of his right ear.

He ran towards the darkness, conscious of leaving the lights of the compound behind him. He found the barbed wire and scrambled through it. Back inside the main *Lager* he stopped for a few seconds to regain his breath. He felt sick and dizzy but he picked himself up and kept running until he felt safely out of range of the guard at the warehouse.

The loneliness of his predicament overwhelmed him. He became engulfed by a wave of nausea. Not knowing what to do, he walked in the direction of the central blocks. He made for one of the bigger ones and entered it.

His way was barred by an unusually sturdy looking *Häftling*. Miklós explained in German that he had just run away from the transport of prisoners rounded up two days beforehand. '*Da*,' said the *Häftling* and nodded. He was in a Russian block.

The *Häftling* led Miklós to an occupied bunk and indicated that he should hide underneath it. He gratefully obeyed and a few seconds later the Russian returned with a piece of bread. Miklós bit into it but fell asleep before he'd finished eating.

Some time later, the Russian came back to wake him. 'You must leave before roll-call,' he told him. Miklós roused himself and made his way to the next hut as the damp air began to clear.

This was a French block. Miklós made his explanations to the *Stubenältester*, a kind-faced man who told him to wait at the door. He returned a few minutes later, having discussed the matter with his colleagues.

'You can come here,' he said. And again – 'But not when it is roll-call.'

'Thank you. Please, do you have any food? I am very hungry.'

'Here,' said the *Stubenältester*, bringing some bread. 'Now go. It is almost roll-call.'

As Miklós turned to go, the Frenchman called out to him. 'Don't worry,' he said. 'You'll be all right.'

He walked to another block, where he found some Hungarians. They had very little food but, they told him, there were empty bunks, any of which he could occupy for the purposes of roll-call.

'Why don't you stay here for roll-call,' suggested one of the inmates, 'and go back to the French block for your provisions?'

The SS man taking roll-call did so quickly and casually. Afterwards, Miklós duly returned to the French *Stubenältester* who welcomed him warmly. 'Stay here,' he said, patting the surface of a bunk near his own. 'Just don't go forward when the rations are issued, or you might be discovered.'

Half an hour later, coffee arrived. The *Stubenältester* brought some over to Miklós in a small tin can. It was gravelly and its dirty brown colouring was compounded by rust from the tin. It tasted like nectar.

The Frenchman smiled and put a hand on Miklós's shoulder. 'Listen, young man,' he said. 'If you can keep going for a few more days you will be all right. We will all be free.'

All at once Miklós felt the emotional strain of the past couple of days surge inside him. He closed his eyes and sighed deeply.

'Don't worry,' said the Frenchman. 'We can hear the artillery. The Americans are very near now.'

'What if someone asks me which block I belong to?' asked Miklós.

'Say nothing. Ignore them and they will ignore you.'

Nevertheless, when Miklós went back to the Hungarians he persuaded them to absorb him into their block as if he'd been there all along. He had his own bunk and before long was lining up with the others for bread, soup and coffee.

After roll-call on the morning of 6 April, the *Lager* alarm sounded. Once again, the SS were preparing for a mass evacuation. All the members of Miklós's adopted block were marched out. This time, however, he didn't have the same feeling of danger. His comrades were a mixture of Jews and Gentiles.

They were issued with half a loaf each and lined up in ranks of five. 'Am I never to be liberated? Is that my fate?' Miklós thought to himself as they trudged towards the main gate. There was none of the sense of triumph he had experienced on leaving Auschwitz. And the Russians hadn't seemed so close then as the Americans did now.

The massed columns filed out of the *Lager* accompanied by armed guards stationed at fifty-pace intervals. Although this evacuation wasn't as big as the 18 January exodus from Auschwitz, the roads were still lined with thousands of prisoners.

This was a much more disciplined march. There was no question of breaking rank. The weather was cool and fair and it was far easier to march than it had been in January. They covered ground more quickly, too, and German ground at that, not Polish.

By about three o'clock in the afternoon, they came to a sign telling them they were approaching Weimar. 'My God!' Miklós cried out to his neighbour, 'we are marching into the town of Goethe.' In spite of the circumstances, in spite of himself, he felt awed.

They were skirting the centre but there were still plenty of local inhabitants in evidence. They gazed at the prisoners in horror. Women at windows half hid behind curtains as they looked out in mingled terror and fascination.

Miklós turned again to his neighbour. 'What feelings these people must be having at this moment,' he said to him. 'They must know the Americans are on their way and now they know about us, too. Look, some of them can't believe it and others are pretending not to notice. Well, they'll have to take notice now. And the fact that we are being led away through their town will make them realize their army is retreating; that the *Amerikaner* are almost here.'

The columns were halted a short distance beyond Weimar. Then they began edging forward slowly. Their destination was yet another railway siding. Along the track stood a seemingly endless line of covered, wooden cattle wagons.

The *Häftlings* were counted into the trucks roughly in groups of 100. An armed SS man was stationed inside each one. In Miklós's truck the guard was a man in his late fifties. He had a stool while the *Häftlings* squeezed against each other across the floor. As soon as the truck was full the guard stood up and passed round a bucket of water for each man to take a drink.

When it became dark, the doors of the trucks were closed. At this point the guard rose from his stool and spoke. 'From time to time on this journey,' he announced in high-pitched, nasal tones, 'we will be stopping for water and for the purpose of relieving ourselves. If anyone here tries to escape, the whole truck will be eliminated.'

Miklós found himself sitting quite close to this guard. There was just one man between him and the stool. The guard looked miserable and uncomfortable in his heavy clothing. He stared into space, occasionally stifling a yawn. Throughout the night there were discussions, squabbles and mutterings in several languages. The guard ignored it all. Neither did he react in any way when some of the *Häftlings* on the far side from him hoisted each other up to look through the iron-barred windows.

Miklós sat reflecting upon his previous transports, to Birkenau and Buchenwald. Hideous images clung to his mind until he finally fell asleep.

When he awoke, he noticed for the first time that his wagon contained a group of about thirty or forty Ukrainians, collected together at the end opposite where he sat. They spoke loudly and their dialect was the dominant one amid the early morning Babel.

In mid-afternoon the train came to a halt in the middle of a bleak stretch of land. At once there were SS guards outside, flinging open the doors and ordering groups of prisoners off the train with the repeated cry, '*Raus, raus!*'

As they climbed down, the *Häftlings* were given water to drink and then were allowed to relieve themselves at the side of the track.

When they went back to their places inside the wagon, the

guard opened his rucksack and produced a piece of bread and some dried vegetables, which he stuffed hungrily into his mouth. The attention of the entire truck was focused upon him as he ate. He simply stared ahead of him as usual, though he did appear a little flushed in the face.

As the journey progressed, the *Häftlings* at the window described what they could see to the others. They were travelling eastwards at about twenty-five miles per hour, past the edges of many small towns, extensive areas of which had been devastated by bombing.

The man situated between Miklós and the SS guard was a bitter individual called István Weisz. He had been in Auschwitz despite having been brought up as a Christian. His father was a Catholic but his mother had the misfortune to have been born Jewish. He held a deep grudge against Jews, which he made no secret of when Miklós introduced himself.

'You think the Jews are responsible for all this?' Miklós asked him.

'You call attention to yourselves. Always pushing yourselves forward. Running the show. The *chosen people!*'

This last phrase was spoken with ill-disguised contempt.

'It seems,' Miklós replied, 'that you are one of the chosen, my friend. And you certainly did not push yourself forward. And, let me assure you, neither did I. This horror is not the result of any "pushing forward". The quietest, most obscure of Jews have been rooted out by the Nazi machine. Old women, young girls and boys, babes in arms – none of these pushed themselves into the gas chambers.'

This attack made Weisz open up a little. He responded with a scathing denunciation of religious doctrine, and Jewish religious doctrine in particular. Miklós agreed that religious teaching had shown itself to be bankrupt in the face of unprecedented evil, but argued that it could hardly be blamed for the emergence of that evil.

On Miklós's other side was a man of an altogether different character from István Weisz. Imre Bárber was an old-fashioned gentleman. A Jew from northern Hungary, about six or seven years older than Miklós, he was round-faced and wore spectacles. He had light-coloured hair and a reddish moustache.

Bárber tried to remain polite in his dealings with those around him. Every so often, however, his eyes would mist over and he would sigh, 'I can't stand this hunger.'

Similar cries became commonplace as time went on. Though they were provided with water at the various stopping places, they were given no food. As they went into their second day, two men in the truck died. Several others were delirious. Miklós again experienced the inner scorching sensation he'd felt on the Buchenwald transport.

Although everyone was growing weaker, the Ukrainian group remained boisterous. They would elbow their way to the front at each watering stop. Their language was close enough to Polish for others in the truck to recognize the phrase 'bloody Jews' in the consequent jostling.

On one occasion the guard intervened to prevent a fight as the bodies crammed together at the door, struggling to get to the water. Still the Ukrainian prisoners railed at the 'bloody Jews', even though half of those they were threatening were Gentiles.

While István Weisz kept to himself at the stopping places, Miklós would walk the few permitted paces with Imre Bárber and one or two of the others who joined in their conversations aboard the truck.

In the face of the stark extremes of hunger, food was again an inevitable topic. Miklós and Imre talked about the fanciest and most exotic of dishes. They dwelt upon the delicate qualities of pastries and cakes, sauces and succulent meats.

Literature gave them another means of escape. Imre and Miklós spent hours reciting to each other, most often from *Tragedy of Man*, the great Hungarian epic by Imre Madách:

> *No do not ask*
> *To burrow deeper into the great secret*

The hand of God, for the very best of motives,
Has hidden from your hungry eyes.

The third night was punctuated by screams, moans and frenzied disputes. The SS guard awoke a couple of times and called for silence but he, too, was near exhaustion. The noises continued throughout subsequent nights and the guard ceased to care.

Some men were too weak to get out at the stopping points. Others lost control of their bowels and their bladders. Death claimed more and more, the bodies being removed while the survivors were drinking water. In between stops, the stench of decay became overpowering. A week passed, during which a dozen men died in Miklós's truck.

Despite the physical effort involved, those *Häftlings* who were able to continued to haul each other up to the window. They lost all sense of direction. The train appeared to be taking a circular route. Miklós climbed up to the window as they were navigating the perimeter of Dresden. The sight was shocking. Grey and desolate, with large tracts of destruction, the whole area was a waste land of impersonal walls and empty doorways.

As the journey entered its second week, István Weisz fell into a coma. The guard ordered Miklós to push Weisz aside and take his place. Miklós himself could barely stand by now and it took considerable effort to move Weisz's body. Having done so, he sank to the floor alongside the guard's seat. To his astonishment, the guard began to speak to him, asking him his name, age and where he was from.

It was about one o'clock in the morning. The darkness reinforced the unreality of the conversation, which culminated in the guard's words, 'Here you are,' as he threw down some potato peelings.

Miklós was speechless. As men around him screamed in the last agonies of starvation, he stuffed the sweet, moist peelings into his mouth and felt the unutterable pleasure of the chewed, pulpy skin sliding down his throat into his stomach.

The guard was having to survive now on a fairly primitive

diet of bread and raw potatoes. Each night, he exchanged a few words with Miklós and tossed the peelings to him as if to a pet dog. And, like a dog, Miklós — pausing only to whisper an urgent 'Thank you' — greedily swallowed these scraps before anyone could interfere.

The *Häftlings* now tried to sleep during the daytime to ward off hunger pains. Imre Bárber was deteriorating rapidly. At the watering stops, he and a number of others took to eating grass. He dismissed Miklós's entreaties not to, and his — accurate — predictions of dysentery and a slow death. By the end of the second week, both Imre Bárber and István Weisz were dead.

They passed through Leipzig, and more acres of destruction. Inside the wagon, men were dying amid pools of their own waste matter, unable to move. Everybody, including the guard, was riddled with lice.

Nobody had a trace of fat on his body. There was no more fighting to rush out when they stopped. It was as much as any of them could do to climb down and remain standing while they drank or urinated.

Miklós felt constant burning pains and nausea. He was burning in his head, his bowels and behind his eyes. He kept going purely because of his regular supply of potato peelings from the guard.

The train slowed down, making its way along the Czech–German border. They passed through the stations of Eger and Karlsbad. At Eger the train stopped for a while and the guard slid open the door to let in some fresh air and stark, spring sunshine.

On the track next to them, facing the opposite direction, was another train of cattle trucks. They were packed with young soldiers in SS uniform. The *Häftlings* in Miklós's truck were amazed to hear these soldiers speaking in Hungarian. They called out to them: 'Are you Hungarian?'

'Yes,' came the reply.

'Where from?'

'Budapest. Where are you going? Who are you?'

'We are prisoners.'

'Ach! You stinking Jews. What are you doing still alive?'

The guard closed the door upon a crescendo of abuse and the train slowly pulled away. An hour later it stopped again, this time for water.

When the men climbed down from Miklós's truck, and their guard went to collect his rations, another SS man came over to them and signalled for Miklós and some others to follow him. He collected more *Häftlings* from other trucks until he had a gang of twenty or thirty men.

The thought flashed through Miklós's mind, as the officer led them towards the end of the train, that this was a selection for execution. Logically, however, he knew this was unlikely. The SS man had carefully picked out men still able to walk.

They arrived at the last wagon. The SS officer stepped forward and pulled back the door. The inside of the truck was packed to the roof with dead bodies. Maggots burrowed and crawled all over them. Flies hovered in the air. Most of the faces were puffed up and distorted. Mouths and noses were sticky with congealed blood.

The train had stopped in flat, deserted land between large, sparsely sown fields. The air was sharp and clear. A light breeze puckered flaps of clothing and wisps of hair that hung down from the mass of bodies.

The SS officer issued each man with a shovel and divided them up into teams. They dug a square in an adjoining field, just deep enough for the bodies to be covered when laid down next to each other, end to end.

As the work progressed – dragging the bodies off the wagon, carrying them into the field and laying them in the ditch they had dug – Miklós felt himself becoming like an automaton. At first, the physical effort of lifting the bodies drained him, and their smell and gruesome appearance was sickening. Gradually, however, he slotted in with the other members of his team, moving in a very slow but co-ordinated rhythm and handling the corpses like so many planks of wood.

It took several hours to complete the task. Every so often they'd be urged on by one or other of the SS officers. At the end, they were ordered not to tell anyone about what they had just seen and done.

When Miklós resumed his place in the truck he collapsed gratefully into sleep. It was dark when he awoke, and the guard was throwing him his peel. It had a small piece of potato in it.

The next day a man crawled across the truck into the space next to Miklós vacated by Weisz and Bárber. He was of medium height, with light brown hair and still-alert, intelligent eyes. He greeted Miklós in German, and smiled.

'Hello,' Miklós nodded. 'Miklós Hammer. And your name?'

'My real name?'

'Well, yes,' said Miklós, puzzled by this reaction.

'It's Peter Howard.'

'You are English?'

'Yes.'

'And Jewish?'

'No.'

'Then how do you come to be here?'

Peter Howard shook his head. 'It's a long story,' he said.

They sat in silence for a while until first Peter, and then Miklós, fell asleep.

In his sleep, Miklós could see the face of the man with the knife on the Buchenwald transport, slicing off pieces of flesh. He awoke with a start, his head running with sweat, lice tearing into his scalp and his back.

Peter was still asleep. Miklós lay down on his stomach and thought about the burial he'd taken part in the previous day. As dusk began to claim the light inside the truck, he felt his natural determination ebbing away. 'Why me?' he said to himself as his eyes smarted. 'God, why me?' Perhaps it would have been better to have died at the beginning of it all, in the *Arbeitsdienst* or Nagyvárad, or even on the transport to Birkenau.

He closed his eyes and clenched his fists. He felt a hand patting his arm and looked up. It was Peter Howard: 'Miklós, do you speak English?'

'Yes.'

'Good, then we can talk without anybody understanding us. And it's a relief to me to be able to speak English again. Please, tell me about yourself.'

Miklós heaved himself up into a sitting position. 'Well, I was a medical student in Budapest. Then in the forced labour battalion, ghetto, Birkenau, Auschwitz, Buchenwald – the usual story,' he said, encompassing the rest of the passengers with a sweep of his hand.

'Ha, I was a medical student, too. In London,' said Peter. 'And I've also been in various camps, ending up in Buchenwald.'

'But what did they want with you? How did they get you?'

'As I said, it's a long story. Perhaps I'll tell you in the course of time. I was picked up in France in '42.' He looked away from Miklós at the floor of the truck, plainly reluctant to go into details.

'Do you have family?' Miklós shifted the topic.

'My parents live in Chelsea.'

'Chelsea? Where the football team comes from? Is that in London?'

Peter smiled. 'Yes, that's right. In the south-west part of London. My folks have got a place in Flood Street.'

'*Flood?*' asked Miklós, disbelievingly.

'That's right. It isn't far from the river, as a matter of fact.'

In between sleeping, Miklós and Peter spent several hours in conversation. Miklós avoided referring to the circumstances of Peter's arrest and they talked about their families and home life. Peter spoke with great affection about his mother. His father, he said, was a civil servant. He had a married sister, and a girlfriend to whom he'd become engaged shortly before departing for France.

Miklós found himself speaking quite dispassionately about his own parents and his sisters. He'd long ago acknowledged to himself that he would never see them again.

The guard always waited until Peter Howard was asleep

before he spoke to Miklós. He gave away nothing about himself but asked Miklós about Budapest and how things had been in Auschwitz. He didn't appear to know where the train was heading.

One morning they stopped just beyond a station. They could see the sign – Passau. 'Look, Peter,' said Miklós. 'We are on the Austrian border.'

By now, nobody but the guard was strong enough to step down and walk from the train. Even some of the robust Ukrainians had died, and those surviving were weak and subdued.

Miklós and Peter sat by the side of the track after they had dragged themselves to the water. Miklós picked up a piece of old newspaper that was lying on the embankment. It was part of the front page of a German daily, published a week or so earlier, on 13 April 1945.

Its main headline read, '*Roosevelt ist tot*' – 'Roosevelt is dead.' 'A boost for the Germans,' said Miklós.

'Many more will have died since,' said Peter, huskily.

Back in the truck, Miklós felt faint. The faces around him were blurred and seemed to sway with the movement of the train. Day and night merged. He was aware occasionally of the voice of the guard, and the taste of the potato peel, but of little else.

The train stopped. It was morning and there was an unusual amount of noise outside. Miklós opened his eyes and noticed that Peter Howard was no longer there. About two dozen of the original 100 men remained in the truck.

The door opened and the guard got to his feet. 'This is your destination,' he announced. 'Dachau.'

Uniformed *Häftlings*, in much better physical condition than those aboard the trucks, were running along the side of the train. They beckoned to the prisoners to get down. SS officers joined them, with strident cries of '*Raus, raus!*'

It was a much depleted body of men that made its way from the train to the *Lager* entrance. Nobody was able to walk.

Everyone was forced to crawl the hundred or so yards to the *Appellplatz*.

Miklós pulled his body along like a bag of sticks. His bones seemed about to poke through his skin. He could feel his pelvis; he had no buttocks, not an ounce of flesh anywhere that he could squeeze between thumb and forefinger. He noticed that he was covered in a rash of white spots. When he scratched himself he realized the 'spots' were lice.

A *Häftling* came over to him and, to his utter astonishment, thrust a tin of sardines into his hand. He hadn't seen such a thing since he'd left Budapest. He was just able to lift his head and whisper, '*Danke*.' The *Häftling* then realized that Miklós wouldn't have the strength to open the tin and so he took it back and opened it for him. Miklós slapped the open side of the tin over his mouth and allowed the oily contents to slide in.

He dropped the tin and continued crawling forward on his hands and knees, his head swimming. As the first of this Buchenwald intake reached the main gate, a *Schreiber* came forward with a pad of paper and yelled, '*Juden antreten!*'

'Not this time,' muttered Miklós to himself. 'Even if I had the strength.' Some, however, did obey the *Schreiber*'s call, pathetically crawling over to him.

Then another *Schreiber* appeared with a pad and began to ask people for their names. Not numbers, but names! Miklós shook his head and felt the taste of the sardines rising in his throat. The *Schreiber* stood over him, asking his name. Miklós looked up and answered in English, 'Peter Howard.'

Then he blacked out.

16

The whiteness was blinding. The touch of sheets a reminder of a remote past. The quiet drone of muffled conversation, the clinking of bottles and hiss of boiling water indicated a world so distant from recent reality as to be, perhaps, a miracle.

A dream? Faces flicked through Miklós's mind like pages in a family photograph album. Ede. Klein. Éva offering herself to him in the kitchen at Nagyvárad. Nagel the accountant. Révész. The man in the cattle wagon slicing like old Rozenberg the butcher through the flesh of a fallen comrade.

But these were images of darkness. Fragments of a nightmare that brought with them a sense of foul and choking suffocation. Here was light and air and space. A soft, whispered tone; a harmony.

Could it be the next world? Miklós looked along the bed at his hands: the fingers of a skeleton draped with skin. A rustle of linen and a face was staring into his. A woman's face. Soft and kind. Round, fleshy cheeks; eyes alight with concern.

'Are you feeling better, Mr Howard?' English, with a faint American accent. A starchy, white uniform. Miracle and mystery.

'Yes, thank you.' The answer was automatic, unconsidered, a token English phrase.

The woman was a mirage, and was gone. But no, here she was again, this time with a man who was also dressed in white. He was tall and dark and spoke with a drawl familiar from American movies. He peered into Miklós's face. 'I'm very pleased to see that you are better, young man.'

He took the woman aside and spoke to her privately. From

time to time as they spoke the tall man and the woman turned towards the bed. After a few minutes they both smiled at Miklós and walked away.

He lay on his back trying to collect his thoughts. Peter Howard. The Englishman on the transport! But why did she call *me* Mr Howard?

With some effort he turned his head to one side. A thin, bald man, his face and arms covered in dark brown spots, was in the next bed. 'Where are we?' Miklós asked him in German.

'We are in Dachau. In the hospital.'

'And you? Where are you from?'

'I come from Yugoslavia.'

'How long have I been here?'

'A week. It's strange to hear your voice, I can tell you. You've been lying there for dead.'

Miklós tried to pick his way back through his mind, like a man stumbling on a darkened staircase. A week! He turned again to his neighbour.

'Are the Germans still here?'

'No. The war is finished.'

'When?'

'About five or six days ago. I thought you were going to die. I never expected to be talking to you.'

'So who is in charge here?'

'The Americans.'

'Tell me, while I've been lying here, have I said anything?'

'No. Nothing at all. I told you. You looked as though you weren't going to pull through.'

The nurse returned, carrying a glass of milk, the first Miklós had seen since Hungary. 'Try this, Mr Howard, it'll do you good.'

As she carefully lifted his head to enable him to drink, Miklós smiled inwardly to recall how he'd never liked the taste of milk. And now it was exquisite. Its very whiteness seemed somehow part of the purity of his new surroundings. He felt himself in paradise. And of course! He *was* Peter Howard. He had given his name to the *Schreiber* at the gates of Dachau.

He fell asleep. An exhausted, satisfying feeling suddenly interrupted by a tug at his arm. He opened his eyes and saw an American uniform for the first time. A soldier was sitting by his bed with a plate of semolina and a spoon on a tray.

'Hi. My name's Al Simpson. I'm a sort of orderly around here. I brought you something to eat. You need feeding up.'

The soldier propped up Miklós's head and fed him, gently pushing spoonfuls of the sweet, milky mixture into his mouth as if he were a baby.

'That's it. You're gonna be all right, fellah.' The soldier's voice was soothing, his manner encouraging. Miklós barely had the strength to eat. His stomach quickly felt full.

'What have I had?' he asked the soldier between spoonfuls.

'Typhus. Typhus fever. You had an extremely high temperature. It'll come down now.'

'How high?'

'Well, it was up to a hundred and five. Later on you're gonna have to eat a lot. You are just over seventy pounds. That's about five stones English weight.'

Miklós shivered as he mentally calculated the metric equivalents of these figures before slipping back into a deep sleep.

When he awoke it was daylight, but he had no idea if it was still the same day. After a few minutes, Simpson the orderly walked past. He saw that Miklós was awake and asked him if he wanted something to read.

Miklós nodded and the serviceman brought him an American paper called *Stars and Stripes*. Still lying on his back, Miklós held it up and looked at the front page. He couldn't concentrate and found it difficult to read. All he took in was that there were several items about General Eisenhower. As he put his arms down he realized for the first time that he was wearing white cotton pyjamas.

'May I have some food?' he asked Simpson.

'Uh-uh.' The American shook his head. 'It can't be rushed. You've got to take it nice and steady.'

Miklós spent most of the next four days asleep, waking

briefly for each of his three daily bowls of semolina. On the fifth day, the nurse spoke to him.

'Mr Howard. Are you awake? It's Sister McCann. How are you today? What about trying to sit up? Well?' She turned back the bedcover and Miklós was shocked at the sight of his legs. Thin and immobile, like two broomsticks, they seemed not to belong to him.

The sister held his back and gently but firmly tried to steer him into an upright position sitting sideways on the bed. The slightest movement made his body shudder with pain and the effort quickly exhausted him.

'I can't,' he groaned.

Sister McCann let him down and tucked him into the bed once more. He asked her for a drink and she brought him a glass of milk.

'Here you are, Mr Howard. Drink this.'

'Thank you.' He was still adjusting to the new sensation of being in the care of humane people and having no need of fear. He found himself trembling.

The next day, the tall doctor came to see him. 'I'd like you to try to sit up,' he said. Sister McCann stood alongside the bed as Miklós strained to lever his head off the pillow. She tried to help him, placing her hand behind his head. He became breathless. Sweat dampened his armpits and his legs. His head pounded. Finally, he gave up. 'I can't manage it,' he said, the English words coming with difficulty.

The doctor examined him with a stethoscope and then said to the sister, 'We've got to get him on his feet.' And to Miklós: 'You'll be all right.'

When the doctor had gone, Sister McCann leaned over Miklós conspiratorially. 'Now, Mr Howard. You heard what the doctor said. Don't be a baby. See if you can get yourself up. I'll help you.'

For the next half-hour, she pushed and pulled against Miklós's weary resistance. His head seemed to weigh twice as much as the rest of his body. He could only lift it if she propped him up from behind with both her hands. The act of trying to draw up his knees brought sharp pains along his thigh bones. It was almost as if he was chained to the bed. Eventually the sister, too, tired of the effort.

At least she had succeeded in keeping him awake. Instead of simply dropping back into sleep he tried to read the *Stars and Stripes*. It was full of military argot he'd never seen or heard before. He persevered and began to piece together bits of information about the conclusion of the war. He read about the shortage of basic supplies in Europe. It was reported the Allies had taken a million prisoners on the Western Front that month. There was a paragraph about the liberation of Dachau concentration camp.

As he was reading, a couple of *Häftlings* came in to clean the ward. One of them came over to him and addressed him in German: '*Ich komm' dich waschen*' – 'I'm coming to wash you.' He filled a bowl with cold water and patiently bathed Miklós from head to foot. The gentle, wet pressure of the flannel seemed to give him strength. His mind cleared. He determined to sit up.

Within two or three more days, with Sister McCann's help, he learned to ease himself into a sitting position, his pillow propped behind him.

There was a window facing the end of his bed. Through it he could see constant activity. The noises of the crowd were sociable and full of purpose, unlike anything he had encountered at other *Lagers*.

Each day he made progress. Al Simpson kept him supplied with newspapers and magazines and fed him three times a day. The sister, and occasionally the doctor, urged him on.

At last he climbed down and walked around his bed, gripping it firmly all the way. His Yugoslav neighbour applauded.

The next evening, Al came to him and said, 'From tomorrow, you'll be eating in the canteen. I'll help you to start with, then you're on your own.'

The canteen was a hundred yards or so from the hospital block.

Miklós leaned heavily on Simpson as they shifted slowly along. He swallowed hard as they entered the building. The warmth and animated conversation enveloped him. The smell of cooked meat was almost intoxicating.

'God, the meat smells good,' he said.

'Whatever you do, don't eat it,' Al warned. 'Your bowels are paper thin. Meat'll kill you, for sure. Stick to the mashed potato and such like for now. Small portions. Take it easy, Pete. Slowly does it.'

Having selected some soft, cooked vegetables and a glass of milk, Miklós was helped to a table by the American, who left him on his own for the first time. He ate slowly, taking in his surroundings.

On the table was an old copy of *Stars and Stripes*, with the heading 'Berlin Fights Block by Block' over a five-column photograph of Red Army tanks ploughing their way through the rubble. He read every item, including a description of the preparations for a United Nations conference in San Francisco. 'The State Department,' it reported, 'arranging to show the delegates the factories, vineyards, shipyards and aircraft plants in California, asked the delegates what they would like to see most. The overwhelming vote was "Hollywood".'

When he'd finished, he asked a man at his table to help him back to the hospital.

For the next two weeks he followed the same procedure. Occasionally, Al would come and escort him back to the ward; at other times he'd wait until someone else could help. At the end of the fortnight he began to manage by himself. By this time he was eating three meals a day in the canteen.

A couple of the other patients – a Czech and a Pole – joined him for afternoon walks. One day he was out with the Czech when he heard someone calling to him, 'Hey, you, Hammer! Just a minute.'

He turned and saw a man waving. It was the pastrycook from Birkenau who had fought so bitterly with Klein and his rabbi friend.

'You made it, eh?' He clapped Miklós on the arm. 'What about those others? Klein? The rabbi?'

Miklós shook his head. The pastrycook nodded. 'We've all had a taste of hell,' he said.

'We heard about the forced march out of Auschwitz,' he continued. 'Were you on that?' This was no longer the head-strong young man who'd shown such a fiery temperament in Birkenau. He seemed mature, sympathetic.

Miklós spoke briefly about the march and they told each other about the transports they had been on. The pastrycook described the arrival of the Americans and the liberation of the camp.

'There was a group of Negro soldiers,' he said, 'who just shot the SS guards they captured. No questions or anything. They got one guard to carry away the dead bodies and a young boy prisoner came over and started hitting the guard with the man's own whip. The Negro soldiers stood and laughed and took photographs.

'Many of the SS just ran away when the Americans arrived on the twenty-ninth of April. Some threw away their uniforms and put on *Häftlings'* clothes, but their well-fed appearance gave them away. There were road blocks all around Dachau. I don't think too many of the bastards escaped. I cannot describe my feelings when I saw those Negroes shooting them. I cheered and I cried at the same time.'

Miklós's Czech companion had long since returned to the hospital ward. As Miklós made his own way back, he determined to avoid any more such encounters which might give away his identity. He wanted to forget Hungary, to put behind him the betrayals and captivity of the past. 'From now on,' he said to himself, 'I am Peter Howard.'

By the end of May, he had gained almost a stone in weight. Flesh was reappearing on his arms and legs, and his hair was growing. He was far from fully recovered but he was able to wash himself and to walk regularly and unaided.

One morning as he was lying in bed glancing through the

Stars and Stripes, and reading how Admiral Horthy had pleaded with Allied correspondents to 'understand Hungary's position and help give her a decent place in the post-war world', a *Häftling* dressed in a brown civilian jacket and trousers came into the ward. He looked around briefly and then strode over to Miklós's bed. He addressed him, in English, as Peter Howard.

'Can I please take some details?' he asked, producing a pen and a sheet of paper from his pocket.

'Of course.'

'What is your full name?'

'Peter Ernest Howard.'

'What are the names of your parents?'

'Andrew and Evelyn Howard.' Miklós recalled the details from his conversations with the real Peter Howard.

'What is your date of birth?'

'June the eighteenth, 1920.' Miklós didn't know the real date and gave his own instead.

'What is your home address?'

Here again he could be authentic and gave the Flood Street address. 'In Chelsea, off the King's Road.'

'Religion?'

'Church of England.'

'Thank you. Tomorrow you will be moved from the hospital to the Allied block.'

The *Häftling* left him. Miklós lay back and closed his eyes. He liked the sound of the words, 'Allied block'. He wondered how his English came across. He could speak it with increasing ease and fluency, but was well aware that his accent could give him away far beyond Flood Street, Chelsea.

The next day another *Häftling* brought Miklós a clean uniform and escorted him out of the hospital. He said grateful farewells to Al Simpson and Sister McCann and embarked on a stiff and laboured twenty-minute walk to a two-storey brick building. The *Häftling* accompanying him showed him to a single bed-room on the ground floor. It was austere but clean, and the bed was made up with smooth, white sheets, a pillow and army blankets.

Despite having his own room, Miklós found it far noisier than the hospital ward. This was partly due to the fact that he was now much more alert to his surroundings, but there was also a lot of coming and going and shouting up and down the stairs.

On Miklós's third morning in the Allied block, a short, dapper-looking man with a sallow complexion, black hair and a moustache came in and introduced himself.

'Good morning. I am Dr Sayid.'

Like Miklós's, Sayid's English had the too-correct precision of the fluent foreigner. 'Where are you from?'

'London,' replied Miklós, on his guard. 'Peter Howard,' he added, standing up to shake hands.

They both spoke in an exploratory but evasive fashion as they exchanged introductory facts about each other. Sayid was an Iraqi doctor, educated in England, who had wound up in the camps as a result of 'some political problems'. And, with Miklós wary of expanding his basic biography of Peter Howard, the conversation only eased when they entered upon the neutral ground of life in Dachau.

Sayid had been in the Allied block for some time and was able to introduce Miklós to the rest of the inmates. Besides the 'Schreiber' in the brown jacket, whose name was Heinrich Fulda, a Czech of German origin, there was a distinguished-looking Canadian airman, a jovial, bulky Polish-Canadian soldier, and three Australians, a man and two women. Everybody had his or her own room.

Miklós and Sayid spent hours together wandering around the Lager. Sayid pointed out the separate Russian, Hungarian, Belgian and other blocks where the different nationalities were awaiting repatriation from what was now termed a 'Displaced Persons' camp.

Soon after his arrival in the Allied block, Miklós developed an egg-sized boil in his armpit. He pointed it out to his doctor friend, who told him he needed an operation and took him to another building – not the hospital – where there was an operating theatre. This was manned by a tall, expressionless Lithuanian–Jewish doctor, who gave Miklós an anaesthetic there and then. When he awoke, his armpit was packed with dressing and Sayid took him back to their block.

They became even closer after this but still neither gave away any personal details. Sayid seemed pleased to attach himself to an 'Englishman'.

Miklós learned more details of the liberation from him. The Americans, Sayid explained, had requisitioned everything from local farms and villages – chicken, pigs, sheep, cattle – to provide food for the thousands of starved prisoners. And, as more *Häftlings* streamed into Dachau at the end of April, they had found themselves without guards and had gone into nearby homes and stripped them of food.

One day, as Miklós and Sayid were walking along the *Lager* street, a *Häftling* raced up to Miklós and greeted him excitedly in Hungarian. '*Szervusz, Miki!*' – 'Hello, Miki.' It was Imre Friedman, his old colleague from Hirschberg. Miklós recognized him instantly. But he responded by turning to Sayid, asking him in cool, measured English, 'Do you know this man?'

'No,' replied the Iraqi. 'It is you in whom he appears to be interested.'

'I've never seen him before,' said Miklós as he turned away.

'Miki,' protested Friedman, hurt and confused.

Miklós grabbed Sayid's arm and the two men walked back towards the Allied block. Miklós made a mental note to avoid walking near the Hungarian block in future.

On 11 June, Heinrich Fulda came into Miklós's room carrying the paper on which he'd written 'Peter Howard's' details ten days or so previously. 'I just wanted to run through your particulars with you,' he said, 'to make sure they're all correct.'

He read them aloud and Miklós confirmed they were in order. 'Right,' said Fulda, 'tomorrow you'll be repatriated. I wish you all the best.'

Miklós hardly knew how to react. He smiled, whispered a quick 'Thank you', and scratched awkwardly at the operation scar in his armpit as he contemplated the prospect of being 'repatriated' to a country he had never even visited.

When Fulda had gone, Miklós went to tell Sayid his news.

'Good luck, my friend,' said the Iraqi. 'Perhaps we'll meet in London one day. I'll come and see you in Flood Street.'

'It has been a pleasure to have met you,' said Miklós in the tone of polite formality which had characterized their exchanges.

'Please,' asked Sayid, 'would you mind doing something for me, old man?'

'Of course not.'

'I would like to write a letter to my father to let him know I am safe. If I write it tonight and give it to you in the morning, would you be so kind as to post this when you are in London?'

'I should be delighted.'

When you are in London. The words echoed in Miklós's mind. All he knew of London, apart from the few sketchy details he'd picked up from Peter Howard, was from books and the BBC.

He couldn't sleep that night. He had a sense of foreboding about his impending journey. What would he do when he arrived in England? He remembered his friend Vicky Sternberg, who had gone there in 1938. Perhaps he would be able to find him.

One thing he was sure about was his loathing for his birthplace. He thought about his parents and his sisters, what tortures and deprivations they must have suffered before their surely certain deaths. He recalled the white-shirted colonel in Nagyvárad, the interrogations, the peasant delivering his 'two Jewish prostitutes'. He never wanted to see Hungary again.

In the morning there was a knock on the door. A smartly uniformed young American with sandy-coloured hair and freckles came to tell him to be ready to leave the camp after lunch.

'I'll have to find you some clothes to travel in. You can't go back home in your pyjamas or your *Häftling* outfit, can you?' He grinned and was gone before Miklós could reply.

The young American returned about half an hour later, a tunic and trousers over his arm. He was still grinning. 'I'm afraid we have no other clothing in the warehouse.' He held up an SS uniform, cleaned and folded and stripped of its insignia, but instantly identifiable. 'I'll leave it with you.'

Miklós changed into the uniform as soon as he came back from lunch. It fitted him better than his *Häftling* clothes had done. He bundled up his 'souvenir' coin and piece of soap with his Auschwitz trousers, took his toothbrush and was ready.

At about three o'clock, a jeep drew up in front of the block. An American lieutenant stepped briskly out of the front passenger seat and came into the building calling for Peter Howard and another, Canadian, inmate to go with him. As Miklós emerged from his room, the lieutenant looked at the SS uniform he was wearing and frowned. 'Is this the best they could do for you?' he asked, slapping Miklós's breast pocket with the back of his hand. 'Jeez, what a set-up!'

They drove for almost two hours, passing through various checkpoints, at each of which the guards eyed Miklós suspiciously, though no one challenged him. The Canadian sitting next to him made the odd comment about getting back home to start a new life in a new world. Otherwise, Miklós was content to shut his eyes and doze.

Eventually they came to the town of Augsburg, where the driver pulled into the courtyard of a drab 1920s block of flats. The American lieutenant got out and told his passengers to wait. He went inside the building and returned a few moments later with two British soldiers. One of them, a flame-haired Scot, gave a start when he saw Miklós's uniform.

'Christ,' he exclaimed. 'What are you doing wearing that?'

'It's what they gave me,' replied Miklós in slow, deliberate monosyllables.

'You just stay where you are.' Miklós had trouble understanding the man's dialect, but could follow his facial expressions easily enough.

Both British soldiers disappeared into the building and came out again with a British battledress uniform similar to their own. 'Now you put this on, laddie,' said the Scotsman, handing it to Miklós along with a tin of fifty Players cigarettes. Miklós thought of the immense value the latter would have had in Auschwitz. 'I could have bought the entire *Lager*,' he laughed to himself.

Miklós wasn't allowed to take a single step without changing uniforms, so he peeled off the SS tunic where he stood, in the open air, much to the amusement of the British soldiers.

He picked up the tin of cigarettes, and the Scotsman's colleague took him into the building and led him along a corridor into a small room with a bed and a bare table. On the plain, white wall above the bed hung a large wooden crucifix. 'Right,' said the soldier. 'Now I'll get rid of that nasty uniform,' and Miklós was left alone.

Shortly afterwards there was a tap on the door and another soldier appeared. 'I've come to take you to the canteen,' he said, 'and then later on to see the commanding officer.'

'What is this place?' Miklós asked him.

'This is the transit post for all British Empire prisoners. Right, are you ready?'

They went into the corridor and stopped at another door. The soldier rapped lightly. 'Are you ready, Private Mostyn?' he called out. 'Yes, mate,' a voice answered and the door flew back to reveal a short, khaki-uniformed man with a round, red nose like a cherry, and a happy grin punctuated by a cigarette curling smoke from the corner of his mouth.

Mostyn chatted to Miklós all along the corridor and into the canteen, where they ate overcooked meat and potatoes. It tasted exquisite to Miklós.

'Gotta see the bloody CO afterwards,' complained Mostyn in between mouthfuls of potato. 'Bloody nuisance, if you ask me. I could do with some bloody sleep.'

In the mainly one-way conversation with Private Mostyn, who said that he came from Jersey and couldn't wait to get back to get his hands on his 'bloody cheating girlfriend', Miklós quickly came to learn that 'bloody' was an English swear-word of common usage.

He laughed at Mostyn's routine grumbles about seeing the commanding officer. He knew he had more reason to be anxious and, when the escorting soldier left him at the door at the appointed time, he entered very nervously.

'Come in,' a deep voice ordered.

Miklós stepped forward into the temporary office. A man of about fifty, with a neat, silver moustache, looked up from the table at which he was seated. 'Mr Howard. I'm Lieutenant-Colonel Fitzpatrick. I have to process your papers. Please sit down.'

Miklós recognized the accent. It was similar to that of his companion in the jeep. Fitzpatrick was a Canadian. Perhaps he wouldn't see through Miklós's own accent.

Fitzpatrick looked up again from the papers on his desk and stared at Miklós for an uncomfortable minute or so before speaking again.

'So you're from England,' he said at last.

'Yes.' Miklós's voice was too high-pitched.

'When did you leave?'

'Nineteen forty-two.'

'Where are you from?'

'London – Chelsea.'

'Your parents' names? Father's occupation?' Fitzpatrick went line-by-line through the details that Heinrich Fulda had written down in Dachau. Finally, he signed the authorization documents, shaking his head as he did so. He handed them over to Miklós with a wry smile. 'OK, you can go,' he said, in a manner which led Miklós to feel that he had signed the paper more through charity than conviction.

17

On the bus the next morning, 13 June, Miklós found himself
with two Australian women, possibly mother and daughter, an
English army captain, and the Canadian with whom he'd come
from Dachau. As they entered Augsburg airport through a fine
drizzle they could see on the runway a DC3 aircraft with
camouflage markings. Within half an hour they were aboard it
and in the air – Miklós for the first time in his life.

His head reeled with the strangeness of his situation. 'Who
would have imagined this?' he thought to himself, remembering
how he used to translate the BBC broadcasts for his family.
'What will happen to me when I get to England? But then,
what can they do to me? They certainly won't put me in the
Kamine.'

They stopped off at a military airfield near Paris to refuel.
The passengers were given no food, however, and Miklós
began to feel very hungry. After an hour or two they were
airborne again.

As the English coastline came into view, Miklós stared down
at it. Was this land to be his haven? He felt apprehensive but
pleased to be coming to the country that had fought Hitler
from the outset. At about 4 p.m. they touched down at Croydon
airport. He sighed heavily. 'God save me from Hungary, at any
rate,' he said under his breath.

They stepped out under a blue sky broken only by a blazing
sun and the slightest wisps of fluffy cloud. A uniformed official
ushered them through the customs barrier and directed them
into the reception hall where, tired and hungry, they were
made to wait. Miklós was finding it difficult to walk and eased

himself into a seat. He longed to ask for some food but felt constrained in these surroundings, so far and so different from Dachau.

The English captain was quickly called away. After a quarter of an hour a man brought over a tray to Miklós and his three remaining companions. On it was a plate of about a dozen biscuits, some cups, a jug and an urn of steaming tea. Miklós could have swallowed the biscuits in one gulp. Instead, he politely handed the plate to the elder of the Australian women, who took two, as did the younger. The Canadian took one and Miklós felt a vacuum form in his stomach as he followed suit.

Meanwhile, the man who had brought the tray was pouring out tea. Miklós was astonished to see him put milk into each of the cups beforehand. He had only had milk in tea at home as a child when he'd been ill. He took a second biscuit and tried to make it last.

A uniformed official came to collect the Australian women and the Canadian man. A few minutes later it was Miklós's turn. He got to his feet slowly before being led outside to an ambulance, in which a soldier and a driver were waiting. Miklós sat down as the soldier greeted him with a nod and told the driver to get going.

They drove for almost two hours. Miklós craned to look at the people, shops and traffic. Everywhere there was a post-war drabness. The men and women looked weary, their clothes lifeless, the shops sparsely stocked. Even the buildings seemed sombre. He found it comforting.

Finally, they drove into a compound containing a row of military-looking huts. Miklós was helped down from the ambulance and welcomed by a middle-aged man and a young woman whose plump, rosy face reminded him of Sister McCann. They were both taken aback by Miklós's physical condition. The man offered his arm and took Miklós to a shower, under which he threw back his head and closed his eyes with pleasure.

When he emerged, the man had taken away his battledress

and shoes and was waiting with a pair of pyjamas, slippers and a dressing-gown. As Miklós put these on, the man gave him two half-crown pieces to put in the pocket of the dressing-gown, 'with the compliments of His Majesty'. He was then led to a bed in what seemed to be an unoccupied hospital ward. He removed his dressing-gown and slipped immediately between the sheets and into a long, unbroken sleep.

He was awoken the next morning by two young nurses, one bearing a tray of breakfast. Both watched aghast as he bolted it down. 'Where have you come from?' asked one, girlish, with blue eyes and curly blonde hair.

'I am from the concentration camps,' Miklós replied.

A look of shock passed over both of the sweet, pretty faces as they registered the fact that this bag of bones before them, wolfing down his toast, was a piece of first-hand evidence of the hearsay horrors beginning to be revealed in the newspapers and the newsreels.

The blonde girl's companion, a freckled redhead with the kind of warm, sympathetic human smile of which Miklós had long been starved, went out of the ward for a moment. She returned carrying a large bar of chocolate.

'Here,' she said to him. 'Take this, but eat it slowly.'

As he held the purple-paper-covered slab in his hand, Miklós nearly cried. It was as if he had been handed a key to a lost Utopia. Even before the war, the chocolate produced in Hungary had been adulterated to avoid the payment of cocoa tax. He couldn't remember when he'd last seen real chocolate.

'Can I have a piece now?' As he looked up at the two nurses, the redhead about his age and the blonde two or three years younger, his attitude was that of an imploring child. 'Sure,' said the elder, 'but just the one piece for now.'

His fingers shook as he unwrapped the paper and snapped off a square segment of the dark brown bar. As he bit into it the sweetness that oozed around his teeth and over his tongue was almost unbearable. The slightly bitter undertaste of the plain chocolate blended with the initial sweetness into a soft, trickling elixir.

The nurses looked at him in astonishment. Thereafter, they indulged him like a baby, bringing him glasses of water, slices of soft, white bread, and more inestimably delicious chocolate.

He slept for the greater part of the next two days. After that he began to take in his surroundings. He was told he was in Stanmore, in Middlesex, north-west of London. He climbed out of bed and wandered to the window. As he stared outside, the blonde nurse came and draped his dressing-gown over his shoulders. 'What is that down there?' he asked her, pointing to a railway track with strange red trains passing each other along it.

'The Underground!' She laughed and gently ushered him back to bed.

On the fourth day, at about five o'clock in the evening, an orderly came to tell him that the CO wanted to see him.

So. The moment of reckoning. Miklós sighed and felt somewhat relieved as well as anxious. He wanted to talk. He wanted to unload some of his burden to somebody who could understand.

The commanding officer was a captain, of easy, public-school charm. He invited Miklós to take a seat without addressing him as 'Mr Howard' or anything else. He had Miklós's papers in front of him. He looked up from them, smiled and asked, 'Where did you stay in Paris?'

Miklós invented some addresses, locating them near landmarks he'd heard or read about.

'I understand you were also in Zurich,' said the captain suddenly. 'Would you mind describing Zurich to me as you recall it?'

As he spoke, Miklós had an image of the previous Christmas Eve in Auschwitz in Levitzky's hut, when the inmates had stirred up the night with their singing. He had spoken to some Frenchmen there who had talked longingly of Switzerland, and in particular of Zurich.

He drew now on those few hazy impressions the French prisoners had lodged in his mind as he described the main street, the lake, the people and the food.

As the captain's questions grew more searching, Miklós's replies became more vague and faltering. After a few minutes the captain handed him a sheet of paper and a pencil. 'Perhaps you would be good enough to make a rough drawing of the centre of Zurich for me,' he said, as patiently as a teacher coaxing a small child.

'Well, here,' said Miklós, gingerly tracing a pair of parallel lines across the page, 'is the main street – the Bahnhofstrasse. Houses, shops and various buildings.' He scribbled an assortment of shapes above and below the lines.

'How about the church?' asked the captain.

'Oh – somewhere around here, I think.' Miklós indicated somewhere central.

'No,' smiled the captain. 'Not there. Can you remember anything special, anything unusual about the church?'

'Well, it was big,' hedged Miklós.

'It has two steeples,' explained the captain.

Miklós's brain was racing. Somehow this did not seem the moment to reveal the truth. He was too tense.

The captain dismissed him. He went straight to bed and lay there panting and turning things over in his mind. How much longer could he keep up the pretence?

He fell asleep and his dreams took him back to Auschwitz. To the *Lagerstrasse* and Kadouk. Miklós had been walking with Ede and Levitzky. They'd turned a corner and come face to face with the cross-eyed brute. They ran from him into a room where Cyrankiewicz was addressing the members of the *Lager* 'underground'. He had a map of Auschwitz pinned to the wall and was referring to it over and over again with a pencil.

'Don't worry, young man,' he said to Miklós. 'It will all be over soon. It can't last.' Meanwhile, Kadouk was looking at them through the window. 'One of you,' he was yelling, 'one of you will have to die today. One of you is concealing a boil under your arm. Don't think I won't be able to discover it.'

As Kadouk's macabre eyes searched out their victim, Miklós dived under a table to avoid his gaze and awoke in a sweat beneath the blankets of his bed.

The next day, he was told he was leaving. After breakfast – at which the red-haired nurse gave him another large bar of plain chocolate – he was given his bundle of belongings and, still in his pyjamas and dressing-gown, taken out to a waiting car.

He sat in the back, next to an army sergeant, and was driven into London. They stopped at a red-bricked building surrounded by mature lawns and flower-beds. He was ordered to follow the sergeant into the office. A sign at the entrance told him he was at a school called St Patrick's.

In the office, his papers were silently examined by an orderly, who then led him to a small bedroom furnished with a single bed, a cupboard and a night table containing a pile of magazines. He was brought some tea and sandwiches at lunchtime but otherwise left alone for the rest of the day.

Towards evening he fell asleep and didn't wake until the morning, when the orderly appeared with a plate of bacon and eggs. Miklós savoured each hot, salty mouthful.

For three days or so his only contact was with Jack, the orderly, who brought him his meals and escorted him on occasional walks around the garden. Miklós shared some of his cigarettes from the Players tin with the man and, when this was nearly empty, gave him one of his two half-crowns to buy some more.

'It was one and eleven,' said Jack on his return, as he placed a packet of twenty Players on the table and pressed the change into Miklós's palm. Miklós was surprised to see that the little silver coin was worth six times the big copper one.

On Miklós's fourth morning at St Patrick's, a young officer walked into his room and greeted him with the short, shocking phrase: 'Guten Tag!'

It was the first German Miklós had heard since leaving Germany. He responded in kind and the officer proceeded to conduct a conversation in German. He asked Miklós to tell him 'what part of Austria you come from'.

The dialogue became farcical, veering from Miklós's English to the young officer's insistent German, in which he fired a

226

series of seemingly disconnected and menacing questions at Miklós. He asked him what his favourite sport was, whether he'd had a German girlfriend, if he had ever been to Amsterdam and if he understood Dutch.

Miklós eventually explained in German that he was exhausted and asked if he could go and rest. 'Of course,' said his interrogator. 'We will call you.'

The next morning Jack told Miklós that the CO wanted to see him. This commanding officer turned out to be a man in his late forties, short, dapper, with a kind-looking face distinguished by greying temples.

'Sit down, please,' he said, indicating a chair facing him across a desk. 'Would you prefer this examination to be carried out in English or German?'

'English,' Miklós answered softly.

'Very well. First of all, let me inform you that I am perfectly aware that you are not who you say you are. You are not Peter Howard. We have a number of options about what to do with you next, but to begin with I'd like to hear the truth.'

'If I told you the full truth,' he replied, 'I feel you wouldn't believe me.'

'Try me,' said the officer in a friendly tone.

Out it poured. For three hours or more Miklós described his experiences with hardly an interruption. When he came to talk about Auschwitz, he rolled up his sleeve to reveal his tattooed serial number.

Here, the officer did interject. 'Tell me,' he asked, 'which block were you in?' Miklós told him and he asked for more details. Which *Kommando*? Who was the *Kapo*? What was written on the main gate? Where was the kitchen? The punishment block?

The officer was remarkably well informed. He took notes as Miklós was speaking.

'It's clear you know the camp well,' he said, his manner seeming to soften a little. 'But as a prisoner or as a guard?'

'Please, sir,' sighed Miklós. 'You've seen my number. Surely you can tell from my appearance. Do you really believe I could have been an SS guard?'

The officer remained silent for a moment or two, then smiled gently and said, 'No, I don't think so.'

'Mr Hammer,' he said, once Miklós had concluded his story, 'you have my total sympathy.' He rose from his chair and shook Miklós by the hand. 'I shall make my report to the Home Office and it is now up to them to decide how to deal with you. But before that,' he said, his eyes steeling a little, 'we are going to check everything you have told me.'

'You'll have to call me Miklós from now on. Peter Howard is dead.' It was an hour later and Miklós was back in his room smoking with Jack. Having given his story to the commanding officer, his tongue was loosened. He couldn't stop talking, thinking aloud to the taciturn orderly, who simply sat in his chair, his face expressionless except to register the passage of smoke up the back of his throat and out through his nostrils.

'I'm not worried,' Miklós went on. 'Poor old Peter Howard. May his memory be for a blessing, eh, Jack? You don't understand what I'm talking about, do you? Never mind, neither do I really. All I know is I've committed no crime and an English officer has shaken my hand. I'll be out of here in a couple of days, looking for a job or emigrating to America.'

'*Hammer?*' Miklós's 'couple of days' had duly passed and now he was being called from his room by a burly army sergeant.

'Do you have any civilian clothes?'

Miklós replied that he hadn't.

'Right, come with me.'

He followed the sergeant into Jack's office, where he was given a white shirt and a pair of dark grey trousers.

'Put these on, Sonny; get your things and follow me.'

It was a rainy evening and Miklós felt cold as they went outside to a car. The driver whistled American dance tunes as he slowly negotiated the wet London streets before coming to a halt in front of a building that looked like another school. Several men were wandering disconsolately around what appeared to have been a playground.

'All right, Sonny. Out you get,' said the sergeant.

He led Miklós into the building, where an orderly, just as morose-looking as Jack, took him into a room with half a dozen pairs of bunk beds in it.

'This will be your quarters,' said the orderly.

'For how long?' Miklós inquired.

'Now that's not up to me, pal. I should get a good night's kip if I were you. If you can, that is. We've got all sorts in 'ere. All foreigners. Noisy lot, some of 'em.'

He turned away abruptly and was gone. From a radio somewhere, a voice announced it was ten o'clock British Double Summer Time. Then a slight, stooped man with thick black hair appeared in the doorway.

'Hi,' he said, smiling. 'My name is Cjeka. Welcome to Oratory School.' He sounded American.

'Hello, I am Miklós Hammer. What exactly is this place?'

'It's an internment camp. For suspicious foreigners.' Cjeka smiled.

'What part of London is this?'

'This is Chelsea. A smart part of town, they say. Though there's not much that's smart about this place.'

'Chelsea,' said Miklós, almost smiling. 'It's almost as if it were home.'

'Rise and shine!' The bizarre, unfamiliar cry cut through Miklós's dreams. He awoke to see a uniformed man standing in the doorway, clapping his hands to urge the sleeping bodies into life.

The occupants of the dormitory breakfasted together along a massive wooden refectory table. Cjeka sat opposite Miklós and introduced him to some of the others. 'This big fellow next to you is "Smithy",' he said, indicating a man with a large head, covered with a twisted mane of dark hair.

'You're Jewish, eh?' said Smithy, abruptly but approvingly. 'Me too. I was born in Germany but I joined the Foreign Legion. I was interned in France also.'

'Miklós was in the Nazi concentration camps,' Cjeka informed him.

'My God, that's terrible,' said Smithy. 'And now they've locked you up here, eh?' He shook his huge head from side to side, clucking his tongue.

Seated on the other side of Miklós was a tall, lean man called Vilner, a Polish Jew with deep-set, serious eyes. There were two Italians, one around Miklós's age, who was called Cappucelli, and an older man whose name Miklós didn't catch.

All the rest were Germans, who kept to themselves at one end of the table. Among them was the man who occupied the bunk above Miklós's in the dormitory. A thin, ascetic type, about fifty, with wire-framed spectacles, he wore a smart grey suit and seemed totally absorbed in his breakfast, pecking like a bird at several small pieces of bread and butter.

The first few days passed in aimless relaxation. The internees had access to radios and newspapers, chess and other board games, and were free to wander around the walled courtyard. The food was meagre and poorly prepared, however, and smoking was prohibited.

Cjeka was originally from Prague but had lived for several years in Chicago. He took a protective interest in Miklós, shocked that this frail young Hungarian Jew was unable to enjoy freedom after his ordeal in the camps. He urged him to seek the assistance of the British Chief Rabbi and various Members of Parliament.

The school had a typewriter at which Miklós and Cjeka sat for hours at a time, composing letters. Cjeka drafted an appeal to 'Miss Eleanor Rathbone MP' asking for help 'in the name of human compassion'. Miklós typed this out laboriously and then another, to Chief Rabbi Hertz, describing the situation in which a 'poor, punished Jew' now found himself.

Both letters were given to a guard to post. Perhaps he never got around to it. In any event, Miklós received no reply.

On 25 July they were all taken by motor coach to a new location – Beltane School in Wimbledon. *En route* they had to stop for some sort of procession. A crowd of people was cheering, though some were booing and a few waved their fists in the air.

It was a General Election meeting. And there, on a rostrum, doffing his hat to his audience, was Winston Churchill. He began to make a speech. Miklós and the others on the coach strained to hear him. His words were lost in the general noise but Miklós was exhilarated by the experience. 'Here,' he said to Cjeka, 'is the man I admire above all human beings. What a marvellous moment, a privilege to see him.'

'But did you see,' asked Cjeka, 'a lot of the people were against him?'

Beltane was a large, three-storey building, set in much more extensive grounds than Oratory. The gardens were fenced in with barbed wire and a number of military staff were in evidence. Sergeant 'Rise-and-Shine' led his charges off the coach and into their new quarters.

Fifty or so inmates were already in occupation. Most of these were German. Miklós's bird-like bunkmate and the rest of the German contingent from Oratory quickly fell in with them.

Miklós spent much of his time speaking English with Cjeka and Vilner, or Italian with Cappucelli and some others, but he sometimes sat in an armchair listening to the conversations of groups of Germans. One day his former neighbour from Oratory turned and stared at him through his wire spectacles and addressed him in German.

'I heard rumours that you are a survivor of the concentration camps,' he said.

'Yes, that's right.'

'Perhaps you would care to join me for a walk around the gardens?'

Miklós was a little suspicious, but accepted the invitation.

'What is your name?' the German asked, friendly but a little aloof.

'Miklós Hammer. I was born in Hungary. And you are . . .?'

'Doctor Otto Dietrich,' said his companion, astonishingly revealing himself to be Adolf Hitler's former press chief.

'What?' Miklós was shaking. Blood rushed to his head. 'Are you joking?' he asked, knowing from the man's demeanour that he wasn't. A matter of weeks after his release from Dachau, here he was strolling with an important representative of the Nazi machine responsible for delivering him there.

'I would like to talk to you about the concentration camps,' said Dietrich in a dry, academic tone.

'Oh, really?' Miklós felt his face blazing.

'You see,' Dietrich went on, 'we heard all sorts of rumours about them. That many prisoners died, for example.'

'Many prisoners died.' Miklós repeated the phrase, nodding in almost automatic affirmation.

'This was the fault of the vulgar brutes unfortunately placed in charge. You'll find such men everywhere, especially in time of war,' said Dietrich. 'Some of the guards here at Beltane could equally well serve at such institutions as Dachau and Buchenwald.'

'No, no, you are wrong.' Miklós contemplated the images of Kadouk and Mengele, balancing them against those of Jack, his smoking companion at St Patrick's, and the sergeant in charge of his present dormitory, Mister Rise-and-Shine.

'You think so? You think the British are so wonderful? So universally humane?' Dietrich's eyes narrowed with bitterness. 'If the British are the great champions of freedom and democracy, then tell me what you and I are doing, walking here together in captivity, you a Jew and I a Nazi?'

'So, you still call yourself a Nazi? Most of the German internees are keen to resist such a label.'

'*Ach*, I have served the party with honour and the highest aims. It all became corrupted in the hands of such types as those SS members of whom you have such recent experience.'

'And did you remain loyal to Hitler?'

'I believe he was an instrument which went out of control.'

'An instrument? Of what?'

'Of a higher destiny. It was National Socialism I believed in. It had within it the power and vision to transform society. To lift civilization out of the mire. If it could have spread without the war it would have placed Europe – and in time the whole world – on a higher plane. For a short time man had before him the opportunity to raise himself to the nobility of existence envisaged by Schiller and Goethe, with the inspiration of Beethoven and Wagner.'

'And is murder part of this noble existence?'

'Death is inevitable. It is part of life. Yes, some had to die. Those who embodied the baser qualities. Lost causes.'

'Like the Jews?'

'Not in my view. The Jews are realists. Clever. They are capable of education, of conversion. They can make a valuable contribution.'

'Then what of the Final Solution?'

'This again is a term we keep hearing rumours about. Only now. I never heard of it during the war. I came to Britain to negotiate with political leaders. It was they who threw the Final Solution in my face. I assure you such matters were kept from the German intelligentsia.'

'Thousands upon thousands of Jews were murdered,' said Miklós. 'And not just Jews – gypsies, Poles, politicals – the cancer was unstoppable. There was dreadful brutality, unspeakable deprivation and cruelty. The Final Solution was a policy of systematic extermination carried out with enthusiastic barbarism across Europe.'

'Such things were the work of Himmler. An obsessive psychological cripple. This was not National Socialism, my friend.'

'Ah, but it was, *my friend*. Like all "pure" doctrines and ideals it makes demands upon that most impure of commodities, human nature. And Nazism demanded cruelty. Stripped away the civilized values. Deadened sensitivities; encouraged torture. "Purity" demands rejection. Mass and bloody rejection. There

233

is nothing noble about Nazism. On the contrary, it is totally inhumane.'

They had completed a circuit of the yard. 'We must continue our discussions tomorrow, my dear young Hammer,' Dietrich said loftily. 'Until then we have to submit ourselves to our democratic, freedom-loving jailers.'

As Miklós stepped back into the building, he was met by Cjeka and Smithy. 'What,' asked the latter, 'were you talking about to that pig, that Nazi?'

'It was a fascinating conversation, Smithy. I am trying to look into the mind of an intelligent exponent of a barbarous philosophy.'

'If you take my advice,' retorted Smithy, 'you'll look into your own mind. At the injustice of your imprisonment here. You should be thinking about how to get out of here. Not about the diseased minds who started the war.'

'He is right,' added Cjeka. 'Forget that Nazi. Concentrate on getting out of here. Let's write some more letters.'

But Miklós did not forget Dietrich. He continued to meet him. He was stimulated by the intellectual sparring. It distracted him from the other internees' constant, frustrating preoccupation with getting themselves out of Beltane School.

'Are you a believer in the idea that might is right?' Miklós inquired one day in his dialogue with his new Nazi acquaintance.

'There is a pattern in nature,' Dietrich replied, 'which is very much akin to that notion. You have to be careful. I am not an advocate of purposeless violence – any more than was Nietzsche. Nietzsche was for me the great observer. And he saw how nature really works. You see, Hammer, there are in nature predators and victims. Gradually the world is streamlined and improved. The fittest to survive are precisely the ones who do survive. It is nature's way of balancing life in its true order. I see parallels here for nation-states. The *Herrenvolk* would know better what was right for the people around them.'

'So even among the Germans the weak would have to fall by the wayside in the thousand-year Reich?'

'A harsh fact to swallow, I agree, but nature is harsh. That is how it keeps from going soft and rancid. Hitler was the genius with the vision to realize this. His ideas misfired on account of the functionaries who surrounded him.'

'But don't you believe in morality? Nietzsche asked how murderers could possibly comfort themselves. How can there be such a thing as a noble, higher existence without reference to morality?'

'Morality is relative. Again, look at your precious British, whom you seem to think possess a monopoly on morality even though they have locked you up.'

'But I can look forward to freedom here. It exists outside the camp. My internment is due to some bureaucratic blunder. Human error – which you cannot eradicate.'

'You will see, my friend, how moral Britain is, and America, as soon as they realize that an alliance with the Soviet Union is no longer in their interests. They will turn against them, I'm sure. Let me assure you that your hero, Mr Churchill, understands all about the relativity of morality. And he is right. Morality is a matter of self-interest. You think the Communist ideology doesn't allow the strong to dominate the weak? Indeed, to eliminate them?'

'For my part, I prefer to be a captive of a people that professes moral values than to be a "free" citizen of an inhuman state. Your distinction between the strong and the weak is mistaken. The analogy with the different species of nature is false. We are all the same species. All humans are weak. Power is exercised simply to protect that weakness. Those who wield power most absolutely have the most to protect. If your voice is naturally loud you don't have to shout. As a human being, Adolf Hitler was one of the weakest. Your "natural selection" would have cast him out with all the other deviants.'

Another circuit was completed. Another parting, Dietrich to the recriminating German prisoners, Miklós to his escapist friends, Cjeka, Smithy and Vilner.

In time, the two groups came to mingle a little. Though no

actual friendships were formed, Vilner and one or two others began to speak to individual Germans. Miklós was no longer isolated in his conversations with Dr Dietrich.

Closer contact between the nationalities was cemented by the arrival at Beltane School of an even more illustrious former member of Hitler's entourage.

Putzi Hanfstaengl had been a successful publisher in Germany and had printed the Nazis' literature for them. He had come to know Hitler personally and had introduced him to Thyssen and Krupp, the industrialists who pumped large amounts of money into the Nazi Party. Hanfstaengl also claimed that it was he – and not, as many believed, Hofman the photographer – who had brought together 'shy, polite' Adolf and Eva Braun.

In consequence, he frequently referred to himself as the 'conductor of Hitler's two grand operatic duets'.

In 1934, however, following the unsuccessful Roehm putsch against Hitler, Hanfstaengl had fled to the United States with his American wife. Friends at the Führer's table had reported a joke Hitler had made about 'fixing' Putzi Hanfstaengl along with Ernst Roehm. Hanfstaengl had taken it seriously.

By the time he arrived in Beltane he was describing himself as a refugee and 'the first ex-Nazi'. Portly, fiftyish and flamboyant, he made much of the fact that his son was serving with the American forces in Japan.

He attracted cosmopolitan groups of listeners as he relayed the 'kitchen gossip' of Hitler's inner circle. He was also an accomplished pianist and entertained the inmates with impromptu recitals on Beltane's old black upright.

On Christmas Day 1945, in Wimbledon, south-west London, the Beltane internees gathered around the piano to be led by Putzi Hanfstaengl in a lusty rendering of 'O Tannenbaum'. Twelve years before, he had played the same song at a party for Adolf Hitler and Eva Braun. Twelve *months* before, Miklós – now celebrating with the others – had sung another German carol with another group of prisoners.

Christmas was a festive time for all the inmates. But another celebration, three months earlier, for Beltane's dozen or so Jews, had not gone quite so harmoniously.

In September, as the Jewish New Year approached, Vilner and one or two others submitted a request to the commanding officer, Major Hindmarsh, for a room to be reserved where they could conduct services. He sent back a note granting their request but asking them to ensure that the other internees were not 'disturbed by any noise'.

Miklós was present when Hindmarsh's adjutant delivered this message. To everyone's amazement, he snatched the note and stormed after the man. 'Excuse me,' he called after him, 'but do you not think this instruction is a little unreasonable considering who *we* are and,' pointing in the direction of a group of German inmates, 'who *they* are?'

The adjutant, a mild-mannered captain of about forty, smiled sympathetically. 'Well, perhaps the CO was being a little heavy-handed,' he said.

'Yes, he was, in my opinion,' Miklós replied, still enraged. 'I would like to speak to him about it, please.'

The adjutant promised to arrange an interview at the earliest opportunity.

A few days later, Miklós was called in to see Major Hindmarsh. Beltane's commanding officer was a white-haired soldier of considerable experience, who sat square and secure in his chair with the adjutant standing behind him.

'Well now,' said the major, with a professional smile, 'what's all this about?'

'Sir,' Miklós replied, standing to attention on the opposite side of the desk. 'I am an inmate of this camp through circumstances of the war. Treated as an enemy alien while the Home Office considers my case. In Hungary, Poland and Germany I was taken to concentration camps simply because of my religion. I escaped death by sheer luck.'

He felt himself losing control. His voice wavered, rose and fell. One of his eyes began to twitch. The adjutant looked a little alarmed but Hindmarsh listened on, his lips pressed together.

'By a fluke,' Miklós continued, his body trembling, 'I find myself locked up with Nazis. Enemies of this country, the country which I believed fought the war for my freedom. I am here because the Allies liberated me.'

Miklós had been nervous about his meeting with Major Hindmarsh. But as he'd waited to see him, he'd told himself that whatever punishment he might receive for voicing his criticism, there were no *Kapos* here, no Block 10, and no gas chambers. And he determined to speak his mind.

'I have heard your request not to disturb these other internees. In this country, of all countries, we Jewish people are being asked not to disturb the Nazis.' He was screaming now. The self-control that had carried him through Birkenau, Auschwitz and Buchenwald had snapped. He felt himself speaking for the millions who had perished.

The adjutant, white-faced, intervened: 'Young man, calm down. Do not raise your voice.'

The major, too, spoke for the first time. 'Take it easy,' he said, but his smooth, confident tone set Miklós off again. He pointed at the ribbons on Hindmarsh's breast. 'What did you get those for? Having consideration for Nazis? Or for defending the liberty and democracy I understood Great Britain to stand for? It's a mockery. And furthermore, why are all the best jobs here in the camp given to the Germans? Not a single Jew is employed in the office or the workshop or the kitchen. The cushiest jobs go to the biggest Nazis!'

He waited, expecting to be dispatched to the 'glasshouse', a room at the top of the building set aside for offenders to be placed under lock and key. His head hung on his chest and he was breathing heavily.

The major rose from his seat. 'I'll look into this matter immediately,' he said crisply. 'Now, do take it easy.' He turned to the adjutant, who escorted Miklós from the room and back to his anxious colleagues.

238

18

The next day, Miklós was summoned to the office by Sergeant Rise-and-Shine.

'As from today, Hammer,' he said, 'you will work here in the office as assistant to the secretary.' Vilner was given a job in the workshop, Smithy in the kitchen.

Cjeka did even better. He was discharged, taking with him a batch of letters from Miklós – to the Home Office, the Chief Rabbi, and the Jewish Refugees' Committee.

By now, Miklós was keen to get to America. He wanted to put as much distance as possible between him and the death and devastation of Europe. He had a relative in Washington whom he'd asked the Jewish Refugees' Committee to try to trace. A few days after Cjeka's departure they replied. They had made contact with the International Red Cross in an attempt to discover the fate of his family in Hungary, and sent a telegram to the American authorities for information on the whereabouts of his cousin, Alexander Hammer.

In his letter to the Chief Rabbi's office, Miklós had included a note for forwarding to Vicky Sternberg, the one friend he knew had come to London. He gave the Chief Rabbi's office details of Sternberg's family history and asked for their help in finding Vicky and giving him the enclosed letter.

Some time in mid-October, a young rabbi, Daniel Wiesenfeld, came to see Miklós. Miklós recognized him as the helpful young man who had brought along the prayer books and prayer shawls for use in the New Year devotions.

'I have greetings for you,' said a smiling Rabbi Wiesenfeld. 'From your friend, Mr Sternberg. He has received your message and will do all he can to obtain your release. In the meantime, Mr Hammer, is there anything I can do to help?'

'Only one thing. Get me out of here.'

'People are trying on your behalf. Good people. Have faith. Be patient. All that can be done, will be done.'

A day or two later, Josef Karski, a Polish captain, was admitted to Beltane camp. He was a chess enthusiast. On the strength of this, Miklós befriended him. During the hours spent hunched over the chessboard, they gradually told their stories to each other.

Karski had been in the Polish underground and had somehow found himself caught up in Budapest at the end of 1944. He even had a smattering of Hungarian, though they spoke together mostly in German.

He described to Miklós how one day he had seen the Hungarian Nazis, the Arrow Cross, herd together scores of Jews on the bank of the Danube in the early morning. Women, children and a few, mostly elderly, men stood huddled for a while in the biting December cold. Dark, wretched and sombre except for the occasional high shouts of the children, they seemed like wraiths hovering above the icy water. Within minutes the river ran red as the last echoes of machine-gun fire bounced off the bridges.

Karski had witnessed, too, the Russian advance into Pest and the fierce battles with the Germans across the water in Buda. He had seen the liberation, entered the ghetto and run back into the city, repelled by the stench of decomposing bodies on the streets.

Miklós listened, horrified, to the captain's account, convinced now of the extinction of his family. He felt hollow inside but never shared his thoughts with anyone.

From his privileged position in the camp office, Miklós was able to engage in a torrent of correspondence. He exchanged several letters with a Miss Fellner of the Refugees' Committee. She told him they had managed to locate Alexander Hammer and that 'at the instigation of your friend Mr Victor Sternberg', she had written to the Home Office taking up his case. But there was still no word from Budapest.

In December 1945, the postal links were restored between Britain and Hungary. On the 24th, Miklós wrote direct to the secretary of the Board of Deputies in Budapest, giving Victor Sternberg's address for reply.

A few days later Miklós was sitting with about twelve other inmates listening to Putzi Hanfstaengl. He was making fun of Hitler's leather clothes, and his attempts to be fashionable to impress Eva Braun. Miklós was laughing along with the others when Rise-and-Shine came to tell him he had a visitor.

'A *visitor*?'

'Yeah, the old sky-pilot.'

'What?'

'The sky-pilot. That young Jewish priest who came before.'

Rabbi Wiesenfeld was smiling. Miklós was relieved.

'I have some news for you,' said the rabbi. In his hand was a piece of paper. 'Here,' he said, and placed the paper in Miklós's hand.

Miklós held it, stared at it but couldn't focus. His eyes blurred with tears as he tried to read what was written on the paper.

At the top was a date – 14 December 1945, Budapest. It was written in his father's handwriting. The rest of the page, too, neat, tightly-packed paragraphs, was unmistakably written by his father, even though Miklós was unable to take in a single word.

He turned over the page. At the top was a line in his mother's handwriting. Beneath that, Ibolya's; and at the bottom, two lines from Alice.

Clutching the letter in both hands, Miklós closed his eyes tightly against the tears. 'This is proof that there is a God Almighty,' he cried out to the rabbi, who was looking concerned.

'Please, Mr Hammer,' he said. 'Sit down calmly and try to read the letter. I got it from Mr Sternberg. News of your family, he said. I didn't realize it would have such a powerful effect.'

'Rabbi,' said Miklós, in between sobs, 'I didn't think I had a family any more. This is a miracle. They are all alive. *All* of them!'

'I didn't know. What wonderful news. I wish you *mazeltov*.'

The letter was in German. Miklós's father had worried that, had he written in Hungarian, nobody in London would understand it and would perhaps automatically reject or censor it.

Several minutes passed before Miklós felt able to read the words on the paper:

My dearest son Miklós,

I write to you just a few lines because we have to dispatch this note immediately.

Ibi and I have returned from the deportations and when we came back a lot of tears have been shed because of you, but thank God that we have heard about you. We have heard from the Board of Deputies who informed us.

We have also heard from our dear aunt, who received a cable from England, that you are there and you are interned and you are well.

I would like you to know that your Mother, Ibi and Alice are all healthy.

From your loving Father.

I send my love to you and my kisses.

Your ever loving Mother, Rosa.

My beloved Brother, thank God we are together. I have been home for two months and I kiss you and send my love.

Your sister Ibi.

My Dear. I am sending my love and kisses.

From your ever loving sister Alice.

As Miklós sat reading and re-reading the letter in the garden, Smithy came along the path in front of him. Noticing Miklós's emotional state, he placed a hand on his shoulder. 'Miklós, it is the biggest scandal that you are locked up in here after your experiences,' he said. 'You must make it known. Give it publicity. Let me tell you, if there is one thing that puts the fear of God into the British it is *scandal*. Scandal is their Achilles' heel. And scandal is the way to describe your situation.'

Miklós was undeterred by the lack of response from the Home Office. Smithy and other inmates spurred him on and even Rise-and-Shine became a willing accomplice. A career soldier with an inbuilt respect for decency and fair play, the sergeant sympathized with Miklós's plight and agreed to post letters for him outside the camp. It helped that Miklós spent a significant portion of the small wage he was paid for working in the office on Rise-and-Shine's favoured tobacco.

Miklós read most of the newspapers thoroughly. From them he picked out the names of various Members of Parliament and other officials at whom to target his appeals for help. He tried to discover which MPs were Jewish, which interested in the problems of refugees, which tended to speak up for the underdog, and which were simply awkward thorns in the side of the Government.

On 29 January 1946, Miklós painstakingly typed out seven versions of the same letter. As he worked, Smithy's words repeated themselves in his mind: 'Scandal is their Achilles' heel.' His case thus stated, he handed over seven envelopes to Sergeant Rise-and-Shine. Each was addressed to the House of Commons from 001 Camp, Deltane School, Queensmere Road, Wimbledon, SW19. The recipients were R. F. Boothby, W. F. Brown, Tom Driberg, Quintin Hogg, T. L. Horabin, D. N. Pritt and R. R. Stokes. The message to each was identical.

Miklós spelled out the details of his experience. 'Nobody,' he wrote, 'would believe that a man from Auschwitz, Buchenwald, Dachau etc. is kept secretly together with Nazi war criminals for nearly eight months.

'I am appealing to an Englishman who can understand what it means to be imprisoned by the Nazi beasts and now more painfully misunderstood by the saviours of liberty and freedom.'

243

He wrote slightly different letters to the Jewish MPs F. D. Mack, Dr S. Segal and Sydney Silverman. A few days later he wrote a long and more detailed letter to the chairman of the Labour Party, Professor Harold Laski, and a short letter to the Lord Chief Justice. He also maintained his barrage upon the Home Office.

The camp became much more active during the early weeks of 1946. A regular flow of inmates came and went. Even some of the Germans were released on temporary permits. Many of Miklós's original colleagues were discharged, as was Karski, the Polish captain, but Vilner and Smithy remained. Smithy continued to encourage Miklós to publicize his case, but Vilner grew increasingly despondent.

Several Italians passed through Beltane in February and Miklós welcomed the chance to practise his Italian, Cappucelli and his friend having long since departed.

His optimism about his chances of release was dented each time another Jew was admitted to Beltane – four or five came through the gates during January and February. He became friendly with a Polish Jew called Stefan Balsam, who arrived in January. Balsam and another Pole, Krakowski, a Gentile admitted at the same time, were visited each week by representatives of the Polish community in London. They brought tins of food as well as news of the outside world.

On 7 February, while Miklós was playing table-tennis with Stefan Balsam, Rise-and-Shine brought him a letter. It had been opened but otherwise not tampered with.

> *Royal Courts of Justice*
> *London W C2*
> *6th February 1946*

> *Dear Sir,*
> *The Lord Chief Justice directs me to thank you for your letter of*

the 4th February and to say that he is inquiring into the
circumstances mentioned in your letter.

> *Yours faithfully,*
> *P. Stephens Esq.*
> *Secretary*

'At last, Stefan,' said Miklós, 'the bubble has burst. They
didn't dare intercept the Lord Chief Justice's letter. Now I will
receive a flood of replies.'

The first was from Laski. It was handwritten and dated 9
February. It promised support and counselled patience – 'The
scale of the refugee problem presents great administrative
difficulties.'

He heard again from the Jewish Refugees' Committee regret-
ting the Home Office rebuttal of their representations, the
Secretary of State being 'unable to authorize your release from
detention pending completion of arrangements for your return
to the Continent'.

They also told him that his friend Mr Sternberg had heard
that Miklós's family were all well.

He wrote again to Harold Laski asking for his 'speedy represen-
tation to prevent my repatriation to Hungary'.

In February, a letter arrived from Budapest.

My dear son,
*   You have no idea how it feels to write to you, to put your name*
on the envelope and know that you are alive and well to receive
and read the letter.
*   In the past few months we have been visited by two of your*
former fellow inmates from the Nazi concentration camps. The first
visitor was a studious young man called Löwy. As it happened, his
visit proved to be one of the most painful experiences of my life,
feelings that I cannot convey to you, certainly not in a letter.
*   Löwy was very polite and serious. He asked me to follow him*
into the street because he did not wish to talk in front of your

mother and sister. He told me that you had been in a big round-up and that there had been no survivors. You can imagine how I felt and the weight of the responsibility of whether or not to tell Mummy and Alice. As there was no direct proof that you had died I decided to keep quiet about what Löwy had told me. For many months it was a torture not to share my pain with another living soul.

During that time we had another visitor. Josef Stern. Another scholarly type. But he was smiling and assuring us of your survival. He told us how you saved his life by feeding him toasted pieces of bread when he was suffering from dysentery in Buchenwald. 'Most people wouldn't have bothered, but your son was very determined. I know Miklós will have survived,' he said. Your mother was very reassured by this and chided me about my gloom and pessimism — not knowing, of course, the knowledge I had to carry in my heart.

Well, some weeks later I was sent for by the secretary at the Board of Deputies. Something very important, I was told. I went to the office as quickly as I could. 'Sit down,' said the secretary as soon as I walked through the door. 'I want to wish you mazeltov!' And he got out two glasses and filled them with brandy.

What could this be? Had I been made Chief Rabbi of Budapest?

'Rabbi Hammer,' the secretary went on, pressing the glass of brandy into my hand. 'This is truly a toast to life. We have news of your son Miklós. He is alive. Lechaim.'

Well, my son, I don't know if it was the brandy, which I was certainly unused to, but on my journey back to the ghetto apartment people in the street were staring at me. I was not running so much as dancing my way home. I burst into the apartment. Your mother was sitting there. I cried out to her in jubilation. 'Miklós is alive! Baruch Hashem — praise the Lord.'

You will understand that the tears I shed then were partly through relief when I tell you that your mother's reaction was so much more down-to-earth than mine had been. 'Of course he is,' she said. 'What did I tell you?'

Please write soon. We are longing to be reunited with you.
Mummy, Alice and Ibi send their love.
    Your loving father

On 19 February, Miklós was sitting at his desk in the office, carrying out some mundane tasks for the secretary, when Rise-and-Shine breezed through the door.

'Hammer, pack your things! My orders are to see you off the premises in a quarter of an hour.'

The two exchanged smiles. Miklós dropped what he was doing and raced out of the office. He pushed his few belongings into the military sack his sergeant friend had handed him along with his 'wages' for the month and was back in the office five minutes later. An immigration officer sat at the place Miklós had just vacated.

The man held up an official-looking document. 'This,' he said, 'is a temporary permit enabling you to stay in this country.' He gave the permit to Miklós, who quickly read the words typed across the top: 'Restriction Order for three months from today's date, granted to Miklós Hammer alias Peter Howard, to reside in the United Kingdom. Dated this 19th day of February, 1946.'

19

A cold, watery sun stood high in a cloudy sky as Miklós went out of the gate. He turned to look at the inmates ambling around the courtyard. A couple of Germans were watching him through the fence. He laughed aloud at them and stepped on to the pavement outside. A pair of pigeons fluttered out of his path as he walked to the car waiting to take him to the address he had given the immigration officer: 2 Clissold Court, Green Lanes, London N16. Victor Sternberg's home.

The car pulled up outside Clissold Court shortly after noon. Miklós got out and looked around him. An old woman shuffled past him dragging a small black-and-white dog which took a great interest in Miklós, staring up and yelping at him.

The driver pulled the car door shut and leaned his head briefly out of the window. 'All right, mate?' he said, and without waiting for an answer drove away whistling 'Moonlight Serenade'.

Miklós hugged his bag of belongings to his chest before seeking out flat number 2, where a brass nameplate beneath the doorbell announced 'Dr Hackenbroch, Dentist'.

Miklós heard the bell jangling somewhere inside the flat as he pressed the button. A receptionist in a white blouse opened the door.

'May I speak to Dr Hackenbroch, please?' inquired Miklós.

Before the receptionist could answer, he saw a large red-haired man shambling towards the front door from an inner office.

'Can I help you?' he asked in a deep German accent.

'I understand Victor Sternberg lives here. I have come to see him.'

'Who are you?'

'I am Hammer from Budapest. I just came from the internment camp.'

'What! You are the friend from the camps? Come in! Sit down. Have you eaten?'

Hackenbroch told him that Victor and his brother Charlie were partners in a carpet shop in South Molton Street in the West End of London.

'Is he there now?' asked Miklós.

'Yes. I'm pretty sure. He should be.'

'Then I'll go and see him. Please can you get me a taxi?'

The reunion with Vicky was unforgettable. The two men embraced and laughed and shook each other's hand. For a while neither could speak, then Vicky introduced Miklós to his partner, Sidney Afia, and to his younger brother Charlie, whom Miklós could remember only as a gangling bar mitzvah boy in Budapest.

Vicky took his old friend to a kosher restaurant in Soho, where they recalled the Sunday morning football matches of their youth and where Miklós tasted smoked salmon for the first time.

After lunch they went straight back to Clissold Court – Vicky rented a bed-sitting-room behind the dental surgery – and talked into the night. Vicky gave Miklós a letter which he'd received two months earlier from his Member of Parliament, David Weitzman, whom he had contacted on Miklós's behalf.

In it Weitzman explained that his representations had been in vain and enclosed a copy of the reply he'd had from the Home Office. 'Dear Mr Weitzman,' this read. 'This case has been carefully considered but the Home Secretary does not feel justified in allowing Miklós Hammer to stay in this country where he arrived under the English alias "Peter Howard". Arrangements are in hand for Mr Hammer to be returned to the Continent. We do not consider it necessary to hold him at Beltane School much longer.'

Miklós remained buoyant in spite of this. 'Do you know,

Vicky,' he said over a celebratory glass of whisky, 'this is my first evening of freedom since October 1941. It is very precious.'

Living space was severely limited at Clissold Court and after a few days Victor and Charlie arranged for Miklós to stay with a Hungarian business acquaintance of theirs called Korein, who had a flat in Seymour Place, near Marble Arch.

Korein was a supplier of artificial jewellery to Woolworth's and other stores. He took Miklós under his wing and gave him a range of samples to sell on commission.

'Tell the customers you're from the camps,' he urged. 'Especially the Jewish customers.'

But Miklós felt uncomfortable speaking about his experiences and certainly couldn't contemplate doing so as a trading ploy.

Nevertheless, some of the Jewish clients took a great interest in him and asked him about his background over a cup of tea or coffee. He kept his answers as vague as possible – 'I was born in Hungary. I was imprisoned during the war.'

One such client told him he knew of an opening where Miklós's knowledge of foreign languages could bring him a higher and a steadier income. And, a couple of telephone calls later, Miklós arranged to start work for Matthew Thorn and Company of New Bond Street on 19 March 1946, exactly one month after his release from Beltane. His salary would be four pounds ten shillings a week.

In the meantime, Miklós continued to agitate against repatriation. He heard from the Royal Courts of Justice.

20 February 1946

Sir,

I cannot interfere further in your case. I asked the Home Secretary to consider the question of your further detention and understand he has done so. It is entirely for him to decide whether you, as an alien, should be allowed to remain in this country.

Yours faithfully,
Goddard.

On 21 February, Hansard recorded the following exchange among the day's written answers in Parliament:

> *Mr S. Silverman asked the Secretary of State for the Home Department why Miklós Hammer, a Hungarian Jewish refugee, who escaped from the Auschwitz and Buchenwald death camps, has been for eight months detained in 001 Camp, Beltane School, in the company of Nazi Party members, SA men and SS men; why he is not allowed to communicate with anyone outside; and when he will be released.*

> *Mr Ede: This man was refused leave to land when he attempted to enter under the false claim that he was a British subject. It would be wrong to encourage the idea that persons who reach our ports by false pretences will be allowed to stop here, but as the efforts to dispose suitably of this man have not yet succeeded, I have released him from detention. He was allowed to communicate with persons outside the place in which he was detained and my correspondence shows that he communicated with a number of Hon. Members of this House.*

The same month brought a second letter from Miklós's father.

My dear son,

I do hope that you are well and in good spirits.

Your mother's health continues to worry me and Ibolya is going to take some time to recover from her ordeal in Bergen-Belsen. I'm sure both would recover greatly if only they could see you. I wish you would change your mind and come home and help us to build up our lives here again.

The synagogue is reviving a little. There is little difficulty in raising a minyan, especially on Shabbat. Everybody asks about you. There are even some young men and women around. We have seen your friend Löwy once more. He almost hugged me when I told him about you. He sends his best wishes. Once you

*have settled your affairs in England, you must promise to come and
see us. This much I must be able to tell Mummy. It is unthinkable
that you could go to the United States or Palestine without first
seeing your family.*

*Food here is still in short supply, though none of us is going
hungry, thank God. I am glad that you are at least being fed well.*

*Your old German teacher came to synagogue last week. Old
Greenwald. Remember how you used to dislike him? He was very
interested in your fate and asked me to pass on his greetings. He was
shocked by the behaviour of the Germans in the war and asked me to
tell you that this was not part of the true German culture. He asked
me to tell you to remember that Germany had brought this world a
Schiller, a Goethe, a Heine, a Beethoven and Immanuel Kant.*

*Please let us know of your plans as soon as possible. Love from
your mother and sisters.*

Your loving father.

Miklós turned his father's letter over and over in his hand, re-
reading it. He smiled as he came to the bit about old Greenwald.
'Tell him,' he said aloud, 'that I have only had the pleasure of
encountering Himmler, Hitler, Goering and Kaltenbrunner
from the German pantheon.'

Miklós had moved out of Korein's flat once he had been
offered the job at Matthew Thorn. Victor found him lodgings
in Warrington Crescent, Maida Vale, from where he travelled
into Bond Street every day by bus, taking pleasure in each
journey as a mark of ordinary, everyday freedom.

Matthew Thorn and Company was an import and export
business dealing in a wide range of merchandise. Miklós
worked alongside the owner, 'Sonny' Cooper, an amiable man
in his thirties, and his secretary, Miss Arnold. It was a busy
office sending and receiving items all over the world. Miklós
was quickly able to exploit his linguistic skills.

He achieved rapid promotion. In April, Sonny Cooper made
him manager of the export office and raised his salary to six pounds.

'I asked Miss Arnold to keep a copy of every letter you've written or translated for us,' Cooper told him. 'I was amazed. You are a foreigner and yet you can use the English language so effectively. I can't write letters anywhere near as good as yours and I was born here.'

'Ah well,' said Miklós. 'Who did you learn from?'

'My mother,' laughed Cooper.

'There you are, you see. I learned from the BBC!'

In a short time, the two of them became great friends.

Miklós could feel himself coming back to life. His weight was up to ten stone and his energy was increasing all the time. He read a lot, wrote regularly to his family, and began to build up a fulfilling social life.

Vicky introduced him to the Anglo-Palestine Club, a Zionist society reminiscent of Klal Zion, in which he soon felt at home. Among the speakers there, he met Abba Eban, Richard Crossman and David Ben-Gurion. He joined Poale Zion, a socialist Zionist group based in Eton Avenue, NW3, and was a frequent visitor at the Zionist Federation headquarters in Great Russell Street. Occasionally he gave a talk about the camps, though he continued to avoid discussing the subject informally.

He still had nightmares, in which the same old faces appeared, and one time woke up screaming. But in general his health was good and he was pleased with his progress.

At Poale Zion he met a Belgian-Jewish girl called Sarah Levi. She too had suffered in the war years, having been hidden in a cellar by a sympathetic Gentile family. They went to concerts together, and the cinema, but mostly they kept to Zionist activities.

They heard Liszt's pupil, Frederic Lamond, by then a very old man, play at the Albert Hall. Sitting near them was a group of Hungarian expatriates, some of whom wept at the music. At the close, Miklós grabbed Sarah by the arm and rushed into the night.

Once a week, Miklós had to report to Piccadilly police station to have his permit stamped and to give details of any changes in his employment or living accommodation. Towards the end of May his permit was extended for a further three months and his appearances at the police station cut down to once a fortnight.

At about the same time, he found new lodgings – at number 9 Sandwell Crescent, in West Hampstead, not far from his regular haunt in Eton Avenue.

On 5 July, anxious about the lingering threat of repatriation, Miklós made an appointment to see Dr István Bede, Chargé d'Affaires at the Hungarian Embassy.

He entered Bede's office at three o'clock and, after a brief summary of his life and origins, came to the point.

'In all my life, I have never asked any favour of the Hungarian nation or its government. But I would like to ask now, for the first and last time.

'My survival owes nothing to Hungary. Officials of the country of my birth handed me over to the Germans for extermination. I'll show you my number from Auschwitz to prove what I've told you about myself is true.

'My request is for you to refuse to acknowledge me as a Hungarian subject – I have no papers. Such a gesture would, I promise you, be a favour to me.'

Bede promptly summoned a secretary and dictated a letter in English: 'To whom it may concern. As Mr Miklós Hammer could not produce documents or otherwise prove beyond reasonable doubt that he is a Hungarian citizen, we are not in a position to furnish him with any documents or to acknowledge him as a Hungarian subject.'

He signed the completed text and handed it over, gravely shaking Miklós by the hand.

Miklós sent the letter the same day to the Home Office.

Professor Laski made a number of representations on Miklós's behalf to the American Embassy. Each new step, however, towards his desired goal of obtaining a place to resume his medical studies brought Miklós new bureaucratic complications. Meanwhile, his battle with the Home Office continued. Each of his targeted MPs wrote back to him, enclosing similar rebuttals from the Home Secretary.

None of this interfered with his flourishing social and working life. And there seemed to be no problem in extending his temporary permit to stay in the United Kingdom. This was renewed automatically on its expiry date.

All the time, he was getting used to London. At weekends, he enjoyed visiting museums and galleries and walking with Sarah in Hyde Park or on Hampstead Heath. He had familiarized himself with the Underground and bus systems and could find his way around easily.

He even ventured outside the capital when Sonny Cooper gave him a week's holiday at the end of July. Charlie Sternberg took him to Bournemouth, where they stayed in a Jewish boarding-house and went to tea dances.

He and Sarah were seeing less of each other now. His plans to go to America preoccupied him and deterred her. His father wrote to say that he had found a 'very nice girl' for him. Miklós replied that 'no girl on earth' could induce him to return to Budapest.

He continued to impress Sonny Cooper. One day, towards the end of 1946, Cooper announced that he wanted to send Miklós to Europe to sell some merchandise. 'You'll be terrific. You know the languages, understand the business. It's obvious you should go.'

'But I can't. I have no papers. I'm still under threat of deportation. I'm stateless.'

'Don't worry. I'll put all that in the hands of the company's solicitors. They'll sort it out. You'll be a success.'

Sonny Cooper's optimism was a little dented by the official reply to the solicitors' letter seeking permission for Miklós to travel. 'The sooner Mr Hammer goes abroad, the better,' wrote the Home Office, 'and he should not come back.'

On 23 January 1947, Sydney Silverman MP rose in the House of Commons to ask Chuter Ede, the Home Secretary, why his department had informed the employers of Miklós Hammer that he was an undesirable alien and the sooner they got rid of him the better; why Hammer himself had been summoned to Scotland Yard and there pressed to leave the country; and what offence this survivor of Auschwitz, Buchenwald and Dachau had committed.

Ede got to his feet. 'I have been unable to find any foundation for the first allegation in this Question. As regards the second, the police were recently instructed to ascertain what steps this Hungarian was taking to leave the United Kingdom, and, as he was not at home when the police visited, he was asked to call – not at Scotland Yard, but at the local police station.

'As I stated in reply to a previous Question by my Hon. Friend, this foreigner came here by falsely claiming to be a British subject, and it would be wrong to encourage any idea that foreigners who reach our ports by false pretences will be allowed to stop here.'

'Will my Right Hon. Friend bear in mind that, however false the pretence was,' asked Silverman, 'had this gentleman not made it, he would now be dead? It was his only means of saving his life. So far as the first part of the Question is concerned, if my Right Hon. Friend is unable to find any foundation for it, will he inquire of the reputable firm who employed this man, and to whom the statement was made; and, with regard to the last part of his answer, may I ask him whether it is now the public policy in this country for the surviving victims of Nazism to be hounded by a secret police?'

'No, sir, that is not the policy,' replied an angered Ede. 'During my tenure of office, I have endeavoured to adopt as liberal an attitude as I can towards those people and, I believe, with some measure of success, but I cannot administer the law which this House has passed if I am to allow people who arrive in this country under false pretences to remain here.

'I take particular care to see that no person is compelled to leave for a country where his religious or political views are likely to bring him into difficulties with the prevailing authorities there.'

Silverman persisted until eventually the speaker intervened to redirect the House back to its other business.

Towards the end of January 1947 Miklós was able to meet Sydney Silverman at the House of Commons and to thank him personally for his efforts. Around the same time, Sonny Cooper's solicitor was summoned to the Home Office and, after a short discussion, issued with travel documents for Miklós's business trip.

With Europe devastated and the Commonwealth dominions in a dependent position, there was plenty of scope for British exports. Britain needed foreign currency, too, and the slogan 'Export or die!' was in the air.

For six weeks, from 6 February 1947, Miklós represented Matthew Thorn and Company in Brussels, Paris, Geneva, Zurich, Milan and Rome. He had money in his pocket, stayed at good hotels and ate good food. He established new business contacts, sold beyond expectations and made the firm a healthy profit.

One evening in Zurich, Miklós asked the hotel receptionist to recommend somewhere in town for dinner. He suggested a certain night-club and Miklós made his way there by taxi.

He was ushered into a smoky, subterranean room, glowing red from an elaborate arrangement of lights around a stage on which a six-piece band was playing dance music. Two or three couples danced on a small square of polished floor space. The women wore expensive-looking dresses that became bathed in red light each time they glided past the front of the stage.

Miklós ordered a steak and some wine and lit a cigarette. He revelled in the freedom of the occasion, quietly humming to himself the tune the band were playing. As he waited for his meal to arrive, he overheard a snatch of conversation from the next table. A woman in her fifties was talking in Hungarian to her daughter, who was about thirty.

A little later, the band-leader came over to the women's table. He too was Hungarian, it seemed. The three of them began to discuss the food and the music and the prospects for the Swiss economy.

Miklós hadn't heard his native language for a long time. He rose from his table and introduced himself. After a few formal pleasantries he returned to his seat and the band-leader joined him briefly before resuming his place on the stage. His name was Hajos. He told Miklós he had come to Switzerland before the war and married a Swiss girl. He had settled in Zurich but, he said, he was having to wait twenty-one years to acquire Swiss nationality.

When Miklós later wrote to his father about meeting Hajos, David wrote back: 'That band-leader of yours is Nándor Hajos, one of late Aunty Hannah's sons. Without knowing it you were talking to your second cousin.'

Milan presented a sullen face. Buildings were burned out, with rubble piled up on street corners. People in the street had a morbid, defeated look. As Miklós's taxi left the station, it seemed to be taking him into a cold, bleak expanse.

He was booked in at Hotel L'Ambassadore, which had only recently been vacated by the Canadian army. Inside, it felt several degrees warmer than the street and his room was clean and comfortable. When he entered the restaurant, he stopped for a moment in surprise at the scene before him. Sleek, prosperous-looking diners were devouring lavish platefuls of chicken, fish, pasta and salad, served to them at cloth-covered tables. The sounds of jolly accordion music accompanied the busy to-ings and fro-ings of black-uniformed waiters and waitresses.

Miklós took his place at a table and surveyed the menu. Several kinds of pasta, sauces, cream desserts – the contrast with the austerity of victorious Britain was astonishing.

A waitress came and Miklós ordered pasta and a glass of wine. He spoke Italian with confidence, and was beginning to relax after his harsh introduction to the city. Suddenly, the waitress rounded on him. She put down her pad and pencil and, leaning both arms on the table, tossed her head at him accusingly.

'You bastard!' she screamed, in ringing soprano. 'Through

bastards like you, we have lost the war. You think because you are putting on an accent I don't know you are Italian? You ran away, you bastard.'

'My dear lady,' he replied, embarrassed. 'I assure you I am not Italian.'

'Don't try to fool me,' she insisted.

'I am not, please believe me.'

'*Bastardo*.' Her voice was at full pitch. Heads turned. The head waiter came over and quietly steered her to another table.

'She seems to think I am an Italian,' said Miklós as the waiter returned. 'That I ran away from the war. I was born in Hungary. I was in the thick of things. I couldn't have run away if I'd wanted to.'

'Please forgive us, *signore*,' said the waiter. 'She has lost her family in the war. Husband and three sons. She is bitter. The wounds are too raw. I'll get somebody else to serve you.'

As Miklós left the restaurant, the head waiter came across and spoke to him. 'I'm very sorry for what happened,' he said. 'Your lunch is on the house.'

He returned to Britain to discover that his difficulties with the Home Office had eased. They seemed to have yielded to the pressures of Sydney Silverman and Harold Laski. He was given unlimited permission to stay. He wrote to thank both men.

In September, Miklós was offered another business trip abroad. To Czechoslovakia. It presented an ideal opportunity to see his family. He wrote to his father asking him to suggest a meeting place on the Czech-Hungarian border. David wrote back that the village of Tótgyarmat would probably be the most suitable. Miklós agreed to telephone from Bratislava to fix a date and time.

His DC3 landed in Bratislava on a grassy runway. When he stepped out the morning felt dewy and fresh. He spent a day looking for places his father had told him about from his student days before the First World War. He drank coffee in the market square and tried to picture his father as a young man.

He phoned his parents that evening and told them he was taking a train to Levice and a bus from there to the border.

The train journey provided a view of the landscape of war. The roads were littered with burnt-out tanks, the buildings shelled and battered, whole blocks flattened.

The bus was crowded. Miklós sat down next to a middle-aged woman wearing a headscarf and, despite the warmth of the evening, a heavy black overcoat.

When this woman heard Miklós buy his ticket from the conductor she turned to him and spoke.

'So. You are Hungarian.'

He nodded.

'I thought . . .' She trailed off, indicating Miklós's suit with a shrug and a shake of the head. 'Were you in Hungary during the war?' she asked.

'No.'

'Perhaps you have been fortunate. I and my family have had a terrible time. You know, your clothes are not like Hungarian clothes. Do you want some cheese?'

Miklós politely declined the open basket.

'We have had to put up with the Russian soldiers. Fighting. Shouting, swearing, terrible behaviour. My brother was killed. Are you sure you don't want some cheese?'

'No, thank you.'

'Hungary – and many Hungarians – took a beating,' she said, sucking at a piece of cheese. She seemed to have very few teeth.

'Where we lived there were collaborators,' she went on. 'Arrow Cross people. Some were hanged publicly. A cousin of mine was among those rounded up. But it was all lies. Gangs. Rabble. Foreign elements.'

As they reached the open road the bus picked up speed, jolting them in their seats. It grew dark. Miklós barely spoke. His neighbour continued to talk about the war and eat her cheese.

Miklós took a room at the small village inn. At about nine o'clock there was a knock at his door. A man had brought a note from his father:

'We are stranded here on the Hungarian side. The Czechs are

not allowing Hungarians through. You will have to cross to our side. We await you with love and great excitement.'

'Please tell him I shall be at the border post at seven in the morning,' Miklós said to the messenger. 'Thank you.'

Not possessing a Hungarian visa, Miklós was more reluctant than ever to set foot in Hungarian territory, even though the urge to see his family was overwhelming. He went to sleep battling with this dilemma.

He awoke at six. A clear, bright morning. The window rattled occasionally with an irregular but persistent breeze. He washed and shaved quickly and silently, put on his clothes and took a deep breath before setting out to walk the half-mile or so to the border post.

The border was marked by a grass-covered ditch, about a hundred yards wide. Across it was a wooden bridge, one end in Czechoslovakia, the other in Hungary. Access was through a fenced-in wooden cabin. Inside sat a guard, yawning and stretching.

There were very few people about. On the opposite bank Miklós could see his parents, sisters and Ibolya's newly-wed husband. He waved to them before going into the cabin.

The guard was a friendly-looking man in his forties. He was bald, except for a ring of thick, black hair around the sides of his head. His full lips were pursed into a smile under his bushy moustache.

'Can I ask you something?' Miklós said in Hungarian.

'Sure.' The smile broke out.

'Do you have a mother?'

'Sure I have a mother.'

Miklós had brought some English cigarettes with him. He placed a pack of Churchmans on the table.

'What would you do if you hadn't seen your mother since the war and now you have the chance to see her at last?'

'I would take it,' said the guard, eyeing the Churchmans. 'No matter what.'

Miklós picked up the cigarette packet and gave it to the man.

'Look,' he said. 'A hundred yards from here, on the other side, my mother is waiting. And my father and my sisters. I understand they can't get Czech visas to come here, and I am unable to go over there. Please, is there anything you can do?'

'Well,' said the guard, taking out one of the cigarettes and lighting it. 'I'm on duty until eleven. As far as I'm concerned you can meet in the middle and stay there till then. It'll be all right with the Hungarian guard. After eleven,' he turned up his palms, 'I can't guarantee.'

'Thank you,' said Miklós, vigorously shaking the man's hand. 'Thank you.'

Miklós ran down the slope towards his family. The Czech guard telephoned his Hungarian counterpart, who let Miklós's family through so they could all meet on the patch of grass separating the two countries.

Everybody was crying. Miklós was introduced to his new brother-in-law amid hugs, kisses and shouted greetings.

'What happened to your hair?' cried Rosa. David and Miklós laughed, while Ibolya took a long time to recover from her tears.

They sat on the ground and ate food that Rosa had brought along. All of them tried to persuade Miklós to go back with them to Budapest.

'At least,' said David, 'come and stay in the house we have put up at in the village here.'

'No, father. We'll stay here and talk.'

After a couple of hours, the Hungarian guard came down to them. 'Don't worry,' he said. 'You can stay here as long as you like. I have spoken to my colleague.'

And so they sat and talked into the afternoon. Miklós described a little of his experiences and heard from his father about relatives who had died. But mostly the mood was one of rejoicing as Miklós talked of his prospects in England. Alice and Ibi pressed him with questions about fashions and famous people and places in London.

At about four o'clock they eventually said their farewells, but not before Rosa and David had again urged Miklós to stay one night with them in the lodging-house on the Hungarian side.

But he walked away and retraced his route to Prague, and then London. And while he made his way back, his family were robbed of their money and papers during the night at the Hungarian lodging-house.

By this time Miklós had met his future wife. After months of persistent matchmaking by one of the manufacturers' agents who regularly called at Matthew Thorn's office, Miklós had agreed to meet the elder daughter of a German-Jewish émigré musician called Joseph Geiger.

The agent was a Mr Kaye who, like Joseph Geiger, came originally from Berlin. Kaye often brought his wife to the office and their joint and effusive interest in Miklós's welfare sometimes caused him to hide when he heard them approaching.

Eventually, in order to silence their constant concern about his 'lonely plight', Miklós said he would let them introduce him to the 'lovely girl' they had in mind.

Sonja Geiger was haughtily resistant to her parents' entreaty, that June, to be 'pleasant to the young man coming to visit us for tea next Sunday'. But when the Kayes explained a little of Miklós's personal history, sympathy and curiosity combined to make Sonja feel some interest in him.

He invited her to see Anna Magnani in *Open City* with him at the Dominion Cinema, and to hear Solomon play at the Albert Hall.

A week later, they went for a walk in Green Park. Seated at a bench, Miklós tried to dissuade Sonja from becoming attached to him. 'I am a cold person,' he told her, 'hardened by experience.'

Shortly afterwards he went on holiday to Torquay with a friend from his office. He sent Sonja an unromantic, matter-of-fact postcard but began to think about whether the time might be right after all to consider settling down.

Sonja's parents were away on a trip abroad when Miklós got back. She and her sister arranged to cook a meal at the house for Miklós and the sister's boyfriend. After they'd eaten, Miklós asked if he could telephone his parents in Hungary.

Sonja sat on a sofa opposite the phone as she listened for the first time to Miklós speaking Hungarian. His face was very serious and she grew pale as she waited for him to finish.

'Thank you, Sonja,' he said at last. 'Do you think you could make me a strong black coffee?'

'Of course,' she replied, concerned. 'Are you all right?'

'Yes. I have just told my father I am unofficially engaged.'

'What! To whom?'

'To you.'

To Miklós's inexpressible delight, his parents were able to come to London for his wedding on 19 October. Sonja's father was a regular performer at the Savoy Hotel and was able to arrange a reception there for 120 guests, including Mr and Mrs Kaye, Sonny Cooper, and Vicky and Charlie Sternberg.

The ceremony took place at Hendon synagogue in north-west London. Rosa Hammer wept copiously as she stood opposite her husband, who closed his eyes during the rabbi's address and in an instant saw again the sombre face of Imre Löwy telling him Miklós was dead; heard again the joyful voice of the secretary of the Budapest deputies: '*Mazeltov*, Rabbi Hammer. We have news of your son Miklós. He is alive. *Lechaim*.'

During the reception at the Savoy, Sonny Cooper stood and proposed a toast to the bride and groom. Somebody whispered to Miklós that he was expected to respond. Slightly shocked, he rose to his feet.

'Reverend Sir,' he began in the conventional, formal style, 'ladies and gentlemen. It gives me great pleasure to see you all here today.' As he spoke he could see Victor Sternberg translating his words for David and Rosa.

'I'm especially thrilled to see my dear parents here this

evening. They have made the journey from the edge of the most devastated part of a devastated continent.

'There are many people who cannot be with us whom I dearly miss and wish could be here. These include my sisters, Ibolya and Alice, Imre Löwy, Josef Stern, Imre Friedman. And many other friends who have shared with me intimately some of the most unspeakable days and nights known to man. I do not expect to see a single one of them again. With your forbearance, ladies and gentlemen, I should like to mention some of their names, so that we may honour their memories.

'Ede Kaller, Tadek Halter, Eva Gross, Dr Reuben Révész, Vanya, from the Ukraine. Roman Levitzky. Weisz, the tailor, whose first name I never knew. Zoltán Klein. David Guttman. A schoolmaster named Gelb. An accountant named Nagel. A brave red-haired boy from Kunmadaras. Miklós Erdös, a "Christian" Jew. Imre Katz, Imre Bárber . . . and Peter Howard. God bless them.'

He then thanked his in-laws for their generosity in organizing such a fine wedding, praised the beauty and human qualities of his bride, and sat down.

Sonja and Miklós planned a short honeymoon in Torquay. But before that, they spent a few days with their two sets of parents. David and Rosa were staying at the Geigers' home in Edgware, as were the newly married couple.

The night after the wedding, Miklós and his father stayed up talking together until almost dawn. They drank numerous cups of coffee and sipped whisky from one of the several bottles brought back from the Savoy.

'I praise the Holy Name for the end of the war,' said David. 'We have had a hard time of it. Your mother and I have between us counted 136 relatives who have perished.'

'You haven't yet told me how you and Mother and Alice managed to get through it all,' said Miklós. 'In your letters you referred to some of the hardships of the ghetto, but how did you keep together?'

'Ah, my son, the ghetto! So many times one or other of us

could have died. I don't know how your mother's health held out, but it did. We saw many friends and neighbours die.

'One day, while I was away, your mother and sister and everyone else in the building on Wesselényi Street were rounded up by the Arrow Cross. They were marched towards the river. Your sister turned to your mother. "Mama," she said, "do you want to die?" She realized what was going on. And she persuaded Mummy to tear off her yellow star and run away to the comparative safety of the ghetto. The Reichmann family took them in for the first few days. Some others escaped with them. Miriam Weisz, for example, Alice's friend from school, but she died a day or so later.'

'But what happened to the rest of those taken away?' asked Miklós.

'They were all gunned down and dumped in the Danube.'

They both drank in silence for a few moments, then David continued.

'My son, it was anarchy in the ghetto. Desperate anarchy. People fighting, bartering jewellery and other belongings for food. The flesh of cats, dogs, horses, rats' – the naming of each animal was emphasized by a chopping movement of the hand – 'was eaten for survival. One time I got hold of some beef. It was when Alice was in bed with a fever. We were desperately worried. She was delirious, almost in a coma. That beef probably saved her life.'

He released a long sigh. Miklós studied his father's face, noting for the first time how much he had aged, how profoundly sad his eyes were. They seemed to stare into some far distance as he started to speak again.

'One day all the men in the street were ordered to the school where you did your training for the *Arbeitsdienst*. We were required to join work parties out East, we were told. We were taken on a train somewhere and then we marched for days with very little food.

'Eventually we reached Hegyeshalom on the Austrian border. To my surprise, one of the Hungarian border guards recognized me. There was this voice asking, "Aren't you David Hammer?" It was János, from downstairs at the Murányi Street apartment. "Don't go with those men," he suddenly said to me. I protested that we were all under orders. "We are going to a work camp at Mauthausen in Austria," I told him. "It is not a work camp," he said to me, very firmly. "Those men are going to their deaths."

'It hadn't occurred to me for one moment that this was some sort of execution round-up. I'd believed what I'd been told. But now this János was tugging at my sleeve. "Come on," he says. "Follow me and I'll get you away." He led me through some trees, along a path, some houses, I don't know. After a while we arrived at a station.

'There was a goods train at the platform. Nobody was about. János, well, he motioned me aboard, into a truck filled with all sorts of materials – boxes, sacks and packets – labelled with the addresses of various factories. And then, "Good luck" he says, as cheerfully as you like, and shuts me in.

'I had only a hunk of bread with me. I nibbled at it, hungry but anxious to save it for as long as I could. The train pulled out. I remained there all the time it made its way to Budapest. I hid beneath a stack of boxes each time it stopped in a station, but no one came.

'It took days and days to get back to Budapest. The train went at a painfully slow pace and stopped for hours at a time. I was starving. But when we did arrive, a miracle happened.

'As I pushed aside the door to the truck, virtually falling out in my weak condition, there almost opposite me on the platform was your mother, with Alice. They and other women had gone each day to the station to await the return of their men from the work detail. That day, my arrival coincided with theirs.

'You know, Miki,' he continued, looking up into his son's face. 'When you left us at the border last month, you never looked back at us. You just kept striding forward and never once turned your head. We were all standing waiting to wave. The women were crying. And you never looked back.'

'I was turning my back on Hungary,' said Miklós. 'Not on you, father.'

They fell silent. Miklós stood up and went over to the window. 'You know now what has happened to me,' he said after a minute or two, looking out of the window. 'You know a little about the hell of the camps. About the death, the pain, the torture and degradation.' This time it was Miklós who sighed.

'Twice,' he said. 'Twice I had the opportunity to get away to Palestine. Twice you prevented me. Just imagine all that I would have been saved from if I had been allowed to go, like so many of my friends.'

Light was beginning to break over the streets outside. Miklós watched a cat dive at something under a fence. A car engine stuttered into life somewhere nearby.

'It was God's will,' said David Hammer.

EPILOGUE

by Tim Rayment

The next day a man crawled across the truck . . . He was of medium height, with light brown hair and still-alert, intelligent eyes. He greeted Miklós in German, and smiled.

'Hello,' Miklós nodded. 'Miklós Hammer. And your name?'

'My real name?'

'Well, yes,' said Miklós, puzzled by this reaction.

'It's Peter Howard.'

So who was 'Peter Howard', the spy whose identity saved Miklós Hammer? Even after half a century, there are clues: enough to search for Howard, if not, perhaps, to find him. Nine months ago I read *Sacred Games*, met Miklós Hammer and decided to trace the smiling Englishman who had been on the death train to Dachau.

The clues came from Hammer, now seventy-five and living in central London. They were few; after all, he was recalling a brief conversation held when he was starving, covered in lice and close to death.

He had thought it odd, he said, that the young Englishman should ask if he should give his *real* name. Years later Hammer would decide that Howard had a double or multiple life. At the time he absorbed merely that he was the same age, the son of a civil servant, had trained in medicine and had parents in Chelsea. The Germans had picked him up in Paris in 1942 and sent him to various camps, ending with this train packed with corpses between Buchenwald and Dachau. That was all. 'You must realize,' said Hammer, 'that in the cattle truck you don't observe things. It doesn't matter whether someone is the son of the king or a civil servant when you are near death.'

It seemed enough to go on. Peter Howard, born in about 1920, possibly in Chelsea; probably a spy, perhaps parachuted into France. I sent a researcher (fittingly, a refugee from the Bosnian war) to the public search room of St Catherine's House in London, which keeps an index of births, marriages and deaths. I asked for every Peter Howard born in 1919, 1920 and 1921; there were twelve, including one registered in Chelsea.

While waiting the minimum forty-eight hours for his birth certificate, we asked the tracing service of the International Red Cross if they knew of a Peter Howard in the concentration camps. I put the same question to Gervase Cowell, who keeps the archives of Special Operations Executive (SOE), the spies who worked behind the lines in Europe. If an agent's work is sensitive, official sources such as Cowell tell you nothing. If it is risky but relatively routine, there is a good chance of being handed the contents of the agent's file.

Within days there came some answers: the Red Cross had registered a Peter Howard in Dachau. He was born in 1920 and was recorded as having been picked up by the Germans in France in 1944. He was alive at the end of the war, but after that nothing was known.

At the Old Admiralty Building in Central London, Cowell was away. Other Foreign Office sources, however, revealed that there *had* been an SOE agent called George Peter Howard. He toured the Middle East researching political books as his cover, and in 1944 he was in Cairo, the SOE's Middle East headquarters, which also ran sabotage operations in the Balkans.

St Catherine's House, meanwhile, produced the birth certificate for a Peter Eliot Layland Howard, born to Lieutenant-Commander R. W. Howard (retired) of the Royal Navy and his wife, Petronel Eleanor. He was of the right age and background: born at 68 Cadogan Square, Chelsea, on 25 July 1920, making him one month younger than Hammer.

I ruled out the Red Cross Howard first. His date of birth was

18 June, the same as Hammer's. The cause of this coincidence was plain: it was a record of what Miklós Hammer had said from his Dachau hospital bed. This was evidence that Hammer's story, as told to the author of this book, is true, but it did not help in the quest for Peter Howard.

We went to Cadogan Square. No 68 is now a school, but the head teacher was able to name the family that had sold the house in the 1950s. We traced to Surrey a member of this family, and she offered a telephone number in South Africa. 'Ask for the Lilac Room,' she said. I dialled the number and, just one week into our search, the only Peter Howard born in Chelsea in 1920 was at the end of the line. 'It wasn't me,' he said. 'In 1945 I was in Burma. I didn't serve in Europe.'

Cowell, back at his desk, then ruled out the SOE's George Peter Howard. Yes, he existed: he was a Hungarian writer and journalist, George Paloczi-Horvath, who worked under the name Peter Howard. Cowell, however, was adamant that he had not been imprisoned in Buchenwald, was not evacuated to Dachau, and 'did not die on any train to or at Dachau'.

I saw part of this agent's file, including a memorandum in April 1944 praising him as 'the only real expert on Hungary remaining in the organization', before concluding that Cowell was right. Later I received a letter from the agent's son, George Paloczi-Horvath (Jnr), who lives in south-east London. 'My father came to London after the Istanbul SOE office was closed in December 1944,' he said. 'Returning to Hungry in 1947, he spent five years in gaol as a political prisoner from 1949 to 1954, and returned to Britain in 1956 after the Hungarian uprising. Thereafter, my father specialized in writing on Communist bloc affairs. He died in London in 1973.'

So I can offer no answers. We have not traced all the Peter Howards born in Britain in those three years, nor the male Howards registered with Peter as a middle name. Perhaps the 'Peter Howard' who smiled on the train to Dachau is among them.

Whoever he was, he is not forgotten. Miklós Hammer,

permitted at last to settle in Britain, married in 1947. He and his wife Sonja, who is from a musical home in north London, had a son in 1951. There was only one first name they could give him: Peter.

The Hammers now live quietly and comfortably in a big apartment in Mayfair. At the age of seventy-five Nicholas Hammer, as he is known today, is still at work, importing and exporting the textiles that allow him his large cigars. I asked him whether he would be alive if he had given his real name at Dachau, and crawled to the Jewish side of the roll-call. 'No,' he said. 'I knew two or three who did. I never saw them again.'

Like many survivors of the Holocaust, Hammer has conformed to the forty-year syndrome. For four decades he denied his memories. He told nobody what he had seen in the camps, not even his wife. Sonja learned the outline of her husband's history from the family doctor, whom she called because the man she had wed was screaming in his sleep every night. Young Peter, sitting with his father in the bath, asked why the number A-12152 was tattooed on his left forearm. He learned that this was Daddy's office telephone number and a tattoo was the only way to remember it.

Awakening his memory to tell his story to Gerald Jacobs had terrible effects on Hammer. The successful businessman began to binge secretly and Sonja, who still did not know the details of what had happened to her husband before they met, would find him in the kitchen in the early hours, stuffing food into his pockets.

I was with the Hammers on the day the contents of *Sacred Games* became public. One of Sonja's most intimate friends telephoned. She was so distressed she could not get any words out. Close to the couple for twenty years, she had never known the story in these pages.

I am glad he told it, and not only because this book is an important addition to Holocaust literature. I have made a friend. When I first interviewed Nicholas Hammer for the *Sunday Times*, I was struck by the total detachment with which he faces questions. There is no visible emotion.

Earn Nicky's trust, however, and he makes you part of his life. He is generous, cultured company. If he likes to be at the centre of things, he is also interested in others. Most importantly, he shares his highest pleasures. Recently he persuaded me that it was not only acceptable but essential for a Jew who loves Mahler, as we both do, to have the recordings of Herbert von Karajan (about whom I had felt uncomfortable). We began to meet to listen to Karajan's version of each of the symphonies, which are a solace to Nicky and Sonja in the early hours. My ears were opened. Nine months later I am no closer to knowing who Peter Howard was than when I started. But I am very glad he existed.

Tim Rayment
The *Sunday Times*
London, October 1995

*

Sacred Games is in every important particular the true story of the first twenty-seven years of my life. It is dedicated to all the Ede Kallers, Tadek Halters, Imre Katzs and Peter Howards and to the countless unnamed men, women and children who perished with them. May their memories blaze through the darkness and indifference.

Nicholas (Miklós) Hammer
London, September 1994